Gerhard Fischer

Disastrous encounters -
Anecdotes and episodes
from the humanitarian aid world

With a foreword of Dr. Michael Feit

Bibliografische Information der Deutschen Nationalbibliothek: Die Deutsche Nationalbibliothek verzeichnet diese Publikation in der Deutschen Nationalbibliografie, detaillierte bibliografische Daten sind im Internet über dnb.dnb.de abrufbar.

Coverdesign: Michelle Hitscherich
Herstellung und Verlag: BoD – Books on Demand, Norderstedt

ISBN 9783756883837

For
Birgit

Preliminary note

I published this book in German in 2019. Many former colleagues had asked whether it would be available in English in the future. Since a professional translation would have cost a fortune, I dared to do it myself.

However, I am neither a linguist, native English speaker nor professional writer. Well, I am no educated translator either, who will never achieve the level of a native speaker anyway.

Some friends as well as one native speaker attested the text would sound somewhat like English, except perhaps „the odd thing ", as Simon coaxingly said. My special thanks go to all of them. Nonetheless, the one or the other native speaker might notice linguistic obscurities or inconsistencies as well as the odd thing.

Simon very likely referred to some strange translations of German idioms as well as sentence structure. Therefore, I omitted the former when I thought the English sounded too weird. Regarding the latter, I tried to do my best. Further, I refrained from including the pictures of the German edition, because their quality was not good at all.

While I translated the text, I actually found many repetitions, which I consequently deleted. Surprisingly, in the end the text shrank of almost 50 pages! Hence, next time I should probably engage a professional lector.

I hereby ask the gentle reader to consider my missing professionalism, to accept sympathetically linguistic deficits and hope that you, dear reader, will still like and recommend the book. The more people buy it, the sooner I can afford a lector!

G.F.

Contents

Foreword

Why read the stories of a Humanitarian Worker? What can be interesting about it, what is new, what has not been told before?

Gerhard Fischer, as a former colleague and boss, but above all as a friend, asked me to write a foreword for this book. I was lucky enough to be able to experience many of these little anecdotes with him, be it as an administrator in Montenegro, Serbia or Moldova, or as the director of international cooperation at Caritas Luxembourg. After reading the first draft, I found myself in the book so much that I was delighted to take on the task of writing the foreword.

In this book, Gerhard Fischer not only tells his story, above all he tells the stories of the people he met. He tells of how people had an effect on him how cultures had an effect on him. The wit, the anecdote mostly arises from these different perspectives, that of the reader and that of the person concerned. Normal everyday things are experienced from two different perspectives; this is what makes the book so charming.

Gerhard Fischer has experienced a lot in his life as a humanitarian worker, seen a lot of suffering, felt a lot of need, and experienced a lot of danger. However, what has remained in him are the people, their stories, their laughter, their friendship. He reports about this in his book.

11

In order to experience these stories in this way, you have to open up yourself to them. Just as Gerhard Fischer opened up to let these stories of these people into his heart and ultimately also into this book, the reader of this little book must also open up himself to both, the heroes of the stories as well as the storyteller, because only if the reader understands both perspectives, the meaning of this book becomes clear.

Gerhard Fischer is certainly much more than a storyteller; he is a professional humanitarian worker, a reliable colleague and a support for many people in need.

I wish you, dear readers, that you will let yourself be carried away by the stories into foreign worlds and cultures and that you will find something of yourself in the stories of other people's needs and suffering.

Have fun!
Dr. Michael Feit

Introduction

As the phrase goes: anyone who goes travelling has stories to tell. In this respect, I have an immense pool from which I can draw on. Since I have been working in the areas of humanitarian aid and development cooperation for more than twenty years, I have been active in various countries, regions and contexts. Whether triggered by the forces of nature, armed conflicts or simply poverty, the common factor was the need for immediate humanitarian action or longer-term support for the people and societies affected by catastrophe.

At a party, someone like me is a hit, at least at the beginning, and can impress others as soon as I begin to talk about my adventures. It is not only my daily work, but also the circumstances that are immensely different from those back at home. Above all, I can score points with funny events or incidents. And: the notion of working in an area that has either been hit by a natural disaster or where an armed conflict has been and is being fought sounds dangerous and spectacular.

Certainly, a portion of love of adventure is part of why I work in these places in countries or regions that are certainly not a normal holiday destination. On the contrary, these were mostly places, for which travel warnings had or would be issued. Who can claim to have been to a war zone, experienced a terrorist attack or witnessed the effects of such at first hand? On the other hand, who travels to countries that end in -istan? Sounds way too much like the dark Orient, suicide bombers, or other such dangers. The same applies to areas that a natural disaster hit. For me, these environments were almost part of everyday life. At the same time, they were always strange to me at first, sometimes surreal, but at times somehow dangerous. In addition, where I worked was usually the focus of international media. When do you ever meet someone like me personally who has a direct connection to these events and who was able to tell you first-hand impressions or stories from such incidents?

How many times have I heard the sentence that I would at least do something useful because I would help other people? It was more or less by chance that I encountered this field of work. Namely as part of a call for volunteer work in refugee camps in the former Yugoslavia in 1994, although I, at that time still a student of political science and history, had actually looked in the newspaper for personal vacation destinations for the coming holidays - what a paradoxical beginning of my career as a humanitarian worker. Actually, I applied more out of curiosity, as it sounded spectacular to me. The organization selected me and a little later, I started to work.

Then it was clear to me that I wanted to work in this area after graduation. What I should do afterwards with my master's degree, I had never thought about it anyway. Some might describe it as naive, others as haphazard. I would describe it as an unforeseen perception: the right inspiration at the right time. Fate? First, my academic degree ended with the fact that I had earn my living as a gardener and truck driver. Fortunately, I then received a tip about another option to study for a Masters in Humanitarian Assistance. I decided to apply and managed to get on the course. Less than four weeks after having graduated, I started to work as a project coordinator for foreign aid at the headquarters of a German aid organization. One year later, the organization sent me to Serbia to open an office and my professional career abroad had begun.

In the meantime, I have learned that there are definitely personal conveniences working in the fields of humanitarian aid or development cooperation abroad: a higher salary due to allowances and having a more senior role that I acquired relatively quickly, and for which I would probably have had to wait years to achieve working back home. After all, I started as a project manager in Serbia, which on the one hand was quite a jump in my career - because there I suddenly had the most responsible position. Above all, that meant that I had to take decisions that I could not discuss with colleagues. I was all alone. On the other hand, at the time I really did not know what kind of responsibility I was taking on.

Even though I was the head of the organization, a very experienced local colleague whom I hired right from the start took me by the hand and taught me many of the tools that laid the foundation for my professional career. In the beginning, I was simply uncertain and excited. Every situation, no matter how small, seemed to be an overwhelming challenge for me. Suddenly I became the one who was responsible, was spoken to and had to answer questions. It took a while for my own tension to subside. In spite of this, I was never able to take it off completely in the period that followed, as I was always the team leader in a new environment in subsequent missions for other aid organizations. Therefore, I kept seeing myself always as a beginner. I have certainly grown professionally since then and have now achieved a certain calmness that, from today's perspective, occasionally makes me smile if I was too excited in one or the other situation at the time. At the same time, I found out for myself that I really enjoy working in this area and that I have personally found a kind of fulfillment, at least in professional terms.

However, it should not hide the fact that behind this there are often serious disappointments or different experiences that I had in the context of disasters. With all my dedication to those in need, I noticed in the course of time that aid organizations also compete in the market of misery and act accordingly in an entrepreneurial manner. My initial naivety that everyone working in this area acted solely out of compassion or humanity and, above all, free of charge (!) for the benefit of those in need, shattered step by step. After all, I have now understood, money counts always. So pure greed for profit? Certainly not at all. Because somehow the assistance has to be paid for. In addition, not only the relief supplies, but the necessary personnel. Aid organizations are not immune to this either. Nevertheless, I experienced the one or the other behavior that I would have expected tough business people to do. Instead of expressing condolences in the face of a death in the family, for which I, working in Sri Lanka at the time, had asked for special leave to attend the funeral, I only received the answer that the desk officer would forward my request to the HR department! Later, only my line manager expressed his condolences. I would like to meet the humanitarian worker on duty who has not yet experienced any frustrating moments - occasionally just encountering disasters.

That is exactly what I want to tell you. Less in the form of a field report, in which I describe what I gradually experienced. Rather, I describe my encounters in different countries based on recurring aspects, chapter by chapter. I particularly focused on anecdotes and other interesting episodes. Because they not only spiced up my own everyday life, but always left me with fond memories. I think they are well worth sharing. Even today, I have to smile about the one other occurrence and then I notice repeatedly that I have not only experienced a lot, but also seen a lot of the world. Besides, they should draw a picture of what my job consisted of. Nevertheless, the individual sections follow a kind of chronological pattern: from deployment to return.

The title disastrous encounters is quite complex, but also to be viewed ambiguously. On the one hand, disasters form the framework in which my various encounters took place. On the other hand, the encounters, whether with people, cultures or objects, were sometimes disastrous, too.

Before any assignment abroad, I had to find an employer, thus an aid organization. Overall, many different relief organizations deployed me. Times longer, up to two years. Sometimes shorter, just a few weeks. I already had bizarre encounters, from my point of view, during the selection process. Later in the field, I had experienced the perfidious way in which people sometimes provided aid. Once on the spot, the story was often about me as a German abroad and respective admiration that I often experienced as a result. Hence, I will raise some peculiarities that are supposedly assigned to Germans as stereo types. In fact, I realized that these were frequently unsubstantiated. Surprisingly, people also assigned me to other nationalities, which always left me smiling. By contrast, it was and is more problematic for me to name an exact job title.

Encounters with foreign cultures and traditions I was not familiar with were also not always easy. Only over time, did I understand and learn that I could by no means expect my own way of thinking and working one-to-one from others abroad. In any case, they have broadened my own horizons. Once, no twice, I even witnessed an actual rain of money (!). How I was always accommodated during the mission also seemed worth to be mentioned. Not only did those accommodation encounters differ in terms of comfort, but also with regard to the odd landlord - in some places even too exotic animal housemates. The primary purpose of all my missions abroad was to implement aid projects of various kinds. During those project encounters, I worked with many international and local colleagues. One even went so far as to say, I would have changed his life!

According to my own perception, I have never been in immediate mortal danger. Yet, I had all kinds of encounters that my adrenaline level suddenly rose and that were dramatic. Especially when I witnessed a terrorist attack firsthand. I evidently successfully ignored such concerns when I was all of a sudden in the middle of a real revolution.

It is true that my craftsmen encounters were far less spectacular. However, no less in terms of peculiarity. The same applied to the bureaucracy in the various countries, which was sometimes practiced surprisingly for us. Unexpected for me were my leisure time encounters. Despite all the misery, I also had a lot of fun. Especially when I was with people who had nothing to do with my work. I learned paragliding in Serbia, but also had a crash. In the end, the return encounters after my missions never turned out to be easy. After a certain period of getting used to it, I kept looking for a new job. In doing so, I had to learn that professional advancement back home was hopeless. Not only once did I hear from the employment agency the following sentence: "Mr. Fischer, you have to be clear about this: we cannot help you!"

After what felt like an infinite number of unsuccessful attempts to gain a professional foothold at home, I always went abroad again. Because of my practical experience, this became easier. At least it gave me the chance of new disastrous encounters.

Finally, I may add that the following is actually, what I have experienced, in a few individual cases also being told by others. However, I do not want to embarrass anyone: therefore, I mentioned neither aid organizations nor former colleagues by name.

1. Encounters with employers

In general, aid organizations enjoy a good reputation in public. In the event of a natural disaster or armed conflict, they deploy personnel to provide assistance as soon as possible. Whether it is a remote country or an ongoing war: aid agencies are not afraid of either the one or the other to alleviate the hardship of the affected people.

Most of the aid organizations I have worked for are non-governmental organizations (NGOs). As the name suggests, they are usually independent non-profit institutions that are neither state nor formally affiliated with state institutions. While more experienced NGOs usually immediately get in touch with institutional donors, such as the United Nations or the European Union, in the event of a disaster, many, especially smaller, aid organizations often finance their projects from collected donations. Sometimes the religious denomination plays a role, where proselytizing is the real objective under the cover of humanitarian assistance. I saw this with my own eyes in refugee camps in Croatia in 1995, where I was a volunteer. One day young American Mennonites came, showed the residents a film about the life of Christ ("In it you can see how Jesus worked!") and provided Bible studies to children. The preacher was standing in front of the young audience, holding a packet of cookies behind his back and only those who had paid attention received one. Just like in the circus - reward after successful exercise. Personally, I perceived such a behavior quite inhuman. Instead of helping people, the Mennonites misused their plight for their own ends. It is true that it was a welcome change in the miserable everyday life for the people in the camp, but afterwards everyone was still somewhat confused. Another volunteer, a retired German Army soldier, was particularly upset. Because he had, a 32-year-old mentally and physically disabled son at home who would never have said "Papa" to him. A Muslim family lived in a nearby house and had a 10-year-old daughter who suffered the same fate. Not only did she look like a five-year-old girl, but also she could not move or articulate at all. Therefore, I admired the way the family cared for their daughter and sister with great devotion. There were five of them in one room and the girl kept making noises that I could never read. The family does. After the film show, my fellow volunteer colleague approached the Mennonite leader and shouted loudly so that all the refugees around could hear. He prompted the leader to pay a visit to the disabled girl in order to see if he could heal her by mere prayers. Of course, it was a provocation that I still found cool. After all the Mennonites refused to come!

In the same year 1995, I worked for a short time during the war in Bosnia and Herzegovina as a volunteer in a refugee camp. The organization deployed me as the first volunteer to find out whether it made sense to expand volunteer work there, even though the war was still ongoing. Later I concluded that this was necessary at any rate, although at the time I was actually not aware of what the real goal of such volunteer assignments should be. Retrospectively, I realized that my mere presence as a foreigner helped people. First, they probably got the feeling that they were not left alone in their miserable situation.

In addition, after I had gained their trust, they told me about their problems and thoughts that preoccupied them every day. In the camps was no one who could listen to them, because they all shared the same fate and similar stories.

In Bosnia, I lived together with comparatively moderate Mennonites in a house whose owner had fled and did not charge any rent! I usually sat in the evening with an American woman, also a Mennonite, but not strictly religious, on the balcony having an after-work beer. One evening a colleague of hers interrupted our conversation with the words: "I think it is great to be here, because I can see every day what is possible through God." Somewhat puzzled, neither of us understood what he meant because we had talked about a very different subject. Therefore, I replied that it would be best for him to tell a woman in the neighborhood who, along with her husband, had lost all three sons in the war. I hope she would kick him out immediately!

Nevertheless, for the vast majority of religious aid agencies in the event of a disaster, the denomination or the belief of the people affected play no role whatsoever.

In addition, there are aid organizations that only focus on certain areas. For example, Doctors without Borders, who are primarily active in medicine, or those who have made a name for themselves over the years in the scene in other sectors, such as water, hygiene or the distribution of aid supplies and have developed the corresponding skills. Those different types apply to foreign as well as local aid organizations, so that their number may well exceed several hundred (!), as was the case in Bosnia and Herzegovina or Kosovo at the time.

Whether an organization already has structures on site or whether it breaks new ground in the event of a disaster often plays a significant role. A few charities, such as the Red Cross or Caritas, are represented almost everywhere in the world, so their advantage is that they already have sister organizations in most of the disaster-hit countries. In an emergency, you can immediately obtain information for which other organizations first have to send teams in order to get an overview. In addition, the local partner often provides staff to help or supports the recruitment of suitable staff. I took advantage from this in several assignments.

On the other hand, often those local organizations were more active in medical care and nursing or pastoral care and not necessarily specialized in disaster relief. Usually, the development of the appropriate capacities will then be part of an assignment on the part of a foreign sister organization. In spite of this, at least in the immediate aftermath of a disaster, they turned out to be valuable resources, especially in logistical terms, giving them a time advantage over others that one should not underestimate, not to mention the local language. However, it can also lead to problems, as I had to experience several times myself.

The local partner expressed demands, which should be met, because supposedly the foreign partner organization had enough funds available. In Sri Lanka, for example, the local director, a lawyer, asked me to get him "kindly" a company vehicle, which I simply refused to do. Further, the local partners always assumed that we would easily finance their own planned projects. Either an intervention should only support a certain population group, for example Catholics, without any evidence of particular need or the planned measures were far outside of our mandate, let alone possibilities. In Kosovo, the responsible project manager of the local partner demanded that we should persuade companies from Western Europe to settle in Kosovo. Because that way we could create countless jobs!

In addition to NGOs, there are numerous so-called government organizations, in Germany for example the German Corporation for International Cooperation (GIZ), which conducts long-term development cooperation. Sometimes they too either act themselves in the event of a disaster or act as donors for other NGOs.

Finally, the same applies to the major international organizations of the United Nations: The United Nations Office for the Coordination of humanitarian Affairs (OCHA); the High Commissioner for Refugees (UNHCR), the UN Children's Fund (UNICEF) or the World Health Organization (WHO), who also carry out their own activities in their respective fields of work, either themselves or together with NGO partners besides their coordinating function.

Most well known in Germany are NGOs in the context of appeals for donations on various television channels, especially after major natural disasters or armed conflicts. Often, they already provide help where others would at best cause a scandal under international law - for example in the absence of a UN resolution. At the beginning of 2013, there were already numerous NGOs based in Turkey, which provided aid to Syria from there. At the same time, the UN had no mandate and was accordingly not (yet) on site. The general rule is that an affected country must ask the international community for help so that aid organizations can take action. However, this also means that the respective state or state bodies usually take on the coordination or decision-making of any activities. This was not to be expected in Syria, since the Assad regime would hardly have agreed to support opposition areas, since, in its opinion, these were areas occupied by terrorists. Therefore, only a decision by the UN Security Council formed the necessary basis for taking action there. Nevertheless, several NGOs had even sent expatriates to Syria beforehand to implement aid projects in the middle of the war.

It remains to be seen whether this always makes sense in view of the great dangers for employees. Nonetheless, it is exactly what makes the NGOs most special: they are all close to people in need. They assist them; mitigate their miserable situation, regardless who it is. They are the megaphone for the victims of war and disasters, the poor, the underprivileged, people with disabilities and, in general, the disadvantaged in the world. At home, they name the victims so that their fate is no longer just one of the many far away, but actually becomes tangible as well as understandable. They stand up for their support, run all kinds of campaigns, collect donations of all kinds and on the spot, they try to do their best for the benefit of those in need. Rightly, many well-known celebrities or politicians make their names available to an aid organization in order to generate even more attention and collect funds. Being on board, whether at home or on site, gives everyone who works for an NGO a feeling of actually doing something meaningful.

Exactly this phrase I have heard countless times. Not products, sales or turnover figures count at first hand. No, it is about people, to help they survive in an emergency or to get them back on their feet in the aftermath of a disaster. That is what humanitarian aid and development cooperation have set out to do: improving living conditions, fighting poverty, and in fact changing and improving the world to a certain extent. Who could mind?

Since the overwhelming majority, especially of the large NGOs, finance their aid operations through government donations or donations from other donors, such as the EU, people sometimes accuse them of merely acting as an extension of politics. Because only very few generate such high donation income that they are not exclusively dependent on institutional support. The latter is often only awarded where appropriate financial pots are set up, where it makes political or economic sense (or is motivated accordingly), where one ultimately benefits or could be affected in the end (German companies?). Keyword: refugee crisis. Unfortunately, those people fall by the wayside who, due to forgotten conflicts, are living a dire existence in the bitterest poverty even after decades - for me the best example is the Congo, although I have never been there. Occasionally the media reports of clashes in the country, but nobody or politicians in the

West seems to care, even though millions of people have died there because of conflicts. Obviously, elsewhere the Western world apparently has no direct geopolitical interest.

In practice, of course, this means that aid organizations are by no means loosely riding a wave of philanthropic sympathy, which make money automatically available to what is meaningful and good. Rather, they operate in a highly competitive market in which, not least, media interest or media attention to the outside world plays a major role.

Internally, aid organizations have professionalized technically as well as concerning personnel in order to be able to intervene, depending on the context of a natural disaster or an armed conflict. That is why it is now much more difficult than perhaps in the past to find even a career entry into this professional field.

As elsewhere, the recruitment process usually follows the same rules for aid organizations: job-posting, application, (hopefully) invitation to an interview and acceptance or rejection. As I said, usually. However, my own experiences in the framework of applications to NGOs are peppered consistently with anecdotes.

For example, as I only found out later, at an evangelical sect specializing in proselytization, which had advertised a very interesting position. Not long after I had applied for the position, the organization invited me to an interview. Although I should have been knowledgeable about interviews at the time, I remember all too well that I went there with mixed feelings. Because my research on the internet about the possible future employer had not been very fruitful. During the interview, four men sat across from me: the president of the organization, the vice-president, the head of political affairs and the managing director. As soon as they introduced themselves with their functions, I had to smile inwardly, because they sounded as if I was sitting in front of the representatives of a huge organization. At first, special emphasis was placed on my religious attitude, which culminated after some twenty minutes in the fact that the President snapped at me, he had now constantly asked whether I believed in Jesus Christ or the Bible, which I still did not answer clearly. Well, I owed a response. After the interview, I was only angry with myself, because I had not had the courage to confront the questioner by pointing out that I assumed I had applied for a job and not for the seminary! Instead, I sat facing the four men putting a good face to the matter and tried to get out of it as good as possible. Inwardly, however, my decision had long been made - namely that this job was out of question for me. Only once did I answer too flippantly. When they asked if I would take part in the daily Morning Prayer before the actual start of the working day. I replied firmly "No, in the meantime, I could go and smoke a cigarette." The clou of the whole story was that they wanted to employ me! I declined by phone and could literally feel the manager's jaw dropped through the phone.

Somehow, I have to be able to identify with the values of an employer, at least to a certain extent. In that case, it was impossible for me. After all, I was and am not a preacher and certainly not a religious fanatic. Apparently, that was what they demanded at the time.

In addition, I experienced that some organizations with a Christian background, especially when the denomination information was expressly required in a job advertisement for a position, also requested the corresponding prayer book. Before I sent an application to an organization based in Germany, I thought it advisable to ask first by phone whether it made sense to apply for the advertised position, even if I did not have the required denomination. Briefly, I got a "No" to hear.

Occasionally, however, in the event of a disaster, aid organizations are desperately looking for personnel and, carry out a rather shortened application process due to the time pressure. Then the focus is generally on professional experience and less on specific knowledge.

I applied for the position of project manager in the North Caucasus at a smaller German NGO, which invited me for an interview. My counterpart, the desk officer at head office, started the interview with the sentence, "if everything is right, what is in your résumé, you can take the job straight away." Somewhat surprised, I replied whether he thought I would cheat. After all, I would have good references to show that my previous employers would confirm. Ultimately, it was just about my experience in managing a project office and the associated team. Experience in the country of the assignment or any language skills played no role at all. After my counterpart had apologized for the overly disrespectful comment, he offered me the job. Since then, we had the kind of friendly and professional relationship, which you wish.

However, it also happened that an organization dispensed any competencies and qualifications as a prerequisite for a specific position, as the interviewer mentioned unexpectedly a completely different position in another country as if pulling a rabbit out of a hat during the interview.

In the early 2000s, I applied to a French aid organization for the job of program coordinator in Tajikistan. I had neither thought about the country nor the conditions there. I just needed to get a job again as soon as possible. After a positive telephone interview, I should come to the HQ in Paris. The travel expenses would be reimbursed, of course. During the interview, the man suddenly asked whether I would be willing to take on a similar position in Afghanistan - the country was still under Taliban rule at the time. What I had heard from there did not sound like a relaxed activity. The same also applied to my own constitution when I asked about the expected salary: around 800 euro gross (!). "This is the internal salary structure", said my interlocutor. I thanked him for the interview, wished the best of luck in finding personnel, and said good-bye. To this day, I have not received reimbursement for the travel expenses that were due.

After all, I experienced, in a way as a cheekiness of all the anecdotes, a flip-flopper when I applied at a German NGO. While I was on holidays abroad, I received an invitation to an interview, which prompted emails back and forth in order to find a proper date. Due to the active exchange of messages, my expectation was naturally aroused being certainly hired. I even cancelled my vacation earlier than expected. As agreed, I then phoned and waited patiently for the call back. Shortly afterwards, to my amazement, the interlocutor expressed a nonchalant rejection of the interview: "Unfortunately, there is no time at the moment and we would get in touch again if relevant positions are going to be published." Of course, such stories certainly happen in other areas as well, but at the time, I considered it necessary to reply. I wrote that I would mention this episode in my book that is still to be written with the title 'Professional Unprofessionalism' and would dedicate at least one paragraph for it.

If you are employed by a humanitarian organization, you usually get a contract that is either limited in time or depending on the duration of the project. Over time, I got used to the fact that an unlimited contract would remain a utopian imagination. Therefore, in principle, I went from one mission to the next. However, these did not merge seamlessly, so that my pension account has a few breaks, which I bridged with the help of the employment agency, if I was entitled to. Hence, I can confidently dismiss a carefree life like 'Florida Rolf'. The German newspaper 'Bild' had reported about him years ago, according to which he, Rolf, could afford excessive twilight years in Florida despite a low pension.

Form the start I adapted to with NGOs right was and is the rather relaxed interaction: to address each other informally was and is part of the normal tone. Unless you have a subordinate superior who, although far more introverted and much less extroverted, insists on the formal 'you' of his subordinate employees due to his position and, above all, management function. Once I was on a business trip with the mentioned line manager and by chance met a director of another NGO at the airport in Berlin, who was well known at the time in the German humanitarian scene. Years before I had completed an internship at his organization. He asked, in the relaxed you-jargon, how I was feeling, including subsequent small talk. Then he turned to my supervisor with the question: "And what are you doing at the club?" The latter blushed and mumbled somewhat embarrassed that he was my boss. Thereupon the director patted him on the back with an appreciative smile, so that my superior stood there completely perplexed.

In general, using the informal tone creates an atmosphere as well as a homelike feeling of familiarity and collegiality, in which, even as a newcomer to an organization, you could find access to superiors more easily. In addition, there was the dress code, which was and is very casual and loose, especially in smaller organizations. Mostly it corresponded and corresponds to anything but a businesslike manner in a suit and tie or fancy dress. In my experience abroad, especially the younger humanitarian workers handled this extreme. Often enough, I met relevant contemporaries whose appearance was more like that of an alternative living community than a serious organization. Admittedly, I was not and still am not a white-collar professional. What I just said about my young colleagues still applies to me today, at least to a certain extent. Not for nothing, I was stared at from time to time when I was working for a governmental organization in Turkey, in which the management position, at least for some visitors from the headquarters, automatically included the appropriate outfit. In all these years, I had only worn a tie once (!) for work, which I had even bought only for one occasion. Namely when I introduced myself as well as the organization to the Serbian Ministry of Foreign Affairs. My local colleague at that time said afterwards that the cotton wool suggested a particularly "hideous taste" on my part!

The sometimes too obvious display of looseness and collegiality should not hide the fact that even small aid organizations function according to certain rules and hierarchies. In my experience, mostly similar: while the head office is more responsible for administration and communication with the donor, the respective field offices implement the projects on site. Depending on the organization, communication therefore usually takes place via a sometimes-sophisticated reporting system, which usually takes place monthly; However, I also had to submit reports that were sometimes weekly or fortnightly.

During my first deployment in Serbia, still under the Milošević regime, I was able to experience those reports were not always read, but sometimes just ended up in a drawer. Slobodan Milošević had been President of Yugoslavia since the late 1980s and many people considered him one of the drivers of the war in Bosnia & Herzegovina (BiH) due to his increasingly prominent nationalism. In the course of the revolution in Serbia in 2000, he was toppled and later transferred to the International Court of Justice in The Hague. There he died in custody in 2006.

For months in my weekly reports, I had repeatedly outlined the political situation in which the Democratic Opposition of Serbia (DOS) had played a major role. Almost every day demonstration marches passed through Belgrade in front of my eyes. When I came to headquarters after nine months, meanwhile the regime changed in Serbia completely, the responsible project coordinator asked me what DOS would actually mean? I was almost tempted to tell her that it was a computer program.

According to my experience, communication between the field and headquarters is a problem in every aid organization and every humanitarian or development worker can certainly tell a thing or two about it. The current possibilities of communication via mobile phone, email, Facebook, Twitter, Skype and the like are probably not entirely innocent, although it is almost impossible to imagine how work and communication was carried out before the Internet age. In any case, I can still remember well when you were not permanently online, but always had to dial into the network first, for example to send an e-mail. Then documents were usually faxed and international calls were reduced to an absolute minimum, as the costs were sometimes astronomical. In Serbia, my employer paid private telephone calls of up to ten minutes per week. Today, on the other hand, one is usually online via mobile phone, sending as a matter of course all kinds of documents by e-mail and even making telephone calls or conferences over the Internet for almost no costs. The permanent accessibility as well as the much lower costs than before naturally reduce the inhibition threshold to communicate briefly with the field or vice versa. In social networks, where aid organizations present themselves and their work in almost real-time in order to attract their fan base and potential donors - all that is missing is the 'Like' button for disasters!

Overall, the tasks here and there are extremely complex. Often enough, however, the headquarters lacked understanding for the field. In my experience, this was often because people did not view the staff in the field in particular as equal members or employees as those in the head office. At first glance, it was even understandable. Because usually an office in the field only exists for a certain period of time and therefore the staff is also only employed temporarily. When I was working in the headquarters of a German organization, my supervisor at the time once said that the foreign employees, especially the German ones, were merely "overpaid vagabonds" who changed employers just as he changed his shirts! It was foreseeable that this would not lead to a friendly relationship with him. He was released shortly afterwards.

Although I have never heard a similar statement anywhere else, I often enough felt like a foreign body when I was abroad who somehow did not seem to belong to the respective organization. Until I understood how the organization functioned at headquarters, who had what task, I usually only found out when my employment relationship was almost over.

On the one hand, it would of course have been desirable for me to have always a longer-term contract. This would at least have secured my regular income and thus made longer-term personal planning possible. In addition, I would have had the chance to get to know one or the other organization much better over time. As a result, I would certainly have been able to develop an identification with the employer and establish closer contacts at work level, especially if there had been a good climate in addition to acceptable conditions. Nevertheless, I was never someone who insisted on the terms of the contract or the tasks set out by the various employers. I always tried to do my best.

On the other hand, that shuffling from mission to mission had quite positive sides. Because over the years I had got used to only being employed on a temporary basis. The subsequent job search was part of everyday life for me, so that, unlike perhaps employees who had worked for a company for decades, suddenly after a layoff, in my case the end of the contract, I did not have any existential fears. From today's perspective, I think that it was even an advantage for me to know different employers. Not only was I able to look at different aid organizations and their working methods, but I also became aware of how diverse the actor landscape was and is. All too often I have met long-time employees of aid organizations who thought that the world was only around them and, in their organization, namely at headquarters - that is why I always told young colleagues that they should change employers once.

The 'somewhat strange relationship' always became clear during visits from the headquarters. Visitors hardly noticed my local colleagues, let alone that they could call them by name. Instead, some visitors saw them only as a kind of service personnel who were just good enough to carry their suitcases. I experienced this particularly blatantly in Sri Lanka, where even the colleagues from the main office in Colombo bossed my subordinated colleagues around permanently.

On the other hand, especially in Montenegro, when I was working for a smaller organization, I experienced an appreciation from my colleagues at headquarters for my employees, which was unique to date.

Overall, I met numerous employers with whom I had both positive and negative experiences. However, this is probably also the case in every other field of work. Nonetheless, the opportunities for advancement that I experienced were unique. Even a beginner at the head office of an aid organization, after only a year I was the head of a newly opened project office abroad - admittedly: apart from me there was initially no other employee anyway. Since then, I have mostly held the management position, once even leading a team of almost one hundred employees without my own secretary or assistant! At home, you might stay in the same position for years or decades before moving up to a leadership position. However, one should by no means imagine that this automatically means that one would get a very high salary. Nowadays, such rapid opportunities for advancement might only be possible in comparatively small aid organizations.

In conclusion, I can probably state that the smaller the organization, the higher the perception of one's own performance. At the same time, however, you also have to deal with a certain unprofessionalism, especially as an experienced person. The larger the organization, the less attention it pays to one's own performance. You are just one of many. However, there the expression of professionalism, especially with regard to all possible processes, is clearly more visible; in other words, the bureaucracy. I do not judge the latter negatively, especially since in one case, as in the other, one mostly deals with public funds, for which one ultimately has to prove their proper utilization. The type or size of the organization does not matter. Although I enjoyed working for smaller organizations, I also noticed that larger aid organizations were not bad at all, whatever difficulties existed. Even when I was working for a government organization, one colleague once labeled me "non-compliant," which I proudly noted. This primarily related to my leadership style, which was more flat than hierarchical. In addition, there was probably my own dress code, which did not correspond to the usual one, and last but not least, my dealings with subordinated colleagues.

Overall, I managed to assert myself in both smaller and larger organizations. Nowadays I think that it is probably better to start with smaller relief organizations in order to learn to deal with all possible 'troubles'. Because in larger agencies, according to my observation, the demands of the employees with regard to a more luxurious life abroad are often much higher.

Even if the employer had turned out to be a disastrous encounter for me at times, somehow, I personally benefited in every respect. After all, one only becomes wise through experience. Nevertheless, as I once experienced with my own eyes, it is despicable that the employees of an aid organization pop the champagne corks (really!) as the bank account for donations grew rapidly in the course of an armed conflict.

2. Encounters with identity

Where do I come from and what am I actually doing? Don't worry, I am neither driven by identity problems, nor do I have a penchant for being philosophical; I have neither forgotten where I come from, nor do I question my work. Quite the opposite: people often not only identified me as a German abroad without even having spoken out, but also mostly surprisingly admired me just to be German. Occasionally, because of my pronunciation, one ascribed me to different European nationalities, especially in Serbia, which always amazed me. After all, my work is so complex and varied that I still enjoy it. Nevertheless, it is not always easy to explain in more detail my job or the exact profession.

Many people had warned me before, back in 2000, I set off on my very first foreign assignment by car from Germany to what was then the Federal Republic of Yugoslavia, now Serbia. "Be careful when you are asked where you come from! Just be careful", was yet harmless: "In any case, never say straight away that you are German!", had made me feel rather more uncomfortable; "Be extremely careful, because people could even get violent as soon as they find out that you are German," which put me in a certain anxiety state. The last days before my departure I received so many encouraging words that I felt like a kind of hero: I, the one who is now heading for the land of evil; on my own, because I was supposed to open a project office there in the first place. After all, Yugoslavia under the Milosević regime played a major role in the outbreak of the Balkan War in the early 1990s and later in the displacement of hundreds of thousands of Kosovars and various other crimes. The latter led to NATO military intervention in 1999.

At least, western media had drawn a corresponding picture. I remember there were reports that Serbian soldiers supposedly barbecued and ate children! In any case, since Germany was directly involved in the military actions against Serbia, I should show a 'low profile' – that is not state to be a German citizen too openly.

Well, theory is one side reality is the other. Because wherever I have worked in Europe to this day, almost everywhere I was one hundred percent identified as a German. Just as if it was written on my forehead.

Whenever I later stayed in a hotel in Serbia, the receptionist would say "Foreigner? German, right?" In Turkey, a man, who was apparently enjoying his digestive cigarette in front of a restaurant, addressed me suddenly: "Hey German! Where from?" I turned around: "Yes and where are you from?" He: "From Hesse (local dialect for Hessen, a German state), you won't forget that! (In German it rhymes with)." In Kosovo, too, people usually immediately recognized me as a German, although I did not even work for a German aid agency.

When I arrived at the border with today's Serbia, all the warnings went through my head again and I felt uncomfortable. However, somehow exactly the opposite happened of what people had foretold. When the police officer identified me as a German not only from my car registration number but also from my passport, he got excited. This completely unexpected reaction took a load off my heart for the first time. On the way, I had previously imagined all possible scenarios of what could happen: would I be allowed to enter the country? If not, what should I do? How do I react if people treated me too rudely? Whom can I ask for help if I need it?

Not only did the officer bombard me with all sorts of questions, a mixture of Serbian and a little English, which I only understood with great difficulty. Rather, he made his colleagues nearby with an appreciative look at the same loud voice that this, that was I, would be a German. Interestingly, not only he, but very often later also his other Serbian and Montenegrin colleagues had repeatedly asked the question during my numerous border crossings whether I had studied, which I confirmed. Then: "Did you really finished your studies?" which always left me a little perplexed, especially since it was just a degree. However, the respective officer reacted just as astonished as if I had been about to receive the Nobel Prize.

Back to crossing the border: The car was packed with personal belongings, additionally with all kinds of so-called visibility material (promotional items), such as pens, stickers with the logo of the aid organization, my employer, for whom I was supposed to work in the country. Thus, the police officer asked me if I had a present for him. I handed him a ballpoint pen, whereupon he let me pass winkingly with a smile. Proud as punch and rather relieved, I started the engine and drove off.

Incidentally, I have experienced the same thing as described here countless times during all of my missions abroad. Not only I as a German, but also Germany as a whole enjoyed such a high reputation elsewhere that it

41

sometimes even made me blushing due to all chorus of praise.

Especially on the Balkans, the countries of the former Yugoslavia or Turkey, either I met someone practically at every corner who had been in Germany himself or had relatives there. Most of the time, some reduced the image to simple platitudes: "Germany is great!" Others, who had never been to Germany themselves, expressed their respect, at least for Made-in-Germany products, against which no other could compete. Therefore, people would even pay a higher price for products. The fact that this had changed in a nuanced way in the era of globalization, when what is written on the outside often does not correspond to the inside, had apparently not yet penetrated in some places – German export industry can be happy.

Whether on the Balkans, Russia or Moldova: I had always bought cigarettes there for a fraction of what they cost in Germany. However, my respective local smoking colleagues thought I had brought them with me from home. The "ones sold in this country are anyway only qualitatively (!) minor copies, while the now lighted cigarette has a completely different aroma, you can feel that immediately", I heard too often - a placebo effect of a different kind.

On the one hand, most of the people I spoke to, especially in Eastern Europe, never gave a damn about the state of their country and even more about their politicians, ("All are corrupt!"). On the other hand, there was always a sense of national pride that struck a German of my generation as completely strange. Countless times, I watched a honking line of cars of a wedding on the Balkans, where people always proudly waved the national flag from the first car. When I asked why, the answer I always received was that "the flag is simply part of it". How things went together in the face of all the complaints about her never became clear to me. The locals, no matter where, were astonished that this was by no means custom in Germany. On the other hand, in the middle of Dushanbe, the capital of Tajikistan. A snobbish presidential palace had been built there, which thousands of residents had to give way through forced resettlement. Instead of hearing complaints about it, those whom I had spoken to replied with swollen chests that everyone could now see what their country was capable! The reaction of my colleagues in Kosovo was even more drastic when I once pointed out that their home country was high up on the corruption world rankings. That could not be true and if it were "After all, there is corruption elsewhere too!" Only gradually did I understand that my colleagues had taken publicly accessible information as a very personal insult. Because of this, the colleagues were of the opinion that I could not stand their country as well as them. That was absurd and peculiar for me I never had encountered before or after.

Often enough, I had to answer questions about a wide variety of aspects in Germany, which frequently caused me to find it difficult to explain: How exactly does the asylum procedure work? How is the social security system organized in Germany? What exactly does the three-tier school system mean? Up to: why are we Germans the way we are? In Serbia, a man once asked me whether there were conflicts between Catholics and Protestants in Germany. This question astonished me, since I or we, apart from perhaps fundamental ecclesiastical questions, would never ever think of such an issue. When I replied that we could not even tell who was a Catholic or a Protestant, he was somewhat amazed. In the former Yugoslavia, you can often recognize from the first or last name whether someone is a Serb, Croat or Bosniac or of the Orthodox, Catholic or Muslim faith. At the latest with such questions, however, I noticed that I was in an environment that had internalized completely different ways of thinking or approaches that I myself did not have on my radar.

At times, however, conversations were absurd when people brought history into play. In 2002, a very young Serbian woman told me that she generally did not like Germans, and even hated them, because they had all voted for Hitler. Why she then worked for a German aid organization, of all things, she answered inexpressively. When I replied what she would say if I said the same about her compatriots, after all, had voted for Milosević, she was quite sheepish.

More often than I would like, I met mainly young men in the countries of the former Yugoslavia, who immediately greeted me with "Heil Hitler" (!), which they probably wanted to use primarily to express their knowledge of German. Obviously, they never understood my harsh reaction.

By contrast, I remember an interesting conversation with a young, highly intelligent civil servant, political scientist and lawyer, in Pakistan. His hobby was German military history. "How did we in Germany deal with war heroes à la Rommel, the desert fox of World War II? Whether monuments were and will be erected to honor him or others and whether they would still play a role of whatever kind today?" he asked me. He himself had never been to Europe or Germany, but would like to visit the theaters of war above all, as they would fascinate him. Although we talked very stimulatingly, the topic he had suggested was not exactly one of my areas of interest and thus, I suppose, he was probably not very much impressed by my sparse answers. He had one more question that would be burning on his nails: why, after the victory over France in 1870/71, did the German Empire only incorporate Alsace-Lorraine and not all of France! Hereby he had caught the historian and conchie on the wrong foot, who could only reply succinctly that there were certainly more burning current topics that should be of interest to him.

By the way, he had also drawn my attention to a supposedly historical incident. Several people mentioned that independently. One evening I went into the dining room of my small hotel in Islamabad, all the employees, without exception, were sitting spellbound in front of the television and watched the prestigious duel between Pakistan and India in a game called cricket. Immediately, everyone got up to leave, whereupon I said that their presence didn't bother me, since I'm not interested in the game anyway. Apart from the fact that the game could sometimes last for five days, I had no idea about the rules and it was more or less unknown in Germany, let alone ever shown on television, I said somewhat impishly. Imagine

45

the same in Germany when Germans play against Dutch kickers. In any case, all of them reacted completely baffled especially when I told them that the sport was widely unknown to us Germans. How come, all of them unison inquired, especially since the following story was circulating in Pakistan - the highly intellectual Pakistani just mentioned had drawn my attention to the same story. In the past, in Hitler's time, the German would have lost against the Pakistani National cricket team and afterwards all German players were summarily shot because of the disgrace they had caused!

In Kosovo, I was able to experience the curious image of Germans several times, especially in summer, when the immigrant workers came home in big cars to spend their holidays in their (former) homeland. My colleagues always only spoke of the 'Schatzis' (a German word similar to sweetheart). Men in Germany always wear white ¾-long cotton trousers and typically consume an energy drink in cafés, apparently those 'returnees' explained to their fellow countrymen who had stayed at home. When I found out about it, I began to pay close attention to it, and in fact, I was able to detect it to a high extent. At least for the trousers I could tell them that it was certainly not true. In view of the fancy cars that were presented up and down the street, especially in the evenings, including loud music, I could only say that none of my friends would drive such 'big' cars, let alone own them. Apparently, people borrowed most of them so that the holidaymakers could show their compatriots at home that they had achieved something. In any case, a colleague said the following to me: an Audi smells like credit, a Mercedes like mafia!

Sometimes it went so far, however, that the actual reality with regard to Germany was either completely hidden or simply not believed. In Montenegro, I had to explain to a colleague that the 'Black Forest Clinic' was just a TV series (in the 1980s) and by no means an actual hospital. In Ingushetia, when I mentioned to a colleague in 2004 that there was a considerably high level of unemployment in Germany, he simply acknowledged this with "That is not possible and thus doesn't exist!"

Faster than I sometimes liked, I almost became a bogeyman when I tried to straighten the image of Germany that strangers had drawn. For instance, that it is not the case as a newcomer to Germany to receive automatically social assistance, as a young Roma in Serbia claimed in 2000. As far as he knew, anyone who came to Germany would receive a lot of financial support. This would still be higher than any salary in this country (in Serbia), he claimed. Therefore, he would try to go to Germany to work in any case. Even my suggestion that as an illiterate he would have no chance there, did not let him abandon his plan. I could not blame him. Because he lived, actually dwelled, with his family in a former slaughterhouse that was completely ruinous and had no sanitary facilities at all. In 2013, a Syrian colleague was visibly astonished that not every German would have a BMW or Mercedes in the garage. Further, the Syrian woman who was told by friends from Germany that every Syrian refugee family would get a "home" (!), she meant a house. By contrast, in 2014 in Pakistan: I met people, who neither knew where Germany was nor even sensed Germany was a state!

Occasionally I heard from my colleagues in Kosovo that I was behaving in a typical German manner. Funnily enough, a few years earlier a young American colleague in Sri Lanka had once told me that I was anything but typically German! It was never quite clear to me what such statements were based on. Only once, when I asked a colleague in Kosovo whether she could do a certain task and I expected a clear yes or no, she only replied that this was now a typically German question. So straightforward. Similar to what we know from Asian countries, the Kosovars maneuver around. Especially when you do not get an answer to a question, people just say something so as not to lose face. If typical shaking of the head is added, namely in contrast to us: shaking the head if one agrees, while slight nodding corresponds more to a negative, the confusion is fully perfect. The same thing, by the way, in Sri Lanka: if a local interlocutor followed a conversation or was asked a question, this was expressed in permanent shaking of his head. At first, I was never able to figure it out.

In Serbia, people not always recognized me as being German. Primarily, it was because I had learned the language to such an extent that, in fact, I could not hold any scientific discourse. However, my vocabulary was enough for more than everyday small talk, whereby I understood a lot more than being able to articulate myself. Within a relatively short period, people assigned me to three different nationalities.

First in a restaurant that was just across the street from our office in Belgrade where I often went for dinner. One day the waiter I knew gave me the menu in Cyrillic, whereupon I asked him to give me the English one, because "I can't read those in my hands", I told him. Completely puzzled, he answered: "How come, as a Russian, you don't understand the menu?" I had ordered it in Serbian and, now completely puzzled, I could not classify at all why he suddenly declared me Russian. Should I have taken this as a compliment or not?

A little later, as usual, I took a taxi to go to an appointment within Belgrade. As is so often the case, I did not tell the driver my destination because, in my experience, very few actually had detailed local knowledge. Therefore, I gave him to understand that I knew the way; he should just follow my instructions. Thus, we somehow got into conversation and the taxi driver asked me where I came from. Foreign countries were clear, but not from which country. When I asked what his guess would be, he specifically replied "France"! I replied, how he came up to such a prompt answer, he said, my Serbian accent would be typical for a French person, whereupon I started laughing aloud. Already then and later, locals had told me that I had a very good accent, which was probably due to my ability to pronounce the rolling 'R'. Once in Germany I wished a Bosnian a good morning, to which she replied in her language and only had to realize much later that I was by no means to be classified as a native speaker, namely her own. After all, her remark made me quite proud of my language skills.

Curiously, I experienced a déjà vu on the later return trip in another taxi. Because, as before, I got into a conversation with the driver. This time that one stamped me as a Hungarian! I would have a Serbian accent that is very typical for Hungary. Then I went over to answering the question about my country of origin with 'European'. In any case, I was not wrong.

Speaking of taxis: after having been in Belgrade for months and going to appointments by taxi in the city many times, I usually asked the driver for an invoice at the end. There was a taximeter, but almost every chauffeur asked what amount to write on the receipt? Then I always said in Serbian that he should write down the amount that the taximeter was showing. The drivers constantly acknowledged this grumbling, astonishing or even furious: "I beg your pardon? ", which, in turn, had initially confused me repeatedly. I thought it was a cultural peculiarity because people reacted so amazed or surprised to a normal instruction. Until the day, a driver told me about it. In Serbian, writing means pišati and the command form pišate, at least that is what I assumed. That is why I always said pišate and the corresponding amount. However, the correct form of command is pišete. As a result, I had always instructed the driver to piss the amount that is to urinate!

After any linguistic misunderstandings, at least my origin was clear. Eventually the question of my profession always arose in such conversations. I would work for a humanitarian aid organization, was my standard answer, which always triggered respect or benevolent recognition from the other person. Most of the time, people could imagine what I was doing. Depending on the type, the catastrophic situation was usually the number one topic of conversation anyway.

In general, the term aid organization triggered a positive reaction from the other person: "Really?" "Honestly?" whereby the tone of voice indicated a high appreciation. Then I always had the feeling that people established immediately a completely different relationship with me, the foreigner. I was no longer the usual stranger in the taxi, but was informally addressed and wished good luck for the work. Admittedly, that always made me a little proud, especially at the beginning. However, hardly anyone knew what the actual job entailed and even I had problems explaining it exactly. Even if people asked at home, what do I do for a living? Normally you might then answer that you are an engineer and work at company X, a locksmith at company Y or a baker and have your own business. Unfortunately, it is not that easy for me, so that I always had and still have problems naming my exact job title.

Personally, I always associate the term 'profession' with an activity for which one is undergoing education and completing it with a corresponding certificate. Although I have a few university degrees, it is difficult to find or use the correct term for them in practice: it is still easy for studying political science that is political scientist. However, I do not work in an academic environment, nor do I specifically deal with politics as part of my job. It becomes more difficult with the Master in Humanitarian Aid. The job of 'humanitarian worker' does not exist as such and may sound like carrying out basic or simple activities. Perhaps you think more of those who distribute food parcels in huge refugee camps in Africa or elsewhere, as you see it often enough on television. In addition, I have not only worked literally in crisis or disaster situations, but also in development cooperation. Crisis worker does not seem appropriate either, as one might think of a psychologist whom married couples or other people consult in crises. When it comes to the term development worker, you tend to think of someone who, for example, supports or guides farmers on site in agriculture and thus has the necessary professional background. The Master of Science in Development Management, which I obtained while working abroad, seems supposedly to be easier. Because depending on the environment, it is more likely to indicate my actual job. However, how do I translate that into German? Development Cooperation Manager? Hardly possible. In addition, the following often happened: when I entered development cooperation as a search term as part of a job search in Germany on the Internet, I usually received technical jobs, such as software or product developer or the like, which was not very helpful. In the meantime, I have switched to always providing project manager as my job title, which is less of a job, but more of an activity. Still, it most likely matches my work. However, experience has shown that I have just as little success with this, at least on the German job market, since a professional background, for example as an engineer or trained business administrator, is usually a prerequisite for project management in the private sector. Yet, my career sounds rather exotic and people did probably not acknowledge too seriously in terms of project management, although the work does not differ significantly from that in the private sector. In my opinion, it is often even more complex in many ways than someone might imagine.

Starting with the environment. Usually, one works in the areas of humanitarian aid and development cooperation abroad. However, you are rarely in such places where German tourists want to relax, let alone could. Especially in contexts of crisis or conflict, one moves in an environment that is not very pleasant. Be it after natural disasters or armed conflicts: the sight of colossal destruction on the one hand, or the latent hassle between different population groups on the other, which as a foreigner usually cannot even be noticed, are constantly accompanying you. That is why you often take oppressive feelings with you into the evening, and people have to find their own strategy to deal with them.

I still remember too well when I came to the affected area in 1999 after two severe earthquakes in Turkey, a few days after the second one in November. Above all, the images of the buildings either completely collapsed or leaning against each other I firmly memorized in my mind. Almost all of them had in common that the former ground floor no longer existed. Erected on supposedly much too thin columns, where either a garage or a small shop had been located, the remains testified that the quake caused the houses and the thin girders to collapse like matches. Good for those who were not there at the time! Within seconds, the earthquake had destroyed not only life but also existences, livelihoods. It is one thing to see such pictures on TV. It is another to see it with your own eyes. Suddenly I realized that this was real. Not only a single one, no, hundreds, thousands, an entire region. At the same time, however, I was also amazed at the strength with which people were able to cope with such blows of fate.

One of my German colleagues, who survived the earthquake at the time only by fleeing the hotel, afterwards stayed overnight for several months in a Mercedes station wagon! Because he no longer trusted any building. I myself, who had not experienced the catastrophe first hand, now in the country, initially, unlike my colleagues, completely lacked that feeling for vibrations. It happened quite often when we wanted to take a short break in a tearoom, for example, and while I was standing there with the cup in my hand, my colleagues suddenly ran out of the building. They immediately noticed even the slightest vibrations, while I stood completely unsuspecting and was only amazed at the small waves in my glass, although I was holding it calmly in my hand: Greenhorn got off cheaply!

In addition, the greenhorn, that is I, committed quite a faux pas back then. I had organized my trip to the disaster area weeks in advance. Then the second earthquake struck and I left from Germany two days after it. Before I took off, a TV team at the airport (Wow) interviewed me! Moreover, a live radio interview via satellite phone from the city center of Düzce was planned for the next day at a set time. The earthquake had hit the city of Düzce severely. At that time, satellite telephones meant you had a small box, about the size of a laptop, and an antenna. This first had to be set up and the antenna aligned with the corresponding satellite. Too bad that we, my colleague and I, had been held up by an appointment on the way, so that we had to stop at a motorway exit shortly before the agreed time, kilometers away from our actual destination, namely Düzce. The city is located about 300 km east of Istanbul and 50 km south of the Black Sea, in the north of Turkey. Of course, I could not admit that we were unfortunately still in the middle of nowhere due to other appointments. Therefore, when asked about the situation, I began to draw an imaginative picture:

Total chaos reigns, people buzzing around, cars curving around rubble, plus the residents who camped next to or in front of their former home and in general there were a lot of people on the streets because there were still constant aftershocks (what my colleague had whispered in my ear). In addition, security forces who would do their best to decrease the existing chaos. After all, the bad weather makes the overall situation even more unbearable for the observer: the cold and the simultaneous rain, thus a weather in which one does not want to send a dog outside, would present a pitiful picture. That is why people needed urgent assistance: in the form of accommodation, but also beds, mattresses, blankets and the like. "Thank you very much for this brief current assessment of the situation," said the moderator, we packed up, got into the car and reached Düzce a little later. Well, there were indeed many people on the streets, but I did not get the impression that it was all too chaotic. In addition, the police had blocked the city center completely so that, for instance, large excavation machines could get into the worst affected parts of the city unhindered.

Fatal, however, were my suggestions as to what kind of assistance was necessary. Apparently, the telephone wires in the headquarters were running hot, as many people actually wanted to donate beds, mattresses, clothing and all sorts of other things. However, such donations in kind were associated with far too high personnel and logistical efforts, especially in view of the distance between Germany and Turkey, to be used effectively and efficiently. That is why financial aid in the form of monetary donations was and is always easier to handle, namely by buying the necessary relief goods directly on site, if possible. It also supports the local economy. Due to the many offers of assistance over the phone at the head office, people there were anything but 'very amused', which I was told rather harshly. Incidentally, I suddenly had to extend my visit in order to replace an older, experienced colleague at short notice. He had experienced the second earthquake up close and decided to leave at once because, in his opinion, earthquakes were too perfidious. One cannot control them or one's own behavior due to their immediate occurrence and be at their mercy for better or for worse. On the other hand, according to the experienced colleague, at least in war or conflict areas one can adapt to the situation by leaving the house or not. Therefore, he decided to leave. I could not blame him.

The safety of employees is the top priority, especially in crisis contexts either that were preceded by an armed conflict or which is still ongoing. The organization for which you work usually has corresponding regulations that have an eminent effect not only on your work, but also on your private life in the field.

Due to the existing danger of kidnappings, for example, we were forced by the authorities in Ingushetia, a Russian republic in the North Caucasus, not only to have the office continuously protected by armed guards, but foreign aid workers were only allowed to move with appropriately armed escorts outside the office or your own accommodation.

Therefore, I was under constant observation, so that a real retreat into private life was hardly possible. If I stayed at home and had visitors, for example, the guards automatically knew who came. Even though inviting someone to dinner may not sound like a disreputable thing to us, the rumor mill started to simmer immediately. The next day, my local staff always knew whether I had spent the evening alone or in company. Who knows what they had imagined? In addition, UN had classified restaurants and cafes in Ingushetia for security purposes, so I could not go where I wanted. Excursions into the city were out of question and local colleagues mostly did even shopping for my own needs. A pleasant way of spending your free time to compensate for the daily stress at work certainly looks different.

Working abroad in disaster situations also means that you usually are in an environment that is characterized by a completely different culture and tradition. In general, people just tick differently than one is used to at home, which was not always easy to accept for me: the political situation, which was mostly anything but flawlessly democratic; all kinds of media that were much more politicized and mostly presented no image of reality; religion, which often played a considerable role and which one should approach with respect, even if one is by no means a believer; the importance of family cohesion, which in some countries leads to a 'clan economy' in which the so-called blood revenge is literally taken and practiced; the widespread marginalization of women who are at the mercy of men in every respect; the importance of a male ancestor, which often leads to the fact that the birth of a daughter initially triggers a certain disappointment; people with disabilities who at first glance don't seem to exist because they are locked away and sometimes even viewed as God's punishment. Even after so many years, I am always amazed at how different people tick. Above all, what was and is visible to me is the careless handling of waste, energy and generally dealing with fellow human beings. People threw chewing gum paper or other packaging away on the street, even if a rubbish bin is nearby.

Even in midsummer, in Gaziantep/Turkey all parks were watered daily - and not too scarcely. The handling of the heating was similar. As soon as it got a bit colder, this seemed to be reason enough to turn the heating up to full capacity immediately.

In particular, I noticed this in Tajikistan: there it can get very hot in summer and equally cold in winter. For colleagues, this meant turning on the air conditioning all day in summer and letting it run to 30 degrees (!) room temperature in the autumn. If, for example, I was shopping in a store, whether in Kosovo, Serbia or elsewhere, or queuing at the bank counter, and it was actually my turn, it often enough happened that someone simply asked in between, and he or she was served immediately. I always found all of this to be quite uncomfortable. While I saw this behavior as a cultural peculiarity, at least initially, I gradually moved on to informing the pushers or the operator that it was my turn.

Mostly, however, the foreign language is the one characteristic that causes the very first difficulties and often leaves an embarrassing feeling when one cannot even communicate in the simplest way: starting with the proper greeting to everyday shopping. Therefore, I was always dependent on translation, which the local colleagues did and they therefore played an important role. In the context of all my foreign assignments, I have never seen German being the 'office language', rather communication was always in English as part of the work in the field, both spoken and written. On the other hand, communication with the head office was usually in German, which frequently caused additional translation work, as only very few of the local colleagues spoke my mother tongue - in all these years, I have mostly been the only foreigner in the office anyway.

Consequently, my role was then to represent the respective organization to the outside world in the context of coordination meetings with other aid organizations and government agencies. It was common for me to come across VIPs that one only knew from television. In Serbia, I once had to cancel a reception of the North Rhine-Westphalian Prime Minister at the time. His delegation had invited me, but I enjoyed a long conversation with the Prime Minister the next day, including having one for the road in a hotel bar! I had been unable to attend the reception because I had promised a friend to attend his event, where a descendant of the Serbian Royal family, a real Princess, had been the main guest. It may sound arrogant in a certain way, according to the motto that Mr. Important, in this case my person, is evidently associated with the highest circles and could even afford to snub the high-ranking gentlemen from Germany. In reality, I had not received an official invitation to the Prime Minister's reception anyway. In addition, the fact that afterwards no one had asked me why I had been absent again testified my unimportance. I was somewhat, no, completely amazed, however, when I met my friend and the Serbian princess when she came to my local colleague and me. She greeted the latter as if they were closest friends. After my colleagues had introduced me officially to her, I was able to talk to her briefly. And? She thanked me for the support we were providing in the country and was generally interested in our work, which I appreciated very much. Because she took time for me without turning into mere small talk. At least from then on, I could claim that I had indeed spoken to a real princess!

Later I experienced a much more amusing anecdote during the opening of a branch of the German embassy in Podgorica, the capital of Montenegro. In addition to local important people and other Germans, I was officially invited. Among the invited guests was the head of the so-called European Monitoring Mission (EUMM) in Montenegro, whose main task was to observe the political situation and to document any human rights violations. I knew the director, a German, well, as we had met several times before. In order to signal a certain neutrality, members of the EUMM were usually dressed entirely in white. Hence, he appeared in 'service uniform'. On that day, my girlfriend from Germany came to visit and accompany me to the event. When I introduced her to that representative of the EUMM, she asked him what he did for a living, whether he was a doctor or a paramedic (because of the uniform). He emphasized his position in a rather offended but determined tone: "No, I am the head of the local EU monitoring mission!" At that moment the German ambassador, whom I already knew from my time in Serbia, stepped out of the building, saw me from a distance and called to our group: "Man, who do I see there?" Actually, his tone sounded rather derogatory, but, in fact, he meant exactly as if old friends met again after a long time. He came straight up to me and hugged me, whereupon the 'paramedic' looked quite astonished.

In addition to all the aspects that revolve around the job at work abroad, it is easy to forget that you naturally also leave your social network, family and friends at home. This is especially true when you go on a humanitarian mission. Because often enough these are so-called non-accompanied positions, which means leaving your partner behind. There should be aid organizations that only send singles to work. Primarily, this relates to the mostly unsafe situation on site and therefore (understandably) has insurance-related reasons.

In fact, especially during my humanitarian missions, I hardly met anyone who was there with a partner. Possibly, it was because that the 'humanitarian community' in the field often consisted of comparatively young people.

In this respect, I almost had a unique selling point, because throughout my career I always had my girlfriend and current wife at home. On the one hand, I then knew where I belonged to and had a point of contact, a home. On the other hand, I always tried to balance life abroad and at home. However, this often triggered not only stress but also frustration on both sides. For example, if the agreed phone call did not come through for whatever reason, or if there was a problem at home and I could not come to help quickly. In this respect, I lived a life in two worlds. The one abroad consisted of work with a smaller amount of leisure time, while the other was exactly the opposite. That meant that even when I was at home, I always had to keep an eye on my e-mails. Switching off properly from the job looks different. Amazingly, my wife knows very little about what I actually do for a living - at least I guess it is. Although I occasionally talk about the content of my job, just like her, we both try to avoid details unconsciously. Ultimately, I am happy about that. Somehow, we have come to terms with this, despite the frequent separations.

Nevertheless, a kind of idealism is the incentive for me, why I was stuck in this field of activity. In addition, there was certainly some sort of love of adventure and constantly new situations that I had to get into. Fortunately, my wife accepted it. Despite the harsh conditions, I have by no means lost the fun of work. To design an aid project and then to carry it out successfully was and is the main driving force for me in professional terms. To see that I was actually able to contribute to a positive change for people who were in dire need, certainly outweighed the associated inconvenience.

Depending on the situation, projects can be relatively simple, but also very complex. In both cases, the project manager is always a developer. Because, he first tries to find out based on the need or problem which type of activity may contribute to the solution. Remember that other organizations want to find out the same thing. Therefore, especially in humanitarian operations, the relief organizations try to coordinate their projects with one another in order to avoid overlapping or duplication.

When it comes to the actual survival of people, for example after natural disasters or armed conflicts, the first thing to do is to accommodate them safely, possibly to provide them with medical care and with the most essential items such as water and food. This can be a relatively manageable number of people, but often there are thousands, tens of thousands or even more people in need. However, humanitarian workers are not always welcome. In Serbia, I once visited a camp that consisted of makeshift barracks, where about two hundred and fifty Roma people lived in inhumane conditions. A man, apparently the leader, approached me and spat provocatively at my feet. He asked if this was again about taking the most terrible photos possible and nothing would happen afterwards. According to him, people had had to endure such visits countless times in the past. "If so, I should run off right away, because the residents were fed up with this type of tourism! "he insisted. I replied that I could not make any promises. At best, I can promise to try my best so that, given the circumstances, we can do something.

Because obviously some kind of help was needed. Indeed, afterwards we found the possibility of regularly supplying the residents with food parcels for at least several months. At the first distribution, the same leader came up to me again. I asked him if he remembered me. Beaming with joy and deeply grateful, he shook my hands and thanked me a thousand times.

Much more complex was the distribution of relief supplies, which I was responsible for in the North Caucasus. There we provided around 75,000 people with hygiene and household items who had fled from Chechnya and had lived in refugee camps or were scattered elsewhere in Ingushetia. It was not only important to find out where the respective people were, but also to organize this months-long distribution in logistical terms. In addition, the action had to be coordinated with other aid organizations as well as the state authorities and the proper purchase of goods had to be always adapted to requirements. People simply look for new, better circumstances in their miserable situation. For us, this meant that the lists of people in need had to be updated almost every week, because suddenly some were no longer there, while others needed to be added to the list. After all, we wanted to prevent the relief supplies from falling into the 'wrong' hands. Because in the end we were and are accountable to the donor.

The longer ago a catastrophic situation was triggered, the more extensive and complex the planned interventions can be. In other words: while, especially shortly after a disaster, whether caused by a natural event or a conflict, when it comes to human survival, mainly material goods such as food, water or medicines are delivered. The distribution is organized in the same way. Afterwards the focus lies more on reconstruction. Then there is a need of specialists such as architects or lawyers. And when it comes to building or 'restoring' institutions that are still half-functioning, or, of course, in a somewhat idealized way, the development of society as a whole towards democratization, even more specialized knowledge and skills are required. Either the project manager brings them with him or knows how and where to use them. That is, he knows how to 'buy' it by means of external experts or consultants.

It is fundamental, regardless of the type of project, that the person responsible has knowledge of the project cycle management. This refers to the entire project cycle from the determination of needs, their written filing in the form of a proposal, acquisition of the necessary financial resources, and implementation of the project up to the evaluation of the results achieved. Aid organizations and donors now generally accept this approach.

Sometimes it is about projects that amount to tens of millions of euro, which corresponds to the turnover of many medium-sized companies. However, only in the rarest cases you do have employees who feel committed to the company's goals through years of service. That is why on-the-job training is part of the project manager's tools, too. This means that not only theoretical knowledge, the rules and processes to be complied with depending on the organization, but also, above all, knowledge of personnel management and, last but not least, the so-called intercultural competence (whatever you mean by this?). In addition, depending on the project at least some basic knowledge is required concerning the content as well as management.

The range of projects for which I was responsible for in all the different missions includes the following: distribution of humanitarian assistance, which were part of normal business, as we organized them in Kosovo, Serbia, Montenegro, Sri Lanka and Ingushetia; Drinking water production directly from a lake in Sri Lanka or the renovation of existing systems such as in Syria and Montenegro; construction projects, whether makeshift accommodation, renovation or new construction of several hundred buildings in Turkey, Sri Lanka, Serbia and Montenegro; vocational or school training in the form of support from local partners or grants for the trainees in Montenegro and Kosovo; income generation by supporting existing or new businesses in Kosovo, Montenegro and Syria; medical interventions from the establishment of so-called health posts in Kosovo to the treatment of tuberculosis for prison inmates in Moldova and Tajikistan; all kinds of agricultural measures in Syria and Kosovo; so-called community development, so that, for example, village communities develop a cohesion that one day they can not only take care of their own problems, but also solve them; and finally the organization of IT training for teachers in Montenegro, training measures for local aid organizations in Montenegro, Syria, Kosovo, Tajikistan up to measures that had to develop or further develop those organizations in Moldova, Kosovo, Syria. When I look back, considering all the different projects I have been involved, I am quite astonished myself: different countries, different contexts, and different measures. At first glance, that might sound impressive. However, that does not mean that I have become a professional in all of this. Rather, what counts is the ability to adapt to all those different situations and to coordinate the actual implementation in order to end all the planned projects successfully.

In addition to project implementation, the responsibility for all financial aspects should not be underestimated. The range here were small projects that comprised a few thousand euro, medium-sized measures in the five to six-digit range and finally more extensive programs for tens of millions of euro.

Overall, over the years I became an all-rounder or generalist, as I was mostly the head of the respective assignment. Therefore, the following statement applies to me: I have somehow done everything before, but actually cannot really do anything specifically.

In general, in my experience, in the area of humanitarian assistance, the contract terms are usually limited to a few months. Either in terms of time or depending on the duration of a project. That means I usually got fixed-term contracts. Over the course of 15 years, I had 13 employment contracts with six employers (some of them were renewals). With the seventh I immediately got an 18-month contract - the longest so far in my professional career!

Over the years, I have learned enough that I could not disguise my origins as a German; even if it was not burned into my forehead. I was also able to determine that the stereotypes that are so often rumored, such as hard work, punctuality, but also the directness of my compatriots abroad are widespread. Sometimes even a lot of fear, like in Montenegro back then: once my colleague in Montenegro at the time reproached his father for having returned home after a few years in Germany as a so-called immigrant worker in the 1970s. Now, it was 2000, "you lived in Montenegro and could lead a "so" good life in Germany". The father replied that his son did not know how things would go there. "Always work and even for a cup of coffee there was no time." He preferred to return home to have it a little quieter. Then his son told him that his new boss would be a German that was me, which his father apparently commented with a desperate "Oh God"! He wanted his son to understand that this would mean nothing but work. Our subsequent collaboration proved extremely fruitful, despite those fears. Not only had I prepared my colleague to the point that he would be my successor, but also since then we are also close friends.

Even more amusing, however, were the appearances, as in Kosovo, with which the immigrant workers who had returned home during summer displayed their 'typical' or new German identity. Since they do not exist, at least as far as I know. In spite of all of this, I have never come across a negative word about the Germans in any of my missions abroad. Quite the opposite: sometimes I encountered such an exaggerated image of Germany that made me blushing, aroused either great amazement or almost triggered laughter when the ideas completely bypassed reality. However, I could not blame most people for it, given their situation. I, on the other hand, was and am in the comfortable situation of being able to return home, at any time. To where I come from and where I am happy to belong.

It was and has never been very easy to communicate briefly my activities to an outsider. Even today, I have difficulties answering such a simple question as to what I would do. When I went to Israel privately years ago to visit a friend, he had advised me not to mention my professional activity when entering the country. Because as soon as you stated that you were working for an aid agency, the Israeli border police would immediately suspect you of working for the Palestinians and thus against Israel. I then indicated 'construction worker' as my profession, which is true in the broadest sense. After all, I help to 'build' changes wherever and whatever.

3. Encounters with culture

Most of the time I worked in countries that belong to a different culture area. Buildings, especially apartment buildings, looked different, as did the traffic signs. People's skin color was sometimes different, just as they were dressed in another way. Finally, the language. What are the people like? How they behave and what traditions they comply with, I believe, you will only be able to recognize if you work with them. Even when I was working in Europe, in the countries of the former Yugoslavia, I gradually noticed that the mentality of my local colleagues was very different from my own. Customs, religion and, especially, political socialization came into play, which were actually completely strange to me at first. Despite globalization and increasing digitalization, these aspects not only had a significant influence on the way people think and behave, but still determine people's everyday lives in many places. The fact that I had to take this into account and accept it sooner or later, no matter where I worked, was and is a learning process for me, which, however, I have still not fully completed, even after decades.

Because, I could not and cannot completely shed my own origin and mentality, which seems to be impossible anyway. However: occasionally I had met colleagues in my own or other organizations, about whom it was usually said that they were in German "verbuscht" (actually this is a reference or exaggeration to people living in the outback where no formal behavior is required); who had been working abroad far too long and had evidently adopted certain modes of behavior. For example, a German colleague in Sri Lanka, immediately after arriving at the field office, ordered the first local colleague rather rudely, an architect, to get his suitcase out of the car. Further, in the North Caucasus, where a representative of an aid organization always wore flip-flops to attend highly official meetings with ministers. There, too, I met an American woman whose mission was finished. Hence, I asked her if she would go home to her family first to relax. She replied, actually, she does not have a home and would probably go to West Africa somewhere, which I found rather sad. Although this has less to do with mentality or culture, it showed me where a long professional life abroad could lead.

After a short time in almost all jobs abroad, my own as well as my colleagues' mentality clashed inevitably.

I got always angry about the tardiness not only of them, but also of others with whom we had arranged a meeting, for instance. Whether initially in the Balkans, the North Caucasus or Asia, people generally seemed to have a different view on this. I was only able to adopt a certain sedateness over time. However, if it went so far, as in Kosovo, that colleagues usually came late in the morning and wanted to leave shortly before the 'official' end of the working day, possibly not completing assigned tasks, then such an attitude still bothers me today.

At the time, the colleagues in Kosovo had to enter their working hours in a time sheet. Calculated over the course of the year, there would sometimes be weeks of absenteeism that could not be tolerated. People had an employment contract stating clearly the required working hours. By contrast, the colleagues got upset every day that nothing works in the country, so as a foreign organization you have to set an example, I told them. Finally, in view of the generally poor work situation in the country, one should be happy to have an above average and, above all, regularly paid job. These were my arguments. However, I often came across a lack of understanding. The working hours are just a formality anyway: a few minutes do not matter; it is by no means a fraud, it is more important that work is done; that possibly more could be done - "what, more work!" - did not seem to make sense to anyone. Obviously, people grew up in an environment that was characterized more by tradition than progress, more by improvisation than organization and more by paternalism than independent action and thinking, where professional promotion depended more on networks than qualifications and where education still does not seem to be as important as it was with us. Although I only gradually understood this, these were always seemingly never-ending discussions.

Nevertheless, the Kosovar colleagues said at the time that I should and must be "a little more flexible". Well, then I would be "a little more flexible" with regard to the monthly salary payment and would transfer twenty euro here in the one month and perhaps thirty euro less in the other. They immediately replied that this would not be possible according to the employment contract (!), whereupon I also took the employment contract and quoted from it with regard to the working hours, which precisely stipulated this. Eventually, there was no appreciation!

On the other hand, in all the other countries in which I have worked, my colleagues were not necessarily on time in the morning, but on the other hand, they did not always keep an eye on the closing time. Especially in Turkey during the war in Syria, this even put me to the test in this regard. My Syrian colleagues, refugees themselves, had nothing else in mind than to help their fellow compatriots in Syria who were suffering. Even under constant pressure, especially from calls for help from their homeland, they did not want to hear about regular working hours. If, for example, a meeting with Syrian compatriots from Syria or other partners took place either only in the evening or on the weekend due to logistical problems, I could hardly claim that it was too late in the evening or on the weekend.

It happened to me repeatedly that I had expectations of my colleagues on the job that they did not meet. Not so much because they did not want to, but rather could not. At first, this always led to frustrations on my part, because things did not go the way I had in mind. My typical comment was always "in Germany it would have been like this ..." Only over time did I realize that I should avoid comparing things with home as much as possible. Because I had to deal with the situation as it was.

If I gave my colleagues whatever task to perform, I initially always assumed that they would carry out as I expected it to be. That meant I could rely on the result to some extent. Unfortunately, however, I always had to review everything, indeed everything. I might as well have done it myself. Especially on the Balkans, I always secretly thought that people could endure any plague, but they did not want to make any effort. When I gave a report to my colleague in Montenegro to read, I could be sure that he would not read it. Or in Kosovo: we had worked out a fairly extensive project, namely a call for tenders for municipalities so that afterwards we could select four that we wanted to support (see below). The whole scheme dragged on for half a year and due to the complexity, I personally thought it advisable to write down the course including the problems, challenges and surprises that occurred, considering that the organization might repeat such a project elsewhere. Hence, I gave my 75-page text to my local colleagues to read so that they could correct possible mistakes and the like. After two weeks, not a single colleague had looked into it.

In Tajikistan, I was supposed to support an aid agency's financial coordinator in organizing his work better. After introducing myself to him at the first meeting, his very first request was to hire an assistant for him. After a short time, however, I noticed that he was everything but busy. In the personal final interview at the end of my three months, I told him that he did not need an assistant at all, because I would do his daily workload in the morning between the first and second cup of coffee. However, he did not want to admit it. "We Germans are simply used to a different pace, which I could not expect there. The Tajiks are different", he replied. I encountered his otherness every day and at one point or another drove me mad. Nevertheless, when I left, he claimed that I had changed his life! Unfortunately, I could no longer determine whether this had also had an effect on his productivity. Still, I felt honored.

No matter in which country I worked, I experienced a hospitality that is amazing compared to ours. Frequently, the invitation to have a coffee evolved to a presentation of all kinds of dishes and corresponding gluttony, after all, they wanted to offer me, the guest, something. This referred less to me as a German, which people still proudly emphasized repeatedly, but more as the responsible foreigner of an aid organization being invited to various occasions as a guest of honor. This happened mostly in the context of a project collaboration or after the completion of it. In 2001, I had the rare pleasure of being the only foreigner in Serbia twice to take part in Roma festivities. On one occasion, a businessperson who had delivered clothes to us invited me. Concerns on my part that this could not only be a conflict of interest, but also possibly some kind of corruption, he brushed aside with an almost indignant reaction. He invited me so that 'his people' could express their gratitude, as we had previously provided food parcels to displaced Roma. We did not enter into a business relationship afterwards, but I found a valuable contact in the town.

I attended his niece's engagement party and later the annual ball of his local Roma community, of which he had been president. Truly experiences that I will never forget. The engagement party, announced as privately, turned out to be an event with several hundred guests and seemed to follow the script of an ancient tragedy. All sorts of pomp and noise, a supposedly happy couple -

although I personally believed that the groom was homosexual, which I kept to myself as much as possible - as well as an impending family drama.

The event took place in a hall that apparently was a kind of community center, which you could see from the outside and, if you took a closer look inside, it had probably experienced its best times in the Tito era, decades earlier: plenty of flower garlands, attached to the ceiling, should probably redirect the dirty floor. In addition, the extended hanging items fixed with adhesive tape on the sides covered the seams of the wallpaper, which had already loosened. The two families of the bride and groom sat opposite each other at long tables, while the other guests sat at individual tables and benches in between. I was also placed there with my colleague. At first, I did not feel very comfortable. Because as the only foreigner present, every other guest not only seemed to recognize me immediately as not belonging to the community, but people seemed to be constantly watching me. I recognized a lot from the expressions of their faces, but I could not interpret them. Was it distrust, curiosity, hospitality or a warm welcome? Thus, for me the motto was to keep my head down and act like a normal guest.

First, plenty of food was served: all sorts of cold platters with cheese, sausage, salads and other starters, while the band played with their typical sounds, which are known from various Emir Kusturica films. The audience got slowly prepared for what was to come. Suddenly the bride and groom appeared and entered the room separately. While the groom was wearing a shiny gray suit, the bride appeared dressed as in a fairy tale from Arabian nights:

white silk blouse, harem pants and moccasins with the front tips pointing upwards. The surprise, however, contained her pinned up hairstyle. Inside were ten to fifteen folded 1,000 Deutsche Mark notes (!).

Not looking at each other, the couple walked through the ranks of those present with thunderous applause to their assigned seats. While the hot meal was served, the music began to play even more fervently. The band walked through the rows and a strange spectacle began. The men present started to cram bank notes, more Deutsche Mark than Dinars, into the musicians' shirts, trouser pockets and even into the instruments! My Serbian colleague and I were amazed, especially since the dancing men wanted to outbid each other filling the pockets of the musicians with money or, due to lack of space, let the banknotes rain over the musicians. The entire floor appeared to be paved with banknotes. A quick count on my part resulted in more than a thousand Deutschmarks just around me! A truly surreal scene entirely to the taste of Kusturica: Roma people, who are not even considered to be second-class people in the whole country, the vast majority of whom therefore vegetated in miserable dwellings with no prospects, celebrated here exuberantly and unrestrained; including a proverbial rain of money, so that one had to believe the end of the world would happen the next day. Until suddenly the music stopped and it became very quiet in the hall. Namely at the moment when the bride's father, already heavily drunk, stood in front of the groom's family table and talked himself in rage. Apparently, an intermediary had arranged the engagement, as my colleague explained to me. However, the intermediary was not present, which was an affront for the bride's family, who, by the way, came from a very wealthy family. Therefore, according to the bride's father, the matchmaker had to appear within the next two hours; otherwise, he would see the engagement as resolved, which led to great applause on one side and resentment on the other. Around me, I could literally see how the previously happy men now sat with grim expressions and seemed to be preparing for an argument. Abruptly the exuberant happiness was overturned. The mood was rather tense that we had to reckon the worst at any moment. My colleague and I therefore immediately decided to leave the event in order to get out of the possible danger zone and not have to attend a possible family feud as curious outsiders. On the following day, the businessperson informed us that in the end everything had turned out well. The matchmaker appeared later and the party continued until morning hours. At the same time, he thanked us for our feeling that we had disappeared at the right time.

Later he invited me to his Roma community's annual ball. This time the party took place in a large hall with more than a thousand guests and me again as the only foreigner. At first, however, the door attendant did not let me enter. Who could blame him; after all, obviously I was not one of them. However, he let me pass after he had received a rebuke from the host, who guided me to the table of the guests of honor, where several mayors from the surrounding communities were sitting. What did that mean? Why was I sitting at that table? At first, I was suspicious because I thought that I had to listen to the complaints and needs of those present in the guise of a party.

Possibly, I should even serve as a potential solver of existing problems. The representative of an aid organization that once provided help and might do the same thing again in the future. Therefore, when he introduced me one by one at the table, I was rather reserved. From today's perspective, I would simply say that you should not worry about it and just enjoy the evening; professional discussions should kindly take place in the office. At that time, however, I lacked the courage, because all of my tablemates were much older. Thus, I limited myself to small talk at first, while all other guests were very excited to see what would happen that evening. Fortunately, everyone around thought the same and was more interested in me as a person than as a representative of an aid organization.

Once again, plenty of food and drinks were served until after about an hour a moderator announced the climax of the event: the upcoming election of Miss Roma and somehow, my name was mentioned, but I did not understand why. Apparently, they had nominated me to be a member of the five-person jury that was to elect Miss Roma. Under thunderous applause, I went to the podium. Little by little, about fifteen women and girls walked by, their age range between about seven (!) and seventeen years, which struck me as a bit strange. All of them strode along the stage, festively, but also quite objectionably dressed - which seemed even stranger to me - , greeted the audience with a curtsy and after the pirouette they strutted out. The decision-making of the five-person committee afterwards, to which I belonged, was by no means in the style of a more in-depth analysis with a cor-responding discussion of the pros and cons of one or the other candidate. Rather, my jury colleagues had passed their verdict in unison after what felt like five seconds. After that, the first girl was clearly the winner, although the others elegantly ignored my personal preference, which was clearly for someone else. The moderator then announced the result of the decision over the micro-phone after less than two minutes. It had become clear to me in the meantime that the whole show was a pre-arranged game. Because even the order of the girls who appeared had been determined in detail beforehand and it was no coincidence that the later winner appeared first, while the last candidate to appear came from the clan of the previous year's winner.

In other words, attention was paid to that Miss Roma al-ways had to come from a different family every year and this time it was the turn of number one - that was the tradition, as the host kindly explained to me later. After all, I had the honor of slipping the 'well' deserved sash on the winner. I might have been too excited because I was doing it the wrong way round, which caused great laugh-ter. Despite this faux pas, every woman present seemed to have been tempted to ask me to dance. Of course, I could not refuse, so that the whole evening was quite ex-hausting in terms of fitness, but also brilliant. I spent a joyful evening that I had never expected at first. Just cel-ebrate a happy event without any ulterior motives or fears. In retrospect, it was an important experience for me.

In contrast, the two weddings in Ingushetia and Tajikistan, which I attended, were downright harmless, albeit with a tradition that was strange to me.

In one case in the North Caucasus, it was tradition that after the actual family wedding celebrations, the coworkers were invited separately to a festive dinner. In the house of one of our drivers, the groom, a banquet table full of food was set up just for about fifteen colleagues, where we sat and were served by the groom's younger brothers. Those apparently enjoyed their job, especially since they were now also able to marry. According to the tradition, the eldest son had to be married first before younger siblings could. Their mother began to explain to me that she was glad that her eldest was finally married. Because she would have believed that he might be "too stupid" (!) to do so. In no way did she whisper it in my ear; rather she said it in such a way that everyone present could hear it. I could hardly believe it and thought to myself that if my mother would say such things about me, I would be anything but enthusiastic. So, I felt embarrassed thinking that she was only telling me this because I was, in a way, the exotic guest. I signaled this to my colleague, who was translating, by opening my eyes, which he understood immediately. He also looked at it with a blink of an eye, following the motto: Just let her, she will know what she is saying. At least we could tell who was wearing the breeches in that household.

Funnily enough, my colleague, a trained psychologist who translated, had often meant precisely this bridegroom when he once again criticized his own compatriots or described them as "simply stupid". Then he, the groom, served as, in the opinion of the translator, a 'flagship Ingush'! Of course, I found that rather arrogant. How can you call all your fellow people stupid? My colleague simply replied that it apparently was so. No doubt, that he was highly educated and, unlike many residents of the region, he was born and raised in Chechnya. He certainly differed enormously from his compatriots or regional people. Even when I could understand his opinion in various situations, I found it difficult to see the motivation behind it. Was he just saying this to impress me and to present himself to me as being smart? Although I trusted him completely, his statements always left me with an ambivalent feeling. However, I had to agree with him on one point. He had told me several times that the population evidently believed that foreigners who were active in the region had already personally cut the largest piece of the financial pie. In other words, all foreigners in the region are corrupt. Therefore, they are anything but welcome. In no way did he mean the salary, but a kind of unwritten law, according to which foreigners would take a large part of the aid money in their own pockets. That was the consensus among the population, according to him. Therefore, the people and local employees would always look grimly. I could never really confirm whether this was true. In the case of our driver, the groom, actually I never saw him smile for a single second.

Back to the wedding evening. According to tradition, he, our driver, symbolically abducted the bride from her parents' house years ago to make it clear that he wanted to marry her. However, the bride's father in person would have picked her up the next day (!), as he probably did not agree with the bridegroom. Her son, according to the mother, would not have given up and not long afterwards 'robbed' his current wife a second time. This time obviously with a successful outcome. When in Rome do as the Romans do…

The bride, wrapped in a white dress with a veil in front of her face, entered the room silently and stood in a corner. I could only recognize that she was still quite young - so after the first kidnapping she would certainly not have been picked up by her father, but by the police, and the groom would have been punished for seducing of minors round here! One by one, my work colleagues approached her and talked to her. The aim was to coax words out of her mouth in whatever way. At first, they tried apparently with flowery words, but this was not successful. Only when banknotes came into play, her tongue gradually loosened. I did not understand exactly what tradition was behind it.

In Tajikistan, too, an employee invited me to a wedding celebration. Not his own, but his brother's and my objection that I did not even know him was ironed out, as was my question of what I should bring as a gift. Well, I did not see the bride there at all, as other women surrounded her, completely veiled, and covered with a cloth over her head in the living room, where various dishes had been available to the male guests beforehand. While only the men began to dance to traditional music in front of the house, inside the bride took a seat on the floor at the head of the room so that she could eat undisturbed. To protect her from the eyes of the strange men, a carpet hung from the ceiling right in front of her head. I watched the dancing outside. Then my colleague, who had invited me, came already very tipsy, a bottle of vodka in his hand, offered me to drink, I refused, and began to complain that he didn't understand what was going on with the other guests. According to him, in the past, vodka would have flowed freely on such occasions; he would have bought several dozen bottles now he was the only one who drank. Not long after, the music stopped abruptly, the men dispersed, and I was told to go to the car because the party was over! There were neither farewell words nor any 'official' announcement, instead all the guests left just as if the movie had ended. Only in the car, the colleague informed me: according to a presidential decree, no more than fifty people were allowed to be present at wedding celebrations and these could not last longer than three hours.

The party, which we were just about to leave, had lasted a little more than three hours and the guests therefore left without a word. People feared that the noise might make the Police aware. Admittedly, at first glance I thought this was a particularly peculiar "tradition". However, on closer inspection, this presidential requirement made perfect sense. Because in the past, in order not to scare anyone away, several hundred guests would have had to be invited to such occasions. The celebration would have been endless and all at the expense of the bride's father, who too often had to sell his own house or take out a loan. The state wanted to avoid those extravagant celebrations lead to financial ruin, especially since everyone there, being financially able or not, tried, possibly thinking or being obliged of having to outdo others!

In general, over the years I have come across all sorts of traditions, rituals, or at least in our eyes sometimes-strange peculiarities during various assignments abroad. When, for example, in northern Caucasus people were praying with a filled glass of vodka in their hand. This happened especially at business lunches, which irritated me the first time. The host greeted the guests, who all had their hands on the glasses, with various empty phrases. Then he raised his glass, toasted everyone and everyone drank in one gulp. He then filled the glasses again and continued with the actual topic of the meeting. Before the discussion, however, he made a toast and began to pray to ask God's help for the meeting. Another to your health! Further, the discussion began and at the end, they raised the glass again in thanks, no matter what the result was. At first, I thought that I had witnessed exactly that prejudice that you sometimes hear about the Russians. Namely, that they drink a lot of vodka. In reality, apparently, it was a kind of protocol, thus ritual, that people would strictly adhere to at such official occasions. After all, I had experienced that ceremony several times, so that the explanation seemed to be true.

It was similar when toasting and then clinking the glass. One should make sure that the glass touches that of the host a little lower. That way one would show respect to the other person. Incidentally, the same was true in Turkey.

In the North Caucasus, I immediately noticed the way people greeted each other. It is true that handshakes were also widespread among men when they did not know each other or were not very well acquainted with. However, friends, man or woman, stood next to each other and greeted by means of an embrace around the waist, something I had always enjoyed watching and nowhere else seen. In Kosovo and Turkey, men greeted each other by bumping their heads.

Those different welcoming rituals already held the first faux pas ready for me, which I could, indeed, had to tap in. For the first time, the director of a local aid organization and his female secretary visited me on the second day. He immediately offered shaking hands, which I did. Hence, I offered my hand to her. She, on the other hand, only reluctantly did it, demonstratively looking aside when I touched it. A dislike could hardly be expressed more clearly, which somewhat irritated me. Well, in Muslim societies the thing is that men should not touch women. I first had to learn that from my local colleague. If a woman still holds out her hand to greet a foreigner, it means that she is used to dealing with western people.

Especially on the Balkans and elsewhere people invited me home very often. The hospitality was always more than generous: only the best for the guest and even if it was a non-smoking household, people even insisted to light a cigarette. Most of the time I let it go. Back then, when I was working as a volunteer in refugee camps, I felt ashamed every time I sat with a family in their cramped room. Because, I was usually entertained by means of food or drinks. Usually, we volunteers hung out with people outside or in the large dining room. Verily, I experienced innumerable opportunities which made me feel embarrassing. Most of the time the room contained all of the residents' belongings, which they were able to take with them on their flight from Bosnia-Herzegovina. Nevertheless, when I sat there, people offered everything what they found. Sometimes they even forced me to try a piece of cake here and a cookie there in addition to various cups of coffee. If I was hungry, they could also prepare something for me. It was almost impossible to refuse anything, even though I did not want to take anything away from people of the little they had. Only over time did I learn that people resent the guest's rejection. Unless he has a plausible explanation or good excuse. More about that later. Regardless where people invited me during later assignments, most of the time it was not just the obligatory coffee or tea, but in cases where a woman from the house was present, she received sometimes the order to prepare at least one little meal in the kitchen. However, the sound usually makes the music. As men sometimes ordered, every woman's rights activist would have been outraged and even I found this not only archaic, but also extremely strange.

I still remember when, during my voluntary work in refugee camps in the early 1990s, another German volunteer demanded that we should especially strengthen women and their role in society. At that time, personally, I was confronted with this topic for the first time; I only replied to her that we could in no way change society. How right she was, however, I learned over the years here and there in particularly patriarchal countries. When I wanted to

87

hand over a wedding present to my language teacher in Montenegro later on, she escorted me into the living room, where I was supposed to chat with her husband, whom I did not know at all, while she went into the kitchen and later stayed away from dinner herself. The main thing I wanted to do was talk to her about everything and not about cars and the like with him.

There, my local colleague, who had invited me for dinner at his home countless times, even ordered in the beginning: "Wife, provide something to eat!" Magic words like "please" or "thank you" did not seem to exist. Moreover, even when I introduced this, both of them made fun of me by overemphasizing them in my presence - at least his wife kept us company while we ate.

For me, different countries, different customs also meant that sometimes people served local delicacies that were far away from being my own favorite foods or drinks. Either I took it as a courtesy or, if it looked too disgusting, I had to have very good excuses. In Serbia, after we had successfully completed a project, as it was custom, the local counterpart invited people to dinner and for me, as the representative of the aid organization, to be the guest of honor. In a village school in central Serbia that we had renovated, we first inspected the completed work as we walked through the building before the director led us into a classroom where almost the entire village community was already sitting together. After all, the aid received, the completely renovated building, people wanted to celebrate accordingly, for which some local specialties were prepared. At first, they served boiling-hot home-distilled schnapps in a tot, but a full glass. Nonetheless, I sipped from it putting up a brave front, while everyone else emptied it in one gulp. Even the few drops were enough for me to get a coughing fit. While everyone else was laughing, I inquired, whispering in my colleague's ear, whether it could blind you.

Further, there was sausage and cheese before they placed finally a complete, cold (!), pink suckling pig right in front of me. Well, it did not look appetizing. Anyway, I was not hungry at all, because my colleague and I had been to a restaurant less than two hours before. Nevertheless, as a matter of courtesy, I took one or two slices of cheese and sausage. Like a medieval knight, the headmaster tore the pig's tongue out with his hands. Only the best for the guest of honor. He offered it to me, which I declined with thanks, pointing out that I was very full. I did the same with the ears and cheeks, which now caused those sitting around me to pluck a piece from the animal by hand and in no time, it was eaten!

On another occasion in Montenegro, when provided a complete, boiled sheep's head to spoon out the brain, I was forced to refer to medical orders not to eat meat temporarily. While I thought I had pulled myself out of the affair, the host obviously took note of this smiling at me. He had read my face, but kept it to himself. Later, I was able to at least offer an exhilarating apology in the region when it came to refusing the obligatory schnapps: every time, whether in the morning, at noon or in the evening, regardless of the occasion, I was always offered a cup of coffee as well as a tot of schnapps, the latter "for health". I then replied, "No, thank you, I had already had a whole bottle for breakfast so that my daily quota was reached."

People accepted my refusal sometimes even vociferous laughing.

In Serbia, at first, I was in no laughing mood, because I had always been the one who had to pay the bill for my colleagues in the restaurant. They never even thanked me. However, much later, when a good-natured driver, father of four, wanted to invite us to dinner. I accepted gratefully, but insisted on paying the bill. Because I knew, that the driver's salary was anything but high. He, the driver, again very seriously and almost offended, explained to me that it was custom there that whoever "calls for dinner" should kindly also have to pay. Moreover, one would not say thank you among friends anyway. Aha! Before, indeed it was always I who was the first to ask the question about hunger levels, which my colleagues automatically understood as an invitation. From then we watched each other mischievously to see who would come up with the crucial question about the meal first. However, in the end I always paid anyway.

In Sri Lanka, I did that with pleasure. Whenever I visited one of our numerous projects that we implemented across large parts of the Southeast, I took an office colleague with me. They were solely responsible for administrative tasks and thus had almost no idea what we were actually doing. At least they gained an insight into the project work and now understood invoice receipts or other documents much better. One of the projects, the production of drinking water, we implemented near Arugam Bay, a place that appeared to have been very popular for surfers from all over the world. Therefore, many restaurants, in addition to local dishes, also offered appropriate meals on the menu for tourists, that is, western tastes. After visiting the project site, we always drove to the same restaurant and each time I asked the local colleague in advance, what he or she would order. I would take the bill. You do not know yet and after extensive study of the menu, everyone without exception, really everyone always chose curry with fish. It was rice with fish, which the colleagues ate every morning, noon and evening anyway! After we left the restaurant, I asked what the food was like and always got the same answer: way too expensive, way too little and way too tasteless - you have to know that their usual curry dish, because of its spiciness, was not eatable for me. In any case, every time was a total letdown for the colleagues.

In Sri Lanka every full moon day, the so-called Poya Day, was a non-working day, on which it was forbidden to drink alcohol, as was the case on public holidays. For example, if you bought alcohol that day, the bottle would be wrapped in a black plastic bag so that you could not see it, which was not easy to hide with a beer crate. Once I was with colleagues on a Poya Day in Kandy, a very important location for Buddhist pilgrims. For lunch we went to a restaurant, took a table on the terrace and my Belgian colleague ordered a beer, although he knew that he was not actually going to get one. To our amazement, the waiter said he could not serve beer on the terrace. However, if the colleague sat down in the restaurant, he would get one. Therefore, we sat his wife and me at the table outside and he was about two meters away inside and enjoyed his beer. A somewhat absurd situation.

We had already experienced something similar at the turn of the year 2005/2006. I went to Sigiriya, a tourist attraction in Sri Lanka, for a few days with some colleagues. There are ruins of a fortress on a 200m high monolith, a huge rock. You can climb it via dizzying stairs and indeed get a fabulous view as a reward.

The day before New Year's Eve, we were in the hotel restaurant in the evening. Alcohol, so the waiter, could not be ordered. We did not find out why. However, we objected that a man at the next table was obviously drinking a beer! Somewhat irritated, the waiter replied that that beer was a "misunderstanding". Well, he agreed, and then we could order beer, too. However, the beer bottles would have to be kept in the kitchen and he, the waiter, would always refill when asked by transporting the glasses into the kitchen. As a result, he kept running into the kitchen with an empty glass and coming back with the full glass. Many guests may have been surprised what strange food it was.

For New Year's Eve, we bought beer ourselves. We spent the evening in a relaxed atmosphere playing the card game UNO and had fun until midnight. Then New Year began and again, as a holiday, alcohol was not allowed to be drunk. Nevertheless, we played until the early hours of the morning and continued our game in the evening. Around 11.30 p.m. on New Year's Day, we were sitting, as before, in the common room of the hotel. I went to the bar to say that a few bottles of beer should be prepared so that we could toast the New Year again at midnight. Back at the table, we played until shortly before twelve. When we then signaled the waiter that he could bring us the order, he simply said, "Sorry, sir, but the bar is now closed!"

In other respects, too, a peculiarity was strange to us. Namely that of the silent protest, the so-called Hartal, which was comparable to a strike. If, for example, a member of a population group - there were Sinhalese, Tamils and Muslims living in our target area - was killed, the corresponding group at the scene of the event called out Hartal, which, depending on the severity, could last for several days. That meant that the streets were empty and all shops closed. You better did not hang around on the street: it happened to a Japanese organization that they drove unsuspectingly through a village where people had announced Hartal and threw large stones on their vehicle. For me, one thing was and always remained incomprehensible: on the one hand, the people on the street were extremely friendly. For example, when I passed other passers-by and smiled at them, they always smiled back. Unfortunately, I did not have the vocabulary even for a mere 'hello'. Nevertheless, I found such encounters fascinating myself. Then I thought of either home, where people pass each other without greeting, or the former Eastern Bloc, where people often enough looked at me grouchily from top to bottom.

On the other hand, the atrocities that people perpetrated in Sri Lanka were all the more incomprehensible to me. Violent crimes such as murders, most of which were probably ethnically motivated, happened almost every day. Once a local colleague called me in the morning, completely upset, saying he could not come to the office.

He was waiting at the bus stop in his village when suddenly a motorcycle drove directly towards a waiting man; the pillion passenger stabbed the man several times with a knife, poured gasoline over him and set it on fire. Panic immediately broke out and all bystanders ran away. The man burned horribly.

Even among my local colleagues in Sri Lanka there were ethnically determined animosities, which I only recognized at second glance. It is true that one or the other got along very well with everyone, regardless of whether they were Sinhalese, Tamils or Muslims. However, that was rather exceptional. On the other hand, there were many where I only noticed, either after a certain time, that they spoke very reservedly or not at all with members of another ethnic group. In my role as Team Leader, I was often forced, actually mostly, to settle disputes among local employees. It was always strange for me how established men suddenly sat in front of me crying. For example, a young colleague, Tamil, threatened one of our Sinhalese drivers that he would kill him (!). In my opinion, the trigger for this was rather insignificant. The driver took the colleague in his village in a tuk-tuk, the three-wheeled taxi moped, and apparently stopped a few hundred meters in front of the house of his passenger, as the Tamils' residential area began there and he did not want to continue for fear for his life. Therefore, the Tamil colleague would have told him that he would kill him, the Sinhala driver, next time if he did not drive him to the front door. Both men were just in their early twenties! When they were now sitting with me in the office and I wanted to find out the background, both began to cry and, in the end, only very reluctantly shook hands in an alleged reconciliation. I by no means believed that they would have made peace and buried their argument. Therefore, I gave them a very decisive say that I would keep an eye on them from now on. At least I did not hear about another argument. The irony of the story was that the very same Tamil colleague who threatened the Sinhalese with death had come to my office only a few days earlier. Because he had apparently received a death threat from the Tamil rebel organization LTTE!

Another time the following had happened: one of our office guards, who was on a late shift, was apparently a few minutes late for duty, but completely drunk. Whereupon a colleague accompanied him home and there, for whatever reason, immediately began to beat up his wife! Colleagues immediately informed me. The next day he sheepishly sat in my office and cried like a baby. In the meantime, I had learned from other colleagues that it was not the first time that the security guard had mistreated his wife. I could only feel sorry for her. Nevertheless, I wanted to dismiss the man for violating his duty, although we could expect that he would then only take his frustration out on her. Nevertheless, maybe that would be a lesson to him. I made this clear to him now. However, the local head of the partner organization, a lawyer whom I had consulted, contradicted the fact that, according to the law, there was no recourse for coming drunk to work. I could only argue that he was late for his work, which, however, is not a reason for resignation! How could that be? A security guard who can obviously no longer carry out his task, caused by himself, must be dismissed! What sign would that be for colleagues? No objections seemed to be an argument. The legal situation is just like that, the lawyer explained to me. Nevertheless, I was able to get rid of my colleague later. Namely by having him split up into different shifts in different places every day. Apparently, that was too much for him in the end and he quit. Unfortunately, that should hardly have helped his wife!

Despite all the cordiality that I undoubtedly experienced abroad as a German people sometimes meant it too well. In northeastern Montenegro, I stopped at a petrol station around lunchtime, whose restaurant (!) was widely known for its good food. However, people rumored that the owner belonged to the Mafia. As the only guest in the room and immediately recognized as a foreigner by the waiter, he asked me whether I was from Germany. I said yes, and he wanted to know where exactly. Since I did not feel like talking, I told him that little place I had grown up in, he would not know certainly. Although this is a similar word, he understood Maybach. Oh, that was strange, because his boss would drive a Maybach! I was just thinking how he would have earned this. So that I could somewhat feel at home (!), he put in German folk music, whereupon I protested vehemently because of the tootling. For my part, he could put in Turbo-Folk, as they called the corresponding national version of hits. At least I would not understand a word. He acknowledged this with a certain lack of understanding.

In general, I found some things quite strange on the Balkans. For example, also in Montenegro, where I worked in the very rural north-east of the country in the early 2000s and had to hear that medical care, especially in the remote mountain villages, was taken care of by a nurse on a horse - once a week. Hard to imagine if there were emergencies. Even with the car it sometimes took us more than two hours to get to some of the villages that were only a little more than twenty kilometers away. In addition, those were as good as inaccessible in winter! 21st century in Europe!

On the other hand, in Kosovo: when I mentioned to a colleague in 2012 that I had bought something at home in Germany and paid with an EC card naturally, he was completely amazed: "How? You go into a shop and don't have to pay in cash?" It seemed to me as if I had just told him about a close encounter of the third kind. He was the youngest of six brothers, five of whom had gone abroad as migrant workers. As 'Benjamin', that is, the youngest, he was evidently condemned to stay in his home country and guard the five houses of the brothers that were directly next to him in a line. I expected that his brothers would at least have kept him informed about such innovations as card payments.

Another Kosovar colleague seemed to be doing nothing but following international football in his free time. He could even easily list teams in German regional leagues. When I criticized the sometimes unbelievably high salaries of the players, he obviously heard about it for the first time. He could not believe it, although I replied, rather irritated, that such information was everything, but unofficial. Everyone would know that - apparently except for himself.

In all the countries of the Balkans, but also elsewhere, I often came across the view that the first-born child must necessarily be a son. If so, the party was frenetic. If not, people announced the birth of a girl more cautiously. This may have been the case with us in the past. It was only there that I learned that such views are still widespread and emphasized today.

Just like the widespread penchant for conspiracy theories. Not only there, but in all of Eastern Europe in general, I have come across this phenomenon repeatedly. Most of the time, however, on closer inspection or listening, it was a question of possible explanations of phenomena that could not be explained; apparently logical patterns that allow a certain behavior to be understood; or just excuses to distract from your own mistakes. What was common to all was the high level of distrust of everything and everyone.

When I worked in Serbia, with regard to politics the Americans were to blame for everything. Even discussions about the most bizarre topics ended with the fact that they, the Americans, were "definitely" behind it. Occasional power cuts only happen because one wants to force the population to support a certain policy. Which? Sure, the Americans. In 1999, the country was hit by air strikes. Who was behind it? The Americans. The supply in the country is so bad that most people have to live on the subsistence level. Why? Because of the Americans. And besides, the fourth plane of the assassins was shot down by the American military on September 11, 2001, only nobody in the world would take note of it - "There is enough evidence"; Tito was an infiltrated Russian spy, "enthroned by the Americans" (!), according to one inter-locutor. Anyway, the whole world was hostile towards Serbia.

Well, one could imagine that a few years after a cruel war had been fueled repeatedly from there, Serbia was not 'everybody's darling'. Even more than a decade later, the locals did not like to hear that. Hence, they picked out arguments that veiled their own actions or guilt as much as possible or offensively, mostly in an almost absurd way, justified their own actions.

At the very beginning of my mission, many Serbs asked countless times whether I would realize how bad the situation of the people in their country is. After hearing that I had already been to other countries in the region, people inquired as to where it was worst in my opinion. Of course, people always expected me to say that the situation was most devastating in Serbia. However, I always replied that the questioner should go to Bosnia and Herzegovina, then, because of all the destruction, he or she would immediately recognize where it was worse. Little by little, I realized at the time that I should avoid political discussions in the future. Because the reality was simply faded out: it could not be as bad as in Serbia anywhere else. After all, Bosnia and Herzegovina (BiH) would get billions from the international community. And Serbia? Nobody questioned the reason why. No matter what political issue it was about. I could never argue rationally. It cannot be what may not be.

With a smile, my colleague in Montenegro and I saw the very first lotto show on television. As in Germany, the numbers were determined using a drawing device in the studio. Previously, people were asked on the street whether they believed the device had been manipulated, to which a man replied "100%!"

In Montenegro, and even more so in Serbia, many of the locals spoke very badly about Albanians, which primarily meant Kosovars. If I ever meet them, I have to be careful because they are dangerous. In southern Serbia, where in some cities the majority of the population is Albanian; my Serbian colleague did not even dare to drive in with me in a car with a German license plate! I should not dare to stare after or even directly at a woman on the street. That could possibly cost my life; after all, people would still practice the so-called blood revenge there. However, no one could explain to me what all those warnings were based on. The only way I could figure it out was by gradually realizing that people based most of such claims on total ignorance. When I asked if there was a Kosovar in your personal circle of friends? Nothing. Have you ever been to Kosovo? Shortly driven through. Similar rumors circulated in Kosovo, where the vast majority of Albanians despised the Serbs. When I asked my Kosovar colleagues if they knew how Serbs would typically greet each other, not even one could answer. Which in turn led me personally to the conclusion that no matter where on the Balkans, any allegations and the like were most likely based on rumors. You knit your worldview the way you want it to be. We know that well enough in Germany, especially among right-wing populists.

A few years later, I was in Albania on a short assignment and visited a family that was actually threatened with blood revenge. A local colleague asked me to interrogate all sorts of questions, which should not be a problem. What happened? Apparently, the father of the family had killed someone. The reason for this was not disclosed. In any case, the murderer was sentenced and served a long prison term. Meanwhile, his wife and her children spent the whole day without exception in their own four walls, as they feared that relatives of the killed person would kill them as soon as they left the house. In the end, I did not ask any questions, because the situation was not only very depressing, but I also did not want to interfere in such personal matters. Moreover, the affected family might have expected support by me that I would never have been able to provide.

Later I worked in Kosovo. Especially at the beginning, when people asked me what impression I had of the country, I always replied with a casual saying "It's the Balkans." Hereby I wanted to express, that in my opinion, the country and its people were not much different to their neighboring countries. As in the surrounding states, there was a lack of ability to accept criticism – there was always someone else guilty for whatever. Self-criticism? Unavailable. The Serbs were always to blame for the whole misery. To a high extent, this may have been the case. However, these accusations comprised everything. Politicians enjoyed the same bad reputation as elsewhere and were all lumped together as a corrupt gang. Nevertheless, one or the other criminals made it into important political positions in Kosovo! Although initially accompanied by foreign colleagues, now, in 2007, Kosovar police carried out traffic controls itself and many seemed to be happy (again) to rip-off now and then; and there, too, one should be careful as soon as someone put the expression "no problem" in their mouth. Because, afterwards in most cases there occurred a problem. On the one hand, somehow familiar stereotypes that I seemed to know from the countries of the former Yugoslavia, in Kosovo it was somehow different for me.

At first glance, the sheer number of petrol stations was particularly noticeable. I was never able to find out whether those operated in a gray area, such as the petrol station mentioned in Montenegro, or whether they followed a common practice. From our office in the city, even those unfamiliar with the area immediately noticed that all of the shops that were right next to each other lined the roadside and offered the same thing. First plumbing, then shoe stores - interestingly, there were not any shoelaces or other accessories in them, because I had rummaged through all of them once. Then came the construction business and finally some pharmacies. You have to imagine that these stores were actually right next to each other. Even the assortment did not seem to differ. Just the name of the business. Why this is so, especially since, in my opinion, the shops mutually competed against each other's customers, a local then explained to me as follows: if a business was going well, the neighbor thought, it must be a good one and thus opened the same and so on. Perhaps looking for or offering a business niche or something completely new seemed to be unknown. Even a Kosovar colleague from another aid organization, who had lived in Switzerland for years, quit his well-paid job overnight to open a restaurant in the capital Pristina: "In view of the many foreigners in the

102

city, it must be a profitable business" he justified his step. Not only was the place very difficult to find, but it offered the same thing as almost all local restaurants: pizza, pasta and meat. He closed after three months.

When I was later in Turkey, I also noticed the phenomenon of shops next to each other with identical articles. There I heard, however, that this was definitely positive. Because, on the one hand, you know immediately where you as a customer should go and, on the other hand, if you do not like the price, you can go next door. Somehow a coherent explanation. In general, a lot in Turkey reminded me of Kosovo. Only it was a lot cleaner there.

In the daily work in Kosovo, three things were most noticeable to me: first, the lack of humor, which a Kosovar colleague frankly admitted to me: "We are simply different to Serbs in this respect". In fact, it happened frequently that ironic remarks by me were completely misinterpreted or not understood at all. Second, the blatant level of education of many, even my work colleagues, although some had a university degree. What we took for granted to know was not the case there: The city of Pisa? "Never heard of it" was the answer of a colleague who had completed a master's degree. Thirdly, what I finally encountered everywhere in Kosovo was a high level of expectations, of which the so-called international community could not have been entirely innocent. The immense aid money that flowed into the country after 1999, at least according to my observation, spoiled many people. Personally, I had the impression that they were simply making demands that foreign organizations in particular would or have to meet anyway. Ultimately, all of this was justified repeatedly with victimhood. Of course, no question that the Kosovar population had suffered considerably in Yugoslav times and even more so in 1999, the year of the Kosovo war. However, even my Kosovar colleagues in 2012 repeatedly argued that one had been a victim of the war, so one, in other words, the international community, had to help the country back on its feet. Even my work colleagues did not seem to want to understand that it was high time that the population or society should also make their own contribution.

It was always amazing to me, regardless of where I had been on the Balkans or other Eastern European countries, how naturally people tolerated rampant corruption. Almost unimaginable for us, everyone in a certain position seemed to rip-off now and then. Not only did it seem well known, but it also seemed to me that everyone accepted it as unavoidable.

In Serbia, the technician did not want to activate the telephone connection at all, but unashamedly demanded an extra fee for it. In Tajikistan, formerly belonging to the Soviet Union, I only came into the country when I paid a slightly higher visa fee, which I only noticed afterwards. In Moscow, I would not have got a plane ticket without flipping in the additional ten-euro note. Further, in Montenegro, where a colleague assured me after he had faced legal proceedings that he knew the judge! A Kosovar colleague took the biscuit by claiming that the entire construction sector in his country was completely free of any kind of fraud, after all, he knew his compatriots. Precisely this sector was under the most obvious suspicion that it had been completely soaked with corruption!

One of our projects there was renovating a school not far from the office. According to our construction specialist, for the comparatively difficult roof construction, we needed very specific wooden beams with a minimum diameter. Hence, we first visited possible suppliers in the city. When asked about the appropriate dimensions, the first replied that he had enough material in stock, which was stacked according to size outside. We went to exactly those woods whose measurements we needed. When we took measurements, however, we found that three centimeters were missing in each case. We made the dealer aware of this, whereupon he declared that it was correct. How come? He said all kinds of wood would be imported into Kosovo. The timbers would be accepted by customs at the border with the original dimensions, although they did not correspond to the actual dimensions. The difference from the actual size would benefit customs. Therefore, one has to label the beams differently in order to be able to collect these expenses again. Nobody answered me why not simply a higher price, the real one, was asked. In principle, it corresponded to the following scenario: suppose you have a carton of cigarettes consisting of ten packs with you at the airport and customs control checks you. The latter takes one pack and afterwards they say that there are ten packets of cigarettes in the carton, although there are now nine or fewer. I was unable to say who actually put the money in his own pocket in the end. It seemed to be a system everyone knew. Except for my colleague, who had claimed that the construction sector was the cleanest in Kosovo.

If I was asked to pay an additional 'administration fee', no matter where and depending on the situation, ranting and raving was not helpful, otherwise I would only have had to endure the anger of the other person or much longer waiting times. Although I might demonize or denounce this practice, in most cases I was by no means immune.

In general, everyone on an assignment abroad will try to avoid such practices as much as possible. Even then, you can be confronted by unsubstantiated allegations. For example, my colleague in Ingushetia explained to me the aversion of the population towards humanitarian aid workers by saying that they assumed that foreigners would only be active in the completely corrupt system if they already had received the largest piece of the cake!

In Kosovo, I once wanted to sell a vehicle of the organization applying a transparent process. Therefore, every interested party should personally submit a written offer in a sealed envelope until a certain deadline and could be present when the bids are subsequently opened. An employee of a local partner organization, who was also the only bidder present when we opened the bids, had secretly hoped that he would somehow be preferred. That is why he initially made a ridiculously low offer, whereupon I pointed out the procedure and the minimum value of the vehicle (according to the Internet) to him again. While his offer was then just one euro above this minimum value, another interested party offered more than two thousand euro more, so that the latter also won the bid. The present colleague from the partner organization had no longer nothing good to say about me and spread the rumor that I had made a "personal deal" with the person who had bid the most. He told this tale to his colleagues, all of whom, without exception, looked at me somehow strangely in the following days. No wonder conspiracy theories were rampant about anything and everything on the Balkans. Somehow, I could not believe all of this. I had applied a completely transparent process, which it was, and yet I remained the scapegoat.

Whenever I experienced similar accusations, I could not do more than emphasize the actual process repeatedly like a mantra. If that did not help, another characteristic that was very typical of the region usually appeared namely the silence or the complete break of contact. Sure, that happens with us, too. However, I had seldom seen that insignificant, in my eyes rather ironic statements, could, in the best-case scenario, lead to complete silence, if not even to a break in a friendship.

In Montenegro, a very good friend of my colleague had made a remark that was, in my opinion, rather trivial in my presence. If I remember correctly, it was all about the arts of skiing. Nothing serious, but flippant among friends. At first, I did not notice, but then it turned out that my colleague has not spoken a word to his former friend since then, almost fifteen years ago! A lot would have to happen before I personally end a friendship. There the inhibition threshold seemed to be much lower. Anyway, I thought it was childish - my colleague, incomprehensible to me, obviously not!

In all assignments, I have always tried to create an atmosphere in the team with a sense of humor. In most cases, I have succeeded. What I first had to learn, however, was the correct use of irony, because depending on the environment people either did not understand or completely misunderstand. For example, when my closest colleague in Ingushetia, the aforementioned psychologist, picked me up at the airport and greeted me, I always replied that I was finally back in paradise. It was he who himself mockingly called his adopted home that way in a personal conversation and actually meant the catastrophic situation in every respect. Then one of the drivers always shook his head. According to the motto, how can I, as the rich foreigner, only speak of paradise when the people there would have problems surviving the day at all? If looks could kill, I would certainly not have survived the mission there. From then on, I had taken to heart never to say anything negative in the presence of locals I did not know.

It was even more difficult for me when religion was the topic. Especially where I worked for a Catholic organization. The denomination played no role in my daily work, but local partner organizations in particular often insisted on preferring them, especially where Catholics were in the minority. I myself have always kept quiet that I had left the Church – putting up a brave front. Instead, I pretended to be Catholic. The fact that I had a Muslim colleague in Montenegro, for example, the local bishop could and would not understand. He also did not want to understand that we would not only support Catholics, but people in need, regardless of their beliefs.

I later experienced something similar in Kosovo, where I had to work much more closely with the partner organization. I always tried to avoid fundamental discussions about religion because, on the one hand, I was by no means familiar with the Bible and, on the other hand, in order not to lose my self-composure despite all the inter-cultural competence and tolerance. A discussion about the sense of divorce with an employee of the partner organization, a strict Catholic, who perceived it as a fundamental prohibition, since marriage is a sacrament, led to a tangible argument with said colleague. I tried to tell him that I generally found the option of divorce a good one, especially for those wives suffering from domestic violence. In this way, those women would have a way out. My interlocutor just could not and, above all, did not want to see that. Unfortunately, my own proselytizing did not work at all in this case to convince him of the advantages of a divorce. Rather, she left me with the question of which tricks religious missionaries might use to induce people to change their beliefs and thus their entire attitude to life using only abstract structures of thought. I did not even manage to convince an allegedly enlightened person of something by means of, at least in my opinion, comprehensible and empirically verifiable reasons. Apparently, Karl Marx saying that religion is opium for the people actually seemed to have caused my interlocutor a certain obscuration of the sense of reality. My conversation partner seemed to be a hopeless case. Perhaps I as a missionary?

In spite of all the surprises at the behaviors or traditions I encountered that were completely alien to me, I can still say that all of this has broadened my personal horizons quite a bit. When in Rome do as the Romans do. Even if it was sometimes not easy for me to accept this myself after a while, I learned that I had to adapt to those circumstances and accept them somehow. Own wiseacre or missionary work with regard to influencing behavior towards German standards only worked to a limited extent. By contrast, the Tajik colleague with whom I had to deal every day claimed when I left that I had changed his life! Despite the exaggerated pathos of this statement, it surprised me a lot, especially since he then hugged me moving to tears. An encounter that I will always remember and that revealed to me that despite all the cultural differences, people, wherever, are emotionally the same.

4. Encounters with accommodation

How was I accommodated abroad? Well, the spectrum ranged from right in the office, mass accommodation, a type of shared apartment, a one-room apartment to an apartment with several rooms that could also have accommodated a small family. I have certainly never lived in luxury, at least by German standards. On the other hand, never as a poor man or a homeless person. I have always found shelter. After all: I never had to buy furniture, except a small desk in Turkey for just 40 euro. In general, there is no accounting for taste. I would certainly never have equipped the furnished apartments that I had moved into in the different countries. The highlight was my apartment in Turkey. There was no space for a stove in the separate kitchen (!) foreseen, only for a washing machine. There was just a little gas stove with two plates on the countertop. In any case, complex menus could not be prepared.

In addition, the respective landlords were remarkable, even better the cleaning ladies. Because I was a foreigner, horrendous rents were sometimes demanded, which I was never willing to pay. In the end, I had always agreed on an acceptable price with the landlords. However, it was not always the case that any deficiencies I had submitted were eliminated by the landlord. Most of the time he ignored or postponed them (see below). Certainly, I was not the type who had to eat off the floor, but the cleaning ability of various cleaners left a lot to be desired. It was either the landlord's or the caretaker's wife. For me this was always the easiest solution because I did not have to look for someone at all. In addition, I had always been careful about who I could or should trust with the keys to the apartment. Nonetheless, the cleaning result was almost never satisfactory. As soon as the accommodation has been cleaned in Turkey, Montenegro or elsewhere, I was always asked to provide admirable confirmation of the efforts made. As if it was an unbelievable achievement. Most of the time I just nodded off the supposedly superhuman strength so as not to get into any discussion. In any case, my wife's testimony would have looked different.

When I arrived in Serbia on my first real assignment in July 2000, I did not have to look for an office first. Because it had already been rented from the headquarters beforehand. However, it still had to be renovated. From the beginning, I had planned to live in the office in order to save the rental costs that I would have had to pay myself. In addition, I wanted to wait long enough to get my work visa before I started looking for a place to live. I also thought that I would be able to do my job even better with it, as it would mean that I would be available and reachable all the time. However, I realized very quickly that I could no longer get away from work in such a constellation. That's why I always tried later to live as far away from the office as necessary so that I wasn't tempted to go back to the office after work if I didn't have to.

In any case, in Serbia I was initially in a hotel not far from the office - in a room that was less than 10 square meters! The renovation work in the office had dragged on for more than three weeks because the artisans had by no means delivered a satisfactory result. Believing that I, especially since I was a foreigner, would accept this, the company also demanded a completely unacceptable amount for the botch. My new employee, whom I had hired on my second day, brought in an architect he knew. He scrutinized the disaster and did indeed discover significant shortcomings. The craftsman threatened legal proceedings, but we weren't intimidated. Rather, we paid him a considerable discount, hired a new one, which then delivered a satisfactory result. Proud as Punch, I passed my first practical test in Serbia.

During all the trouble with the artisans, we had to prepare the distribution of medicines to five hospitals across the country. Therefore, looking for an apartment was beyond all question. When the office was ready to move into, I had the comfort of a 15 square meter, but unfurnished room. Its form was rather oddly: somehow, diamond-shaped, but tapered to a point, so that it almost looked like a triangle. Initially I slept on a mattress. Later I bought a bed. Apart from that, the room served more as a storage room for all those things that we did not need immediately. A homey feeling certainly looked different.

At the time, it never occurred to me that I would have to get away from work. Quite the opposite: Almost every day we were on the road somewhere in the country - in one year there, I drove more than 100,000 km by car. We usually left the office at seven o'clock in the morning and did not come back until around 8 o'clock in the evening, often much later. After that, I always switched on the computer to carry out the necessary office work. Most of the time, however, I had to postpone it to the weekend, so that I actually had a seven-day week, which had not really bothered me at the time.

When the team grew, I decided to look for an apartment, as my room now also had to be used as an office and I had received my visa. I quickly found a three-room apartment through an agent. In retrospect, it was, hard to believe, my most luxurious accommodation in all these years. It was not necessarily set up to my liking, but I have never had high expectations anyway. I had a comparatively large living room with a balcony, kitchen, bedroom and guest room on the fourth floor (with elevator) of a residential building that at least did not come from the communist era. On the contrary, it made a relatively new impression and was relatively close to the office; about half an hour walking distance. At least I was able to enjoy my free time in my apartment back then.

What came over me, when I chose the ground floor of a small house when I started my next assignment, is still inexplicable to me after so many years. I started to work for another NGO in the Northeast of Montenegro. My flat was actually a shabby dwelling in an old house. At first, I had moved into a small room in a kind of boarding house run by a student. I never fully understood her apparently difficult family circumstances. Just so much that her parents must have separated and returned to their villages. In any case, in the three weeks that I stayed with her, I had never seen parents or other relatives. Nevertheless, she gave me the impression that she was a fearless woman who took her life into her own hands. During the day, she worked at the local court and in the evening, she prepared for her final law exams. It is true that her English was not enough for more in-depth conversations, but we both made up for it with hands and feet, as well as my Serbian, which was still rudimentary at the time.

In the 1990s, I had been a volunteer in refugee camps in Croatia and Bosnia and Herzegovina and had learned the language enough to be able to have small talk conversations. Now, however, due to linguistic problems or shortcomings with my landlady supposedly minor problems in the apartment became insurmountable hurdles: which washing program did I have to set on the washing machine if I could only read the temperature switch or where and how did she separate the garbage? After the first puzzled look, she always replied, "Just throw everything together". Incidentally, by which she also meant the laundry!

Now I was in the shabby apartment and could not expect such pragmatic solutions from my new landlady, who lived above me. Physically, one could have considered her a man because of her chunky figure, at least from behind. That is probably why she was nicknamed "Muška Žena" (male woman) by some locals! Nevertheless, she was always friendly and was happy to take over cleaning my place - of course for a fee. Well, she did not really have to clean much anyway. On the one hand, the apartment was so dark that you could not see all the dirt or dust and on the other hand, after a short time, I had only used one of the three rooms. Because now it was November and it had started to get bitterly cold. Only the living room had a wood-burning stove. In addition, due to the weak electricity supply, the authorities had divided the city into four sectors, in which the electricity was turned off four hours a day. In the first sector from 7 a.m. to 11 a.m., in the second from 11 a.m. 3 p.m., in the third from 3 p.m. to 7 p.m. and in the fourth from 7 p.m. to 11 p.m. The times when there was electricity rotated by the week. After all, I knew in advance when there would be no electricity. However, reading by candlelight was anything but fun, so I usually spent the evenings in a café in another part of the city where there was electricity.

I had asked my landlady to light up the stove in the afternoon so that it would be a little cozier when I got home. She had done that until that day, after about a week (!), when I found the apartment completely fogged up. I could barely see the hand in front of my eyes. Apparently, the chimney was blocked and even after asking several times, she did not feel the need to take remedial action. As a result, I moved out a little later because it was just unbearable.

However, the circumstances of the apartment that I moved into immediately afterwards also turned out to be not entirely free of conflict. My Serbian teacher at the time had noticed all the fuss about the clogged chimney and offered me to move into her parents' house on the ground floor. This has just become free. After an initial inspection, I immediately agreed. Again, the constellation was such that the landlords lived above me and the landlord's wife also wanted to act as a cleaning lady for a fee. Not only could I now use all four rooms - it had become warmer in the meantime - but also somehow, I now had a much homier feeling than in the dark dwelling before.

On warm evenings, I could sit on the terrace right in front the house to read a book or the like. However, it soon turned out to be somewhat problematic. Without exception, every passer-by stared at me so much that after a short time, I began to point out to them, to make them understand that I by no means came from Mars, but was an inhabitant of the earth! Since the apartment was on the ground floor, however, it was also unavoidable that I received animal visitors, especially when the windows were open. The little mouse that hanged around on the shelf that was covered by a curtain in a niche next to the kitchen was still harmless. I had stored my food supplies there. Still, she had frightened me when I opened the curtain one day and she suddenly jumped at me. On the other hand, the presence of a rat hiding under the living room couch was scarier. I could see it when I knelt down. However, I could not chase off the beast. Even the most sophisticated methods using pillows, boards, and the like were unsuccessful. Thus, I informed the landlady, who immediately said that only poison would help. She scattered it around the apartment and assured me that it was safe for humans. Unsuspectingly, I went into the kitchen the next morning to put on some water for coffee, as usual. I could already see strange red stains everywhere on the carpet in the living room, which looked like traces and led straight into the kitchen, even along the stove into the sink. I almost fell over in shock, because that was exactly where the poisoned rat lay. I immediately rang the housekeeper out of bed, asked her to remove the whole mess by evening and went nauseated to a café.

It was she, the landlady, who suddenly made me quite angry. Because I had found out that every time she did her cleaning jobs, especially in the mornings, when she obviously had a lot of time as a housewife, she used my landline phone to call her son in Slovenia. Of course, at my expense without telling me. When I confronted her and asked her to reimburse the phone bill, she reacted in the apparently usual manner there. Instead of admitting everything, she began to attack furiously. She would have rented the apartment to me for living and not for storage. Back then, we had about a dozen boxes of relief supplies in a room that I did not use. I replied it was not her business how I would use the apartment, after all I would pay rent. Reluctantly, she agreed to reduce the next rent. However, from then on, I was through with her. Fortunately, my assignment ended shortly afterwards, so I left home. Contrary to usual practice, I had not said goodbye to her. I was just pissed off. When I was already on my way to the airport in the car, she called me and asked me if I would actually be leaving for good. Even though I was still angry, I affirmed and wished her all the best. I can no longer say whether I really meant it honestly.

A few years later, in Moldova, I had a landlady of a completely different type. At least a local colleague who had found the apartment for me had announced her somewhat mischievously: she was a retired former KGB employee. I no longer know whether he wanted to scare me. In retrospect, I think he wanted to draw my attention to possible problems without knowing the woman himself. Maybe also that I had to expect strange things. Well, at least during the inspection and the subsequent signing of

118

the contract, I could not find out anything. I only wanted to rent the apartment for three months anyway and was happy to have found accommodation for this comparatively short period. The landlady showed everything in a friendly manner and was very polite. Obviously, she really wanted to let me have the apartment in which she usually lived herself in order to have an additional income. In principle, there were no problems. Only when it started to get cold. Then it got uncomfortable, as the heating was not working. My colleague explained to me that the government would only turn on central heating in Moldova if the temperature dropped below zero for five days in a row. At my request, the landlady came to winterize the apartment. That meant that she taped all windows, which were anything but heat insulating, all around with adhesive tape so that I could no longer open them! Too bad that a short time later the central heating was actually turned on, which I couldn't regulate manually. Since it was running at the highest level, the room temperature in all rooms rose to almost thirty degrees Celsius! Therefore, I removed the tape in the bedroom. Curiously, from then on, I slept with open window open, while it was freezing outside!

At that time, a colleague from Transnistria invited me to his home. By then I had heard a lot from that part of Moldova, mostly nothing good. That 'republic' belongs to Moldova, but it is not really Moldova. Because the Stalinist regime in power that only Russia feels, it belongs to. According to my colleague, the only recognized means of payment was the Russian ruble. In the 1990s, there was a war, which resulted in the deployment of Russian troops on the "republic border". When we drove there, we had to show the passports, just as if we were crossing a state border. As a foreigner, the police officer gave me special scrutiny. However, they let us pass without further ado.

My first personal impression of the city of Bender in Transnistria was indeed bleak. Somehow, after crossing the border, I had the feeling that I had entered a completely different world. As if, I had switched from a color picture to black and white on the television. It was already getting dark, but before I crossed the border, I had the impression that the landscape still had a hint of color to it. I could no longer recognize a variety of colorful things from the car. A white veil of frost laid over everything and the few people I saw blew out mighty clouds of breath. It must have been bitterly cold outside. The city did not seem very picturesque either, because I could not see anything other than residential silos. You can see the castle back there, said my colleague, but I only saw a veil of fog.

My colleague's apartment was also depressingly small. After all, he had worked as a doctor for more than twenty years, but could not afford more than a two-and-a-half-room apartment. After their two sons moved out to study, he and his wife would feel comfortable! Since then, they have also been able to receive guests, as they now use the living room for its intended purpose. Before, it had apparently served as the children's bedroom. After the woman of the house greeted me, her husband guided me to the living room where a plastic fireplace was turned on. However, it did not get comfortably warmer. In addition, my colleague played German pop music to create a homey atmosphere for me. However, he did not play the music by chance, because he was an outspoken fan of Germany. His German language skills were astonishing, as we communicated without difficulty. He had already told me before the visit that years ago he had been in Germany for only about two months to buy a car - "of course a German make, since they are reliable". He would have learned a little German at the time. Well, the 'little' German was incredibly good. Since then, he has been interested in everything from Germany including music. In any case, I told him we could do without the music. It was, for my taste, just horrible. We sat on the couch and talked over tea. A short time later dinner was ready in the kitchen, where all kinds of specialties were on the table. It was still reasonably warm there, so I could take off my winter jacket! Immediately after the delicious dinner, it was just 7.30 p.m.; the colleague said then that he and his wife would now go to sleep. Because the electricity would be switched off very soon anyway. I had no choice but to cuddle under the three thick duvets at a time when small children usually go to bed in Germany! Somehow, that fitted in with the rest of the desolation.

In terms of climate, I experienced exactly the opposite in Sri Lanka. Even though I got there in December, it was quite summery, apart from the humidity, so that I actually only sweated once a day. Namely permanently. My location was the city of Ampara, in the east about 320 km from the capital Colombo. For the journey, we usually needed some seven to eight hours by car, depending on the traffic. When I arrived in Ampara, my first impression was that I had landed in the jungle. During the trip, the

121

driver had already explained to me that there was a lake nearby where wild elephants came to water every evening. Just two months before, residents of a hut would have panicked when an elephant approached them. Then the animal itself panicked and trampled the hut and the couple! I saw many peacocks and all kinds of other animals creeping and crawling in the city. At first sight, I had to realize that I had by no means arrived at the zoo. While the topic of 'security' had previously only related to conflicts, I now seemed to have to include the animal world as well.

We drove through a tangle of small back streets to my accommodation. This was a small hut with two rooms, surrounded by thick trees, so that hardly any daylight could get in. It was immediately clear to me that I definitely did not want to stay in it. Even my dark cave in Montenegro was a comparatively bright treasure! The kitchen was in a corner in the corridor and contained only two gas burners on a rickety table that served as dining table, too. I could not inspect the toilet because the light was not working, but even at first glance, I could not see anything good. As a protection against mosquitoes, a net was stretched over the bed. The mattress in the bed had certainly also seen better days.

I spent only two nights in the hut. Afterwards I moved to a little house where two colleagues lived. According to them, it had initially served as an office. My room was added later. It had its own entrance from the outside, but not from the inside! Now there was a comparatively large living room, but there was no furniture apart from a large metal desk. The toilet was right in the shower and, to my surprise, contained a plastic washing machine (how cute!) that even worked. A short time later, a roommate left us so that I took over her room in the house.

Due to the warm and humid climate, I was happy about every cooling, even if a cold shower always meant luke-warm. Nevertheless, my American roommate asked me to install a boiler so that she could take a hot shower. At first, I could not understand at all. Only over time did I learn that right after a hot shower I felt like the apartment was cool. At least it lasted for a short time. The kitchen was quite large, had all kinds of cupboards, a stove and a separate entrance from the outside. We used another room to dry clothes, but due to the high humidity, this only worked when the fan was switched on.

A wall surrounded the house and there was free space in front of the veranda to park several cars. Next to the en-trance gate, there was a small shed for the guards, who watched the building in alternating shifts for 24 hours. Mostly they only served as gate openers. They were nei-ther armed nor trained. Several times in the evening when I got home, I had probably woken up one or the other by my constant honking.

Only once in my entire time in Sri Lanka did a guard sound a strong alarm while I was in the house. Com-pletely excited he knocked on the door and shouted: "Sir, Sir, please come!" I should come immediately and when I opened the door, I realized what had happened. Mon-keys had pushed the water tank, which had a capacity of about a thousand liters, from the roof!

Apparently, the house was in a territory of a whole horde of monkeys, which had to constantly defend it against another and the fights, after all, always seemed to be fought on our tin roof. In any case, this hassle made a hell of a noise when the monkeys ran over the roof. I only saw them now and then. Once, I came home from the office, got out of the car and went to the front door. I put the key automatically in the door, as always, when I noticed that less than two meters away to my left, a rather large monkey was stuck to the tree at eye level. Baring his teeth, he hissed at me. Before you can say knife, I was in the house - admittedly going with weak knees!

In addition, I had often seen rather large lurking iguanas and crawling snakes, especially in the back streets of Ampara. Thus, I always had a bad feeling when I opened one of the cupboards in the kitchen hoping no animals would nestle there.

Speaking of animals: As team leader, I had to visit the ongoing projects from time to time to find out how things were going. One was about a two-hour drive southeast of Ampara next to a lake, where we operated a drinking water treatment plant and provided the inhabitants there with about 90,000 liters of clean drinking water every day. The project manager was an experienced Austrian colleague who was staying there all by himself nearby. On my first visit, I had two strange experiences with wild animals: when I arrived, the local employees were sitting at lunch and sipping a soup that I could not define at first. They told me that one of the colleagues had caught, slaughtered, gutted and prepared a turtle that morning - a delicacy. I should help myself. I replied that

I was a vegetarian! Then I went with my colleague to the pump in the lake, which was about 200 meters away from the system. He proudly explained to me that the system was running almost around the clock. As a result, however, the pump would often fail, as algae would frequently clog the intake socket under water. Just as he told me this, the engine stopped and my colleague immediately jumped into the water to see what was wrong. Suddenly a local colleague yelled Watch out there is a crocodile! Where? Pointing at it with his finger, the colleague replied well, there - not five meters away! The Austrian crawled comparatively calmly out of the water and continued to explain the system to me, just as if nothing had happened. Tarzan sends his regards! For me at that moment my colleague corresponded to at least half a Tarzan.

Later we went on a trip to Sigiriya, an impressive tourist attraction in Sri Lanka, where temples and all sorts of other ruins are located on a rock about 200 meters high. On the way, the driver suddenly stopped the car and pointed into the jungle, where a wild elephant was. Before I could see it, my Austrian colleague had jumped out of the car with the camera in hand and ran in the direction of the elephant. I still could not see the animal in the thicket. The driver whispered nervously that the man should come back because it was very dangerous, especially if it was a cow elephant with her cub. Standing at the car, I only now recognized the animal and my colleague a few meters away from it taking pictures – what was still missing that he would have communicated with the typical Tarzan scream (Uaauuauauaaaa). Then I would have named him Tarzan. An appropriate anecdote from my time in Montenegro: I once had a meeting with the mayor in Bijelo Polije, a city in the north. His first name was, no kidding, Tarzan!

Meanwhile, I shared the house in Sri Lanka, as I said, with an American colleague. Lastly, I had shared a flat in my student days many years ago. Hence, I was rather skeptical. Above all, I did not feel like having work as a topic in the evening. Over time, however, it turned out that I mostly spent the evenings alone in the house. Because my young flat mate was out almost every evening. She had been in town for a year when I arrived and had made numerous friends.

For me it was a real stroke of luck, because I actually preferred to be alone in the evening after long and stressful workdays in order to be able to enjoy at least some privacy.

I had already been able to experience in Ingushetia and later especially in Turkey how stressful such a flat-sharing constellation can be at times.

Ingushetia is a Republic of Russia and is geographically located exactly in the middle between the Black and Caspian Seas in the North Caucasus, bordering Chechnya. From there, without exception, all aid organizations operated by means of 'remote control' in Chechnya, as the authorities had forbidden foreigners to spend the night in Chechnya. Thus, aid organizations had local staff in Chechnya who independently carried out distributions or the like without the project office being on site. However, they received instructions on what should be done from Ingushetia. Our office was in Nazran, the largest city in the Republic, in a small settlement that consisted of dozens of identical houses on the outskirts and where most of the organizations had their base.

While the offices of our local colleagues were on the ground floor of our two-story building, the living room on the second floor also served as an office for us expats, my German colleague and me. In addition, both he and I had our own room, which we actually used just to sleep. For security reasons, the building was guarded by armed guards 24 hours a day and we were only allowed to leave the house with two armed soldiers.

Most of the time we spent the evenings together in the living room, unless we were invited to dinner, birthday parties or the like at other organizations. It is true that this had pretty much welded the 'international community' together, because everyone else lived under the same restrictions as we did. However, I was to a certain extent permanently with my colleague: during the day at work and in the evening apparently privately. Personally, we got along very well and tried to give each other a minimum of privacy as best we could. However, the given constellation was not always easy. We also tried to ignore the topic of work after the office closed, even though most of the time we sat at the desk anyway! Occasionally I would go to my room to read and when my colleague was not there, I would sit in the living room or lay down in the bathtub and listen to the music quite loudly. Despite the adverse circumstances, we managed to make the two-person flat share as pleasant as possible for both of us, so that we got through it without conflict. Years later, however, it was completely different in Turkey.

A small German aid organization assigned me as Head of Mission to open an office in Antakya, ancient Antioch in the southeast of the country. Assistance to Syria and Turkey should be organized from there. A German with Turkish roots who, in addition to all the translation work, was looking for an office accompanied me. In the course of the first week, a New Zealander who had lived in Damascus for more than ten years and a Syrian who was initially supposed to be translator and was later assigned to work in the Aleppo office in Syria joined the team.

Initially we foreigners stayed in a kind of pension in the old town, run by a German nun - she said that she had actually been on a pilgrimage 35 years ago, arrived in Antakya and decided to stay there. A typical old Arab building that led from the front door into an inner courtyard, from where you could then get to the individual rooms. Everyone had their own room, while the toilet and shower were shared. In the long run, however, the accommodation would have been too expensive, so we went looking for an apartment and office, which turned out to be not that easy.

In the Province of Hatay, the capital of which was Antakya and which belonged to Syria until 1939, still lived a large number of Alevis, a Muslim religious group. Not to be confused with the Alawis, who include the family of the Syrian President, Bashar Al-Assad.

At that time, there were frequent demonstrations against the refugees from Syria in Antakya. Often, they were even referred to as traitors who neither should be assisted nor their supporters, that is aid organizations. Apparently, a considerable part of the population still sympathized with the Syrian regime. Therefore, it happened often to us, once we had found a suitable building to rent, after the supposed landlord found out about our planned activities, they often suddenly withdrew shortly before the contract was signed. For me personally it was a helpful experience, because now I was able to understand how those Germans with foreign roots felt who had grown up in Germany but who only were rejected when looking for an apartment because of their name. My German-Turkish colleague, apparently, had experienced this quite often. In the end, we found two apartments in two buildings next to each other. One was to serve as an office and accommodation for the female employees, while all male employees shared the other.

Yet both flats were still unfurnished, so we had to get what we needed first. Since the available budget was quite low, we could not hope for luxurious furnishings. The bedrooms were each equipped with a bed, a folding chair, a corresponding tea table and a narrow shelf that served as a cupboard. In the end, in the living room of the men's flat was a sofa set as well as a dining table with four chairs. Well, in the approx. 30 square meter room they still looked a bit lost. Without exception, my colleague bought all of the furniture in the office, including the desks, from the market at sensational prices. At least at first sight, they made a new impression. Only the kitchen equipment and the washing machine were second-hand, with the result that the washing machine not only gave up completely on its very first usage, but also caused a considerable flood in the apartment.

When we had moved into our new home, a neighbor came with a tray of tea and cake as a Welcome and said that she used to live in Pforzheim, a town in Germany. After I told her that I had very good friends near Pforzheim, a village she knew, she felt nostalgic. From then on, I was in her good books and felt almost at home.

At first, there were mostly just two of us in the apartment: The New Zealander and me. Occasionally our Syrian colleague stayed overnight. Later another German joined, whose room was then taken over by an Englishman after his early departure. We had agreed that everyone should pay the same amount into a household budget every week to buy those groceries that everyone consumed anyway, such as water, butter or the like. Everyone should cover other delicacies individually. The joint cash register worked exactly once, namely, when we went shopping together in the supermarket around the corner for the first time. Either afterwards one of them did not have any change on hand or the colleagues were not there. Ultimately, I was the only one who lived in the apartment permanently and so most of the purchases stayed with me. As a result, whenever my colleagues stayed overnight, they consumed the available food. Often enough in the evening I found a looted refrigerator. While they sat together in the living room in the evening, I withdrew to my room and read or watched a movie on my little computer. I made it clear to them from the start that I did not want to spend the evenings with colleagues. In any case, we had comparatively long working days, so that I usually did not come to my room until around 9 p.m., sometimes later, from the office across the street, being tired to death.

On top of all discomfort, however, was the Syrian colleague who spoke loudly on Skype until early morning hours, which often enough stole my sleep. One day I was at the end of my tether. I made it clear to him that if that happened again, he should immediately look for another place to stay. At that time, I had not realized that he was simply worried about his family in Aleppo. The city was the focus of the war. The colleague could only contact his family at night. Apparently, in addition to speaking to family members, he had received many calls from friends asking for assistance. Years later, when I was working again in Turkey, I had Syrian colleagues who were no different.

In the living situation in Antakya, however, the worst thing for me was the fact that my colleagues apparently did not care about cleanliness. Not only did I often find nothing to eat in the evenings. In addition, colleagues had spread all the used dishes around in the kitchen; the shower was left littered with hair; even all kinds of clothes were from here to hell's half acre and back, not to mention the garbage bin, which overflowed immediately every time the colleagues were there. That is why empty chip bags and the like were sometimes scattered all over the apartment. I could hardly believe that I was dealing with adults. They acted more like guests and I, as the permanent resident, had to take care of everything. Somehow, I gave them their head (my own fault!). Because, on the one hand it was anything but easy in Aleppo and thus they wanted to fully enjoy the days in Antakya. On the other hand, the end of my contract was foreseeable. After that, however, I swore to myself: Never again such a constellation!

This kind of living together has always been too much for me alongside all the usual lines of conflict when sharing a flat. Nonetheless, an awkward environment paired with too much loneliness is worse to endure, as it was back then in Tajikistan.

My assignment there was on the one hand to train the local finance coordinator and to support the field office in structuring it. The registered office was in the capital, Dushanbe, where I initially stayed in an apartment belonging to the organization in a tower block on the outskirts of the city. I knew enough of those typical residential complexes from the communist era from other Eastern European countries. At best, you could nestle in your privacy at home. Otherwise, the entrance, the stairway, the elevator, if it worked, as well as all corridors spread a shabby atmosphere that I would probably never have gone into voluntarily. My place was somewhat tidy, but the furniture was not only visibly used, but also more than that, namely dirty, greasy, so anything but comfortable.

The office, in turn, was located in a walled compound consisting of several smaller buildings and was comparatively close to the city center. There were guest rooms, so after a few days I asked to be able to move into one of the two guest rooms. I took quarter in a 20 square meter room, furnished with a bed, a closet, even a small suite and a desk. Internet connection was also available, so I was really looking forward to it. Next-door was the bathroom, which was more like a washing facility for miners. In addition, the wiring from the socket to the boiler had been quite adventurous. At least I had my own bathroom, because apart from me, nobody else was staying overnight in the 'compound'.

After a relatively short time, however, I felt that something seemed to be wrong with my assignment. Almost everyone I encountered in the office was somewhat reticent, some even distinctively negative. My recreational activities as well as my well-being, how I felt in the country I was in for the first time, how I felt about the country; what about the accommodation; what I did in the evening; none of this seemed to interest anyone at first.

Only slowly did I realize that everyone apparently thought my assignment was some sort of controller, whose observations were decisive for the continued employment of one or the other. Being all of a sudden aware of this, I informed the colleagues about my assignment, which at least significantly improved the behavior towards me, but hardly changed anything about my almost lonely living situation. I usually spent the evenings alone, talking to my wife on the phone or reading. On Fridays, expats from other organizations met in a bar. I only went there once. There I even met a colleague from another aid organization I knew from Ingushetia. However, those evenings always seemed to degenerate to collective binge drinking, so that afterwards I did not feel like going any more. In any case, my assignment was limited to four months.

After all, a trip to Muminabad should bring some change to my everyday life, as I was not only able to visit a project there, but also to speak to local partners.

The small town is located about 250 km southeast of Dushanbe not far from the Afghan border. At first, I was quite euphoric to get out of Dushanbe, and the drive went through a breathtaking landscape. However, in the following five days I was able to experience what real dreary loneliness meant.

I stayed in the compound of the organization in a room that reminded me very much of my very first accommodation in Sri Lanka: a bed, a bedside table, a vague wardrobe and lots of darkness. In the room next door was a young Swiss who had lived there as a project manager for over a year. To arrange his accommodation a bit homier, he hammered some pieces of wood together to have come sort of additional furniture!

The whole complex was at the end of a downhill cul-de-sac road, far away from the next tiny grocery store. There was hardly any other way to describe it. Because the range of goods was quite manageable. There was always only one product on the large shelves. Apart from pasta and rice, I could not decipher the Cyrillic script anyway, and no western articles I knew apart from Coca-Cola.

During the day, we went either to the office, which was in a building in the middle of the compound, or to the surrounding villages, where bank reinforcements were about to be built to provide protection against the all too often occurring floods. We then spent the evenings in the compound. On the first evening, I was able to experience the sadness: no electricity and, since the pump did not work, no water, too, in most of the households in the city. Unless you had enough money to buy a generator. However, very few people apparently had that, if at all, because I did not hear the typical noise of the units, as I knew it from Kosovo in particular.

At least the Swiss colleague had a small gas stove to prepare dinner or hot water. Thus, we sat together in the evening by candlelight, ate something, talked, drank tea and went to bed quite early. I only had to experience those evenings for about a week and could hardly imagine that I could have endured there for a longer period. Now I also understood why the Swiss made the arduous journey to Dushanbe every Friday in order to be able to enjoy at least some change on the weekend. Years later, when I met a Swiss woman in Kosovo, we remembered that we had met briefly once in Dushanbe. She told me that not only had she been in Muminabad with her husband for two years, but also, she had a wonderful time there! As is well known, there is no accounting for taste.

Nonetheless, all of the later accommodations were nothing compared to the ones I had to endure as a volunteer when I came into contact with the field of humanitarian aid for the first time. In 1994, I replied to an advertisement in the newspaper looking for volunteers to work in refugee camps in Croatia for three weeks. Actually, I had looked for possible holiday destinations, but then answered without knowing what exactly such a volunteer assignment connoted. Shortly afterwards, I was invited to a preparatory seminar and selected. Less than two weeks later I was in a suburb of Split (Croatia) as one of seven others who were now the second group to replace the

135

first volunteers in two refugee camps. Initially, my assignment was planned for three weeks. I not only extended this by a few weeks, but also later took a semester off and spent several months there.

We lived in the apartment of a Croatian family who had sublet two rooms to the organization. The house was about 500m away from the larger camp. The rooms were only rented after the two tents (!) in which the first group slept had been blown away in the truest sense of the word by the notorious strong wind, the so-called Bora. Because the plan had actually been that the volunteers should camp, which, however, no one had communicated to me at all.

After all, we now had permanent accommodation. Two rooms, one for men and one for women, where we, five men, slept on mattresses. There was no space for clothes, so we actually lived out of a suitcase or backpack. It was no different with the women, especially since the previous group, all women, also stayed a few days before they left when we arrived. There was only one toilet, which initially 17 people used. Consequently, going to the lavatory was always a matter of luck. It was never spick and span anyway that did not bother us much. The family consisted of the father and son, who both slept in one room, and Vinka, the woman of the house, who had become a legend for me. Not only did she have a very high-pitched, squeaky voice, but also her snoring was legendary! She usually had a catnap in the afternoons, and indeed, the sounds of her sleep were so loud that, with the window always open, people could hear from afar in the street.

Still, she was kind of a brand. Everything revolved around money all the time, though the additional rental income meant that she was in a much better position than any neighbors were. I especially liked her way of dealing with people. While the refugees were a thorn in the side of all neighbors, she had no prejudices. She did not care if someone was Croat, Serb, or Bosniak (Muslim). Almost every evening she and we visited three families (Muslims) who lived not far from our accommodation. For Vinka they were neighbors and by no means disagreeable strangers. I, on the other hand, must have been a kind of moneylender for the woman of the house. Because when I was her guest for a long time, she always came to me at the end of the month and borrowed small sums. I never got the money back. While volunteers still came every three weeks, I was the only one who stayed there for a longer period. That is why I felt almost part of the family and I was just embarrassed to draw Vinka's attention to her debts, even though I myself experienced cash flow problems at the time. At least I enjoyed some privileges. Several times, I was the only one who was allowed to accompany her husband on his nightly fishing trips. The first time I tried to fish with a harpoon, I fell into the water with my weapon! Afterwards, they only offered part of the catch to me for lunch the next day. Fresh crabs that, according to Vinka, would normally cost us a fortune!

Once, her 14-year-old-son asked for advice completely desperate. While his parents were at a funeral, he probably wanted to impress a friend and go for a ride in his father's car. The supposed trip had not lasted very long.

It ended at the wall of the building opposite. He had crashed right into it. Together we inspected the damage, which was significant. His father would kill him if he saw the car. Therefore, the son asked me if I could say I had driven! My solidarity with family matters did not go that far. I replied that he himself had to take responsibility for what he did. I offered him to be present when he was going to confess to his father. In the end, he did not kill his son, but gave him, in my opinion quite rightly, a loud lecture.

In the house, Vinka insisted that we could only take a warm shower on Fridays, on our day off, because only then she would switch on the boiler. She allowed us to cook on one of the four gas plates on her stove. In order not to get in the way of the quirky landlady in the morning, we usually had breakfast with the Muslims on the terrace. We also spent most of the evenings with the refugees. If not, we would sit in the living room with our hosts and try to communicate with our hands and feet.

Somehow, I had survived this extreme living situation even for months. However, I was even able to top it. Because first in autumn and later over Christmas and New Year 1995/1996 I spent several weeks in Zenica / Bosnia housed in a refugee camp, a former boarding school.

Around 250 people were penned up in the three-story building, most of whom had fled from the area around Srebrenica, which gained notoriety at the time. Even at first glance, it was noticeable that comparatively few men of all ages were among them. Rather, it was mainly women, children and old people. As known, several thousand men were separated from women and killed afterwards.

We, three volunteers, had a corner room that was no larger than about 20 square meters: an Irishman, a South African with Indian roots, who was well-liked by everyone, not only because of his skin color and long hair, but also because of his character and not least because of his very good language skills, and me. Another two Germans, a woman and a man joined later, so that the five of us slept in the room that also served as a kind of tea kitchen. We used a small wooden box as a refrigerator, which, like all other residents, we placed on the outside of the window ledge. In the beginning, however, birds looted our modest supply constantly overnight. Food was served twice a day in the canteen, where we also stood in line and which was more like a field kitchen without goulash. Overall, the quality of the food was rather low.

It was already very cold outside, while the heating inside was running at full capacity. It is true that you could walk around in a T-shirt, but the whole building was always stuffy and humid. Apparently, people never aired. There were showers and toilets on each floor for everyone to use. Only once a week we had hot water for about three hours, so that you had to queue and worry about whether there would be enough for the longed-for hot shower. When the other German arrived, he went into the shower in the morning as a matter of course, I was brushing my teeth and he asked, already standing in the shower, whether there was hot water. I said yes, but he started screaming because only ice-cold water came out of the showerhead. With an innocent, mischievous expression, I replied, "Oh today is not Friday at all. I completely forgot. "

We spent either the evenings playing cards or in the rooms of other residents who had invited us for a coffee. They were no different from us. Whole families lived in each room, so that it was pretty cramped everywhere, which inevitably led to arguments: some were too loud, others blocked the hallway with all their shoes or various other things people had been able to carry when they had fled. People also frequented our room until late in the evening. We were the exotic ones in the whole house, so that in principle there was never any real peace. In addition, all refugees, without exception, were completely traumatized by what they had been through. Actually, we were there to especially entertain, but also to console or to settle disputes, quietly listening when people disburdened their heart and, last but not least, to organize the people without having been authorized to. Nevertheless, everyone assigned us this task unconsciously which people accepted, too. Probably because we were constantly organizing something: be it kindergarten for the little ones, English lessons for the teenagers, game afternoons and evenings as well as all sorts of other activities for the adults.

At the turn of the year 1995/96, we wanted to organize a special festival for all residents. Songs and small skits were rehearsed with the children. Our South African colleague was in full cry. We decorated the canteen together with the elders and for dinner there should be cold food, but as a kind of buffet with many different dishes. Some refugees even prepared typical local appetizers. Little by little, the hall filled up. Without exception, all residents turned up, even those we had never seen before. Not only was it a success for us, it also showed us that people perceived it a special event. Our plan worked perfectly. Because we wanted to offer the displaced people a change from their dreary everyday life. The buffet was empty so quickly that you could hardly believe it and people applauded frenetically the children's performances. There was a lot of laughter and gossip and when music started, the dance floor was full in no time. People took us volunteers immediately into the dance and tried more badly than right to follow the given dance steps. I kept one bizarre picture in mind: a police officer with a pistol in his back pocket (!) - where he actually came from was always a mystery to me - danced with a mentally handicapped woman, just as if she was his sweetheart. The elation lasted exactly until midnight. When we usually wish each other all the best for the New Year at home and pop the champagne corks, it was suddenly as quiet as a mouse. Almost everyone took a seat, began to cry a river or lay in each other's arms. Apparently, all the memories of what they had been through in the past year suddenly came back to them. Perhaps because of what they had experienced; they could not believe they were happy to spend such a nice evening. It was more likely, however, that most of them remembered earlier New Year's Eve when they could still celebrate lighthearted together with their loved ones.

Now they suddenly sank in the situation the war had put them. They probably also thought of those who could not be there now and of what the uncertain future might bring for them. Despite this sad mood, for me personally it was probably the best New Year's Eve I had ever experienced. At the same time, he showed me the comfortable situation I had compared to these people. I could leave this accommodation for home at any time, but they could not. Moreover, even if most of the apartments that I had moved into in the course of all the foreign assignments did not necessarily meet my requirements, they were always better than the conditions under which those displaced people had to live. An important lesson for me.

5. Encounters with projects

In general, aid is divided roughly into three phases: firstly, directly after a disaster, the emergency phase, the distribution of goods is intended to ensure the survival of the affected population. After that, secondly, the activities concentrate on the reconstruction of the infrastructure and, thirdly, the support and restoration of functioning structures within the framework of development cooperation. The periods of these three different phases range from a few months, a few years in the rehabilitation phase to decades in which attempts are undertaken to 'develop'. The work and the requirement profile of the aid workers are correspondingly different. Above all, in the immediate aftermath of a natural disaster, aid organizations usually send teams of technical specialists to provide medical assistance, set up and operate drinking water treatment systems, search for people buried with dogs or set up camps. Often these specially trained volunteers do a regular job at home and their employers provide them short-term leave for such assignments. In addition to their very special work, they should also train local staff who should later take over the work independently if necessary. A coordinator usually acts at the same time behind the scenes, some also call him a delegate, project or program manager, who maintains contact with local authorities, ministries and other actors in order to coordinate and organize the work of his aid organization with them.

In most of the assignments, I held exactly this position, which required less specialist knowledge. Rather, I think

143

that the following requirements were most important: first, knowing the procedures and processes in order to be able to organize them as effectively and efficiently as possible. Second, to be able to guarantee this, you need a well-functioning team. I also include the ability to create one. The content, duration and budget of the projects in the various phases of emergency aid, rehabilitation and development sometimes differ enormously. However, what they all have in common is the basic procedure. In the meantime, both in humanitarian assistance and development cooperation, so-called project cycle management seems to be the method accepted by almost all actors.

First, the program is determined. Suppose the earth shakes in country X and an aid organization decides to provide assistance after international support is requested. In the next step, the aid organization will send someone, usually an experienced employee, to carry out a needs assessment. This now determines that the affected population in a certain area, for example, is urgently lacking food. The organization will then elaborate a corresponding project proposal and send it to potential donors. In Germany in this case to the Foreign Office or to the EU Humanitarian Aid Office (ECHO). If the proposal is approved, which secures the financing, the implementation can commence and at the end or after completion of the intervention it is evaluated in a last step. The objective hereby is to identify possible deficits, problems and the actual impact of the project carried out, in order to improve them if the organization wants to repeat it elsewhere. This is a somewhat simplified description, because in reality the individual phases contain a large number of further steps. In addition, almost every aid organization has its own internal procedures and processes with regard to responsibilities and communication channels that come into play in the individual phases. For example, the former can relate to procurement of relief supplies, which either exclusively the head office or the field office carries out. Furthermore, the regulations of the donor play an important role, especially when it comes to public institutions. After all, you always have to prove that you utilized the provided funds properly after the end of a project. Mostly it is taxpayer's money!

However, in order to be able to carry out aid projects at all, a well-functioning team, especially local colleagues, is essential. Since you mostly do not speak the language of the country of assignment, you, as a foreigner, are in a certain way at the mercy of your local colleagues. In addition, they do the actual work, but, unfortunately, often enough people do not appreciate accordingly.

In general, foreign organizations are an attractive employer for local people in such contexts. Because the salaries are usually higher than in other sectors. In one case or another, there are additional benefits. Finally, yet importantly, at the end of the month the employee can assume to receive the contractually agreed payment on his account. Often enough I had employees in the Balkans or in Russia who told me that in the past, they often only got their salary months later. Therefore, the rush or the flood tide of applications for corresponding job advertisements is usually very high. However, it is common that a large number of candidates who fulfill neither the necessary requirements nor qualifications, but primarily try their luck because of the advantages mentioned above. It can happen, for example, that an applicant, as I had to experience in Serbia, even though English was written and spoken very well indicated in the résumé under language skills, could neither articulate himself in the foreign language nor understand any word at all. When I was in Montenegro, a colleague from another organization based in Serbia asked me to be there for her interviews. Because she had come to the country all by herself and wanted me to attend. Of course, I said yes. She had organized five interviews in a row in a café, as her office was not yet ready to move in. The aim was to select an assistant for her. Unfortunately, we had to break off the first interview after a few minutes. Because it turned out the applicant neither spoke English nor understood a word at all. Curiously, the candidate interviewed immediately afterwards had submitted curriculum vitae that was identical to the first candidate except for the name and date of birth and he did not speak a word of English either. I could have sworn I had seen them both out on the town together before. The following candidate only provided the standard answer: "I like the job and I like to travel", to every question. She had absolutely no idea of the intended function! Any inquiries were needless.

To date, I have processed countless applications in all of the assignments. I had received by far the most unusual cover letter in Kosovo, which I would like to shorten a bit, but reproduce verbatim including the spelling mistakes (I try to translate it accordingly): "One day, while I was coffee drunk with a friend, someone else came and told us about you that you had come and take some people to work". He then went on to say that, he was currently working in a law firm, but there were enormous problems there, especially since he was a "Catholicer" (sic!). "I can say that I am full and tired of it. My and my friend's way out (rescue) is no longer work with Muslims but at least take a salary but that has nothing to do with Muslims or leave Kosovo. (...) In addition, the motive: "Until I may leave Kosovo or until something is done with Kosovo, I would like to work for you and I guarantee you my diligence." By the way, the applicant was a trained German teacher - poor pupils!

Having received that application, I just thought that it was about someone who did not want to be employed under any circumstances. I could not believe reading it. The crux is therefore to have the right touch to be able to separate the wheat from the chaff, especially since the hiring process usually has to be carried out comparatively quickly.

When I took over the leadership of the office in Montenegro, I had a local assistant who had already worked for the organization for a year and who later showed me his so-called cover letter. Actually, it was just a five-line email. He had a driver's license, knew the area well and had previously helped organize the distribution of relief supplies for another aid organization. The application only ended with "Sve najibolje" (All the best). He had been invited to an interview, although not even a résumé had been attached. Hats off! In my two years there, I could not imagine having a better colleague with whom I am still in regular contact today, even after many years.

In addition, as agreed, after my contract ended, he took over the leadership of the office and achieved successful results.

Whether I composed a team myself or took it over from my predecessor, I had always taken to heart to encounter my local colleagues respectfully, transparently, but also patiently. No matter where, I arrived as a foreigner to a country whose customs, culture and mentality I was not familiar with, initially I found myself in the role of a beginner, even though I had previously worked elsewhere in a similar context. Hence, I never presented myself as the smart-alec lone fighter or undisputed ruler, but rather as the greenhorn who absolutely relied on support of local colleagues.

In general, colleagues accepted my leadership role from the start. Most likely, however, I seemed to have won the respect and esteem of my local colleagues by mucking in myself. At least that is what an ex-colleague in Turkey had told me: Although being Head of mission, I would not only been present when aid was distributed, but I would also have assisted by handing over the heavy flour sacks to Syrian refugees. My successor had not even come to the distributions himself.

Well, what they praised there, I actually always took for granted. I always felt to step in automatically where one or more hands were missing. After all, it was just the distribution of relief supplies and the like that I had organized for days or weeks together with my colleagues and thus could now personally experience the result of all the effort. Even when such never-ending days were very ex-

148

hausting, I could go home in good conscience and a feeling of happiness. I could not miss it, on the contrary: I would even say that these were mandatory dates.

Usually, I was in the management position, especially in smaller teams, the one who spent most of the time in the office doing administrative tasks so that aid projects would go as planned. I was the one who made sure that new projects were elaborated, applied for and, if possible, approved so that the continued existence of the office, and thus the jobs of the local staff, were ensured. I was the one who represented the organization at official appointments or meetings. Last but not least, the one, who was responsible for all this to the head office and the donor. On the other hand, aid distributions afforded the very rare opportunity to come into personal contact with the beneficiaries or recipients. Even when I got my hands dirty or was white with flour in the evening, I was not only happy but also won the respect of the people and, depending on the region, of my colleagues. Admittedly, an exuberant thank you from the people was also balm for the stressed soul. It is true, that I have always taken it to heart wherever I have been assigned, but it may well be that elsewhere it could also be viewed as a sign of weakness or even disregard.

When in Sri Lanka, for example, I had prepared or fetched my coffee in the kitchen in the morning, opened the gate myself when I left, or carried my luggage myself, the cleaning lady, gatekeeper and other local colleagues sometimes were angry at me. Because with this, although by no means intended, I (possibly) intimated them that I did not trust them and ultimately not allow them to carry out the tasks for which they had just been hired. Although I never really liked the constant 'Sir' from my local colleagues there, I had to get used to it, especially since the people there used the same salutations in their own language. Although at times I felt like an antiquated colonial ruler, I simply let them go. This was by no means a kind of master-and-servant relationship, but by letting them do their jobs, I evidenced that I trusted them, even though it was often difficult for me. It took some time getting used to for me and still to date.

Sometimes my colleagues were too humble, because, especially when we did not really know each other, they probably thought that their job could be jeopardized. This perception on the part of local employees was apparently reinforced by my tone. In any case, it happened surprisingly that local colleagues were afraid of me because of sound of my voice, even though I could not find anything negative about my diction. Apparently, the German language sounds quite harsh compared to others. A friend, an enthusiastic dog owner, once told me that the "hard German tone" would generally be used for training dogs everywhere.

Once in Kosovo, it was about our secretary, from today's perspective I should actually have been a little stricter. Because even simple tasks assigned to her seemed to be insurmountable. In the end, I mostly had to do it myself. In addition, as a single mother, she always cited exactly this burden as the reason when she was once again unable to concentrate. Her difficult personal situation was decisive to employ her and we all always considered it when necessary ("My child needs me at home!"). The organization even paid a part for her back operation! However, that did not prevent her from quitting from one day to the next in order to go to Afghanistan alone for several months, where she was supposed to work on an American military base. Afterwards the colleagues told me, that she had been afraid of me, because of my tone. Therefore, she would not have been able to fulfill given tasks. In my opinion, it was only some sort of circumlocution for her incapability.

In addition, the other colleagues there probably thought just from my tone that I was consciously expressing that I would not enjoy working with them and that I could stand neither them nor the entire country. Of course, I by no means intended this. Possibly, they secretly accused me of having worked in Serbia for a year in the past, which I told my Kosovar colleagues about in a too nostalgic way, which might have implied a rather biased opinion. The Kosovars had suffered too much under Serbian rule until 2000.

Admittedly, especially as a beginner, I found it difficult, no matter where, to be transparent and honest with my local colleagues, which seems ridiculous to me from today's perspective. On the one hand, it was certainly due to my inexperience and the associated uncertainty. On the other hand, I was often alone and did not really know whom I could actually trust. Of course, the question arose as to what and whether I actually had anything to hide. Probably it was more about a lack of confidence in that I often thought that colleagues could not do one or the other task assigned to them, as I wanted. At the latest when the work outgrows, you will have to realize that you also have to learn to delegate. That in turn should be a first step towards management skills, in the spirit of management guru Peter F. Drucker: "Organization is a means of multiplying the strengths of the individual". It took me some time to understand all of this.

Only when it refers to finances and especially salaries particular caution needed to be taken with regard to transparency.

The salaries of the individual employees should be kept under lock and key, otherwise you only create an atmosphere of resentment, envy and frustration in which everyone only looks at the other and the actual work falls behind. That is what happened to me in Turkey. The responsible desk officer from the head office took part in our team meeting. In it, she urged that a new, but completely inexperienced, employee, a Syrian, should be employed. The remuneration should happen according to the budget, whereby the salary was a lot higher than that of the permanent staff. With this, she had triggered a less than stellar insurrection, because the colleagues suddenly had the individual salaries in mind and therefore immediately demanded corresponding increases. It was only with great effort that I poured oil on trouble waters afterwards by simply expanding the requirements of the position in question and offering my colleagues at least a slight salary increase. I had experienced something similar in other missions.

A very central element of the management in the field was leadership. Responsible positions could be reached relatively quickly in both humanitarian aid and development cooperation, for which, for instance in Germany, years or even decades of experience must be demonstrated. I myself was able to learn this the hard way during my first assignment in Serbia the other way around, however. After only one year as a desk officer in the head office, I suddenly took the role of "boss" in Serbia the next day. Initially in a manageable team, namely one employee and myself. This quickly grew to seven employees. Fortunately, I had a colleague who was about 20 years older than I was at the time, who, although formally subordinated to me, sometimes literally took me by the hand and gradually took away my feeling of uncertainty. Unfortunately, he died much too early in 2005, because I would describe him as the one from whom I learned almost all of my basic skills. This includes, among other things that you should always keep in mind every employee without exception. For example, when people invited us to dinner after the very first distribution of medicines in Serbia, he pointed out to me that the truck driver should also be there, because without him the medicines would not have arrived in the first place. He was right. I personally would have forgotten the driver back then. Since then, I have taken this to heart and always reminded myself of it in similar situations. Because all too often, in my experience, those colleagues who are not directly involved in the project work are very quickly overlooked: especially the cleaner or driver. As a result, over the years I had got used to practicing a friendly rather than hierarchical relationship with the employees who report to me. Although the local staff never questioned my leadership position, it did happen to me that once a manager blamed me of precisely that kind of relationship. "As a manager, you should act entrepreneurially rather than "a backslapper"!" Personally, I felt this to be ridiculous, especially since I had not only succeeded in building a team that worked well together, but had also successfully carried out all sorts of projects by then. In the end, this is the only thing that matters.

Often enough, especially in the beginning, it was difficult with local colleagues with regard to project management. In particular, I had to learn to be patient. Because I often either hired staff or already worked with employees who had very little experience in the areas of humanitarian aid or development cooperation. In addition, in many countries the professional or, in most cases, university education of colleagues very often did not correspond to the standard that I was used to. This meant that I had often delegated tasks that I had considered easy or took for granted to be carried out. Afterwards, I always found that I had to scale down my expectations from my staff. In Kosovo, I had a colleague who had been working for the organization for years and, at the same time, studied law already for some semesters. However, he was unable to write even the simplest letters.

In general, the written English of my local colleagues usually left a lot to be desired. A good example were the applications that I received to read, regardless of where I was on duty. The same applied to texts, such as reports, that colleagues wrote as part of their work, too. In addition to a general sloppiness, I always noticed that the scientific procedure, as I had learned it, namely that references or quotations must be properly indicated, was apparently conveyed differently elsewhere or not at all. Of course, it could be because we all communicated in almost all of my missions in a language that was foreign to everyone. Therefore, the written English certainly did not correspond to that of native speakers. However, I blamed this more on the respective education system and less on my colleagues. Therefore, in addition to my role as a project manager, I was often also a trainer who had to coach local colleagues gradually. Of course, this was very difficult to practice. Especially in emergencies, the entire project office was under enormous time pressure anyway. Therefore, gradually I acted upon a maxim, as long as no any delay does not physically harm, I just had to be patient. My colleagues thanked me repeatedly.

Although I was always quite involved and stressed in my day-to-day work, I still had to learn to take the time for my colleagues or to take their concerns seriously. Otherwise, it can happen, like back then in Serbia that you lose good people overnight. The colleague, the one I hired first, had asked me several times about a possible contract extension, which in turn I put off repeatedly due to the workload. For me, his continued employment was a matter of course and therefore only a formality. Perhaps I had mentioned it to him, but obviously too casually. Moreover, I had thought he would continue to work with us only. When he pushed for specific feedback before my Christmas vacation, I postponed the matter to the New Year again. However, I had completely misjudged the situation. Because after my return I found his resignation on the desk. Unfortunately, I had lost a very important employee. My lesson learned was that I should not always trust my gut feeling!

In Ingushetia in particular, I recognized the possible consequences of a disrupted mutual trust between foreigners and local employees. In a six-eye conversation, I was supposed to settle disagreement between two employees who report to me. One, a foreigner, had made the other, my most important local colleague, feel from the start that he would not trust him. Actually, the conversation was about, in my opinion, an insignificant argument. Suddenly, however, the local colleague got up and shouted at the other, saying that if he talked to him again in this way, he would kill him! I myself was very astonished. In some areas, and this was undoubtedly the case there, such statements were to be taken seriously. Apparently, the personal relationship between the two of them was completely shattered; otherwise, I could not explain such a statement to myself and had never noticed it before. The coordinator, my local colleague, left the room in a hurry, and I followed. And the one addressed? He visibly pale became self-absorbed with an open mouth. By persuading my local colleague, I managed to pour oil on troubled waters, but the relationship between the two, if you could call it that from then on, remained more than frosty.

I think, retrospectively, I always managed to establish a bond of trust to my local colleagues. I am still in contact with many, even if only sporadically. Admittedly, I also had to learn first that teamwork abroad is the be-all and end-all. Because of the foreign language, I would not have been able to act completely alone anywhere. When dealing with colleagues, I always tried to create a relaxed atmosphere, applying humor paired with self-irony, without forgetting the seriousness of the actual work. In Turkey, other foreign colleagues probably referred to me behind my back as a kind of clown. That did not bother me in any way. Because all local colleagues liked me, and some from other teams, even asked if he or she could work in my team, too! I always had to say no, but it made me feel proud, namely that I was not completely wrong with my style when it came to managing people. A Syrian colleague poignantly complimented me who said that I was by far the best she had come across in this foreign country!

Ultimately, it probably always depends on the personality of the foreigner that local colleagues respect you and you gain their trust gradually. Once you have achieved this, the basis for successful project work is in place. It does not necessarily have to degenerate into the situation where colleagues, as happened to me in Pakistan, even ask me to sign autographs at the end of my mission!

In the context of disasters and conflicts, often-local NGOs spring up like mushrooms, which are, sometimes founded by former local employees of international aid organizations. Because over time they have noticed, how the system of allocation of funds worked and they could supposedly secure a good living in the long term, even though sometimes without any professional qualifications. In Montenegro, we were generally interested in projects in the field of the environment and wanted to carry out a comparatively small awareness campaign in schools together with the local representation of ECHO. Shortly after an initial conversation in which I had presented vague plans, I received constant calls from an employee of another foreign aid organization whom I already knew and whose work his own boss was anything but enthusiastic about. "He can't even fill up the car properly," was his standard sentence. He, the local employee, would have heard of our interest - afterwards I found out that he had a love affair with the representative from ECHO, who had apparently shared our plans with him. However, at that point in time we had no concrete plans in mind. In any case, he would have heard that we were looking for partners for an environmental project (!), for which his own organization called 'Four Pillars' was exactly the right one. Therefore, out of curiosity, I invited him to find out more about his organization. How long has his organization existed, what the name means, what kind of projects had been carried out to date, what qualifications he had, who would finance the whole thing and, last but not least, what environmental project he was talking about? I asked him. He proudly showed the registration certificate dated a few days earlier. The name of his organization just occurred to him - "it sounds good, doesn't it?" Since the organization was only recently established, he could present neither any projects nor any other written documents or donor. His many years of employment with the other foreign NGO should qualify enough and we would certainly find a joint project with him, he stated. I dug deeper, what vision or concept his organization had. Whereupon he kept referring to the registration. At the end of the ten-minute conversation, I did not want to let him go completely disappointed. Hence, I asked him to elaborate a detailed project proposal in English. He should send this to me in the coming week. I am very excited. It was the last time I heard from his organization...

When we as a foreign organization had a longer-term presence in the field, we have repeatedly received a wide variety of project proposals from local NGOs. Though not being that unprofessional as it had been in Montenegro, but I often got the impression that many thought that as soon as the word humanitarian was somehow incorporated into the text, nothing would get in the way of funding. Suddenly school utensils mutated into essential aid supplies in Kosovo; renovation of public buildings (!) in Serbia or a company vehicle for the honorary director in Sri Lanka became humanitarian issues; rhetorical workshops in Moldova became basic needs that have to be met in order to help people in need. In Turkey, I received similar project proposals from an organization in the same format. In one chapter, it repeatedly emphasized that the planned intervention would be in accordance with international humanitarian law, human rights and the like. However, I did not understand what the delivery of cows to farmers that we were supposed to finance had to do with it.

On the other hand, it can also happen that you do not know immediately, how and where to spend your funds appropriately. Especially when a disproportionately high amount of donated funds is available. In 2004, Chechen rebels attacked the secondary school No. 1 in Beslan, a city in North Ossetia-Alania not far from Vladikavkaz, and took hundreds of students and teachers hostage for days. It is known that the rescue resulted in a massacre in which over 330 people were killed. Less than six weeks after that terrible event, I was in that building. A former teacher, still visibly shocked by the events, guided me through and told me what exactly had happened in each classroom. It must have been sheer horror. I could not and did not want to follow his whispered explanations, let alone unpack the camera and take pictures, in view of the many grieving people who walked through this place of horror, weeping in silence. Water bottles were placed everywhere by visitors to recall that the hostages had not been provided with anything to drink. In the end, I did not know who to despise more: the hostage-takers who ruthlessly gained control over children and teachers. The Special Forces, who, according to the teacher, were comparably relentless during the rescue by firing a tank shell into the building, although there were still many hostages inside; or the rampant corruption of the Police at the checkpoints, who apparently let an entire van full of terrorists pass unmolested. Especially since it was common knowledge that two different tariffs were applicable on the two-lane road: those on the right lined up who did not want to pay. Therefore, it took a long time to clear them. On the left, on the other hand, those who were in a hurry queued: 100 rubles including opening the trunk. For 200 rubles, you only needed to present the ID!

In the aftermath of this comparatively manageable, but terrible event, huge amounts of aid supplies and funds poured into the country. An aid organization assigned me to elaborate a project financed by their donations.

Coordination offices set up by the local authorities tried to distribute the aid as best they could, so that as many people affected as possible could benefit. Undoubtedly a useful instrument, especially since the situations after disasters are usually confusing and characterized by chaos. Thus, even experienced aid workers are happy that there are institutions that at least try to keep an overview. For NGOs, it is already a tried and tested means to utilize their available funds in emergencies. The primary goal is to avoid overlapping or duplication of aid.

In the context of Beslan, however, the volume of aid increased to such an extent that the highest government agencies in North Ossetia-Alania took over. In addition to dozens of airplanes full of all kinds of relief goods, spontaneously organized aid transports, philanthropic people who randomly handed over cash at people's front doors, many aid agencies that suddenly had considerable donations earmarked for the victims of the terrorist act. In view of the confusing situation, at least the authorities felt compelled to channel the work of the various organizations and, if possible, to control them by openly demanding that they have the decisive power at every step in the implementation of planned measures. The authorities, of course, had previously suggested these. Further, the foreign organizations were bluntly told that only certain local companies were allowed to be involved in all activities, which had to be approved by the government-set up coordination committees and, of course, how they would ultimately be awarded without the aid agencies. Moreover, of course, only because of the better knowledge of the environment and people as well as the professional expertise of their own staff. Honi soit qui mal y pense. In any case, at the meeting where these conditions were presented, were only quiet protests at first, but later not a single NGO, rightly, got involved.

In the aforementioned meeting, various ministers reported on the needs of the affected people, in the hope that one or the other gap could be closed without becoming more specific. In the end, the Minister of Sport suggested to the 30 or so representatives of aid organizations that they finance a football stadium with a capacity of 30,000 spectators, because that is what the people affected need most!

A short time after, I met the representative of the committee set up by the school's parents and teachers. When I asked what they needed most urgently, the man surprisingly replied that I should ("please") tell them because I had a lot more experience! After I had an overview of the planned assistance of many organizations, we decided to equip the local blood bank. At first, this caused some sort of astonishment of the donor, because it was a considerable amount and it obviously did not seem to be related to the terror act. However, the families directly affected had not only been lavished all sorts of relief goods and money on, but numerous aid organizations were also planning to set up centers in which people would receive psychosocial support in order to treat the trauma. Certainly, this made sense, but in my opinion, no further center was needed.

Our planning originally aimed at a longer-term project, from which the children, who had survived the hostage taking, should particularly benefit. That is why we worked on the idea of setting up a scholarship fund for them to support them in a future study. Initially, our donor had been enthusiastic. However, this turned out to be too long-term. After all, the use of the fund would only have been possible years later. Further, we needed to assume that our organization would then no longer be present in the region. Hence, the question arose who should manage the fund and, above all, later who should determine the provision of scholarships? Who knows what would have happened to the fund in the meantime? Would it be available at all in the future? Finally, we gave up on the idea and decided to equip the local blood bank so that it would be better prepared for any future event.

The emergency phase usually merges smoothly into the reconstruction or rehabilitation phase. These two phases can best be recognized by the sometimes overly dense forest of billboards in a disaster area, since normally every NGO puts up a sign with project information where it is active. On the one hand, hereby 'claims' are defined of the respective organization. On the other hand, it also fulfills the public relations requirements vis-à-vis the donor and, finally yet importantly, to inform the local population about the aid provided. It is true that not every organization makes its presence known, but the number of aid agencies or NGOs that act in the event of a disaster can in one case or another amount to several hundred (!). For example, when I was driving along the east coast in Sri Lanka a year after the devastating tsunami of 2004, there was a billboard about every 100m - over a distance of dozens of kilometers!

In the event of a disaster, whether triggered by nature or a conflict, the first attempt is always to ensure the survival of the people affected by addressing the basic needs of the people. The interventions are always similar: provision of medical and drinking water supply, shelter and the distribution of food, hygiene items as well as basic household items according to the given situation.

In practice, however, it can be problematic if the needs assessment is not carried out in the field, but from the desk in the head office. In Sri Lanka, for example, countless containers full of blankets and winter clothing ended up after the tsunami occurred, and were stored unopened at the port, because due to the local climate - you can usually enjoy Christmas Eve there in beach clothing - they were simply not needed. Some of the containers I saw with my own eyes. Moreover, you are in a tight spot when the recipient rejects the delivered assistance.

In Serbia, I was supposed to organize the distribution of milk powder to hospitals that had been procured before my arrival. A colleague at the head office had this idea based on television pictures. Too bad that the responsible doctors in the field all refused this kind of assistance, since they gave priority to breastfeeding of mothers. In addition, the powder packaging, although made in Germany, was labeled in Cyrillic script - in Russian. When I asked about this, the only answer was that one would have thought that it was the same language! In any case, the local people were anything but enthusiastic, as they assumed that the powder was actually produced for the Russian market, but that it was rejected there or did not meet the hygienic standards. Therefore, they would only receive possibly rubbish. I did not make friends with it. Instead, I kept looking for excuses on the spot with an innocent expression until we had solved the problem and finally handed the parcels over to a local organization for distribution - should they have arguments with their compatriots.

It can even happen that one has to resort to even more drastic means. An airline had generously donated several thousand small toilet bags, filled with toothbrushes and toothpaste, shaving equipment and all sorts of other small items that the airline normally provided to passengers in first class. For the sake of simplicity and without our knowledge, the head office loaded the bags onto a truck full of school furniture and sent to us in Montenegro. On the spot, customs made us aware that the bags, as they contained toothpaste, required a document of compliance from the authorities. Thanks to our good relations with customs, we were able to receive the truck and promised to get the necessary documents before we would distribute the bags. However, we realized that the toothpaste had already expired – no wonder that the airline had generously donated! Although supposedly harmless, the beneficiaries would certainly not have accepted the bags. So, we were forced to take the tubes out of the bags in a cloaks-and-dagger operation, taking them to a waste container and set them on fire, with which part of the aid literally dissolved into smoke and mirrors.

In general, in-kind donations, especially when it comes to used items, are not welcome anyway, as they involve a tremendously high amount of time as well as logistical and financial expenditures: clothes and shoes, for example, have to be assorted, if necessary, sorted out and thus be disposed of, for which in turn personnel is required. Apart from that, the distribution of such relief goods will always be extremely difficult, as it can never be fair and sometimes it can and will even cause unrest among the beneficiaries, as I had experienced in Croatia.

One day, on behalf of a foreign aid organization, a truck arrived at the refugee camp, in which I worked as a volunteer. It was fully loaded with a wide variety of donated items such as washing machines (!), some brand-new mountain bikes, smaller household items and even dirty clothes - which would otherwise have ended up in the bulky waste. Without talking to anyone, the two drivers simply unloaded all the goods and left. Of course, people pounced on it, which led to a bad fight among the community! Within a few moments, our work with the refugees was obviously ruined. While we had tried somehow to make the coexistence of the people reasonably bearable, now everyone tried to get the best piece of it. On the one hand, it was understandable; on the other hand, we volunteers were quite frustrated. Unfortunately, investigations into where the supposed assistance had come from remained unsuccessfully.

Once we had distributed shoes in that refugee camp. A truck full of shoes that had been donated in Germany was now to be distributed in various refugee camps in Croatia. We had already heard of tumults from other camps, so we wanted to organize the distribution as best as possible so that we would not have to experience any disputes.

Hence, we worked out a sophisticated system that we explained to the refugees before the distribution. First, we sorted the shoes - incidentally, we discovered a whole lot of individual shoes that we had to throw away. Further, we displayed them in the large hall, sorted by size, just like in a shoe shop. Then we divided the approximately 250 camp residents into groups of 20 adults each. We excluded the children because their parents or grandparents should choose their shoes. Those in the first group could choose one pair per person; the following groups then two pairs and finally the first group was allowed to pick up their second pair at the end. It is true that the residents had accepted this procedure and in fact, there had been no arguments. However, we also had days to prepare. The number of refugees was quite manageable and, after all, we volunteers did not have to be paid either. Professional aid organizations usually do not have this kind of capacity.

In my opinion, bringing relief supplies to a country only makes sense if they are either not available on a short-term, or there are other important reasons for doing so. Many years later, I was responsible for buying potato seeds in Western Europe for Syria, and this is only available in Western Europe.

Usually the HQ tendered such goods, selected according to certain criteria and procured. Many companies seem to have specialized in offering their product range to aid organizations without being asked in the event of a disaster. This happened to me as the responsible desk officer at the headquarters of an aid organization after the severe earthquake in Turkey in 1999. Almost every day, I received new offers for shelters. During the selection process, the responsible colleagues excluded me, because I was a beginner. However, pretty much everything went wrong with this procurement, which could go wrong at all, although the supposedly cheapest and at the same time most winter-proof solution had been awarded the contract.

The makeshift houses were procured in Finland (!), which is not just around the corner from Turkey. In addition, they not only consisted of innumerable individual parts, so they were not easy to assemble. Moreover, they were not loaded as whole packages, as actually intended, but in equal parts; that meant one truck only with front elements, another with rear elements, etc. In total, the shipment consisted of 40 trucks, which gradually left Finland. In addition, you could only assemble the elements with specially made screws. Conveniently, these were on the last truck, so that not a single shelter could be set up until the screws were available. Finally, the company had agreed that a professional team would be assigned to support the affected people in setting up their temporary accommodation.

I never knew what nationality that team was - at least it was not Finns! Given the urgency of the situation, their attitude to work was anything but motivated. We had to push them every day to make them do anything at all. In addition, they had never really understood our principle that they should guide people so that they could set up their emergency shelters themselves. Instead, all four always worked on the same emergency shelter. In any case, the pace left a lot to be desired and they could not communicate verbally anyway.

In the meantime, I myself had been there by chance, as I had planned my business trip weeks in advance. Actually, I should just get an idea of the progress of the project. Personally, I had longed for this trip. Not just because it was my very first ever. Especially, I also expected that the team would perceive me as part of it who enabled the assistance. I was accordingly excited. I had already reported on the interview at the airport. Just like about the adventurous radio interview.

As already mentioned, an older German colleague broke off his assignment prematurely. In order to support my colleagues, I simply declared myself a logistician, who received the arriving trucks, depending on their cargo, and directed them to the designated locations in five villages. In addition to the delayed progress of the construction, there was also the fact that all Bulgarian drivers of the trucks apparently took a short break at home on their long journey across Europe to regenerate. That is why one or the other truck suddenly disappeared for days! Even the commissioned company could not provide any information about them.

In my new role, I experienced a rather bizarre situation that was comparable to a comedy show. In one village, a local company kindly provided a forklift to unload the cargo. Before he arrived, I once instructed the truck driver he could already open the tarp so that it would go all the faster afterwards. You know it or have seen it before: the driver usually opens the lace fastening, takes out the first batten, and balances it under the tarp to maneuver it onto the roof. This Bulgarian colleague, however, proceeded differently, which I observed curiously from a distance while sitting in the car: after he had loosened the lacing, he tied a much too long rope to the tarp, at the end of which hung a hook. Like a cowboy, he threw the rope over the whole vehicle. However, the tarp did not rise as intended, but fell back again, so that he pulled on his rope to be able to throw the metal hook again. Too bad that he had parked the vehicle exactly under a power line and before I could take action, the hook had already touched the power cable. Electric sparks hissed zigzag and catapulted the driver backwards. Completely perplexed he stood there in the dark, because all of a sudden, the lights of all the houses around us had gone out.

I quickly asked him if he was okay, told him I had to leave to another construction site all of a sudden, started the engine and absconded. When I returned after a while, a crowd of wildly gesticulating people, including the Police, had gathered around the driver. I, of course blank-faced, tried to calm down the situation motioning with both hands, because I could not speak the language. Sometimes linguistic communication deficits can be very useful. For the sake of completeness, I should add that in the end, everything went smoothly and apart from a power failure lasting several hours, no further damage had occurred.

Usually, smaller, rather unknown aid agencies, if at all, receive significantly fewer donations than the larger ones. In addition, the latter have the advantage that they often already have their own network of local sister organizations in the affected countries. Nonetheless, no matter how big the organization is, in the field, all of them run after institutional donors such as the EU, so that their representatives are flattered and sometimes visibly enjoyed this role.

In practice, I tried to elaborate project proposals, because such donors grant the applicant that is the aid organization, a certain percentage of the total budget as so-called overhead costs. This enables the organization to cover part of its expenses in the head office. That is why I always tried to establish and maintain contact with the respective representatives to explore the possibilities of support. When I was working in Serbia, the organization's headquarters put me under real pressure to get project funding from ECHO. Although the responsible coordinator of the alleged sponsor was German, I just could not get an appointment with her.

One day, a meeting with a representative of the German Foreign Office was scheduled in Belgrade. All German aid organizations active in Serbia were invited. He inquired our experiences with ECHO, especially since "Germany finances 27% of their budget, but only 7% of the money would flow back to German organizations in the form of project funding". Two days later, ECHO, the German, surprisingly called and invited me to a bilateral meeting. Apparently, the representative of the Foreign Office had expressed his opinion regarding the lack of support for German organizations on the part of ECHO. Because she greeted me immediately with the question of whether I had complained elsewhere, which of course I had denied. She then asked me whether we had capacities and suggestions for a project, which, of course, I answered in the affirmative. Then she suddenly offered me a project to support refugees in Serbia, for which we should elaborate a corresponding project proposal and submit it in a few weeks.

To support me, the head office assigned two colleagues, who arrived shortly afterwards. I had arranged a meeting with one of them in the north of Serbia with a representative from ECHO. In the conversation that followed, the colleague said to her word-for-word: we, that is, our organization, would do what they, ECHO, wanted; even if it was a question of the delivery of weapons!

Although it was the last few weeks of my assignment, I put all my energy into elaborating the project proposal. Ultimately, these efforts were successful, although I was no longer in the field at that time. After I had already received a second contract extension, another one, according to German labor law, should have resulted in a permanent position. However, due to the uncertain situation as to whether the project would be approved or not, my employer played it safe. Nevertheless, I later kept contact with the person responsible for the project, who at least informed me that its implementation is successful.

Another type of project award, especially with large donors, was so-called call for proposals, by means of a public tender. Usually it was precisely specified where, what type of interventions, the available budget, and by whom a project can be submitted. UNDP, the United Nations Development Program, applied a somewhat unconventional approach in autumn 2005 in the North Caucasus.

In the weekly coordination meeting of the NGOs, a UNDP representative announced that they still had funds for the current year in the field of income generation activities. That is why they would award five micro-projects as part of a quick process. The deadline for submitting the proposals would be in ten days. The meeting took place in November, so that it was clear to everyone that UNDP compelled to spend their funds to avoid budget cutbacks in their next budget period.

It need to add that the approval process for a project could take several months, especially for institutional donors. In this case, everything seemed different because UNDP put the pedal to the metal. Of course, I wanted to submit at least one project after consulting the head office. The background to this was the assumption that this would enable us to have our foot in the door for the future. However, I had no experience with the donor. Apparently, other NGOs felt the same way.

Back at the office, I asked my local coordinator what he would suggest. The requirements were as follows: maximum duration of the project was three months; Target group: internally displaced persons from Chechnya together with locals; and most of the budget should go to the recipients. My colleague spontaneously suggested cleaning up the area around neighboring apartment blocks and creating green spaces. The residents themselves should do this, as a number of displaced Chechens lived there. We did not have time to assess the needs. That is why we immediately took action. We went straight to the buildings and talked to the residents. They acknowledged our idea very positively. The next steps, especially who would be considered as workers, would be clarified if we were awarded the contract. UNDP provided us appropriate application forms, but no one really knew how to complete them. So, I agreed with the representative of another aid organization, with whom I got on well, that we would exchange the forms. As a result, each of us should check whether the other's project met the specifications and whether it even made sense. Admittedly, a somewhat unusual approach, especially since we were actually competitors. However, we were both enthusiastic about each other's openness. On the one hand, it was not about large sums of money and, on the other hand, we had different project ideas anyway. In any case, we subsequently submitted our project proposals, which UNDP approved within a few days. Once again, it had become clear to me that the cooperation among the aid organizations could sometimes be fabulous.

Nevertheless, even with meticulous preparation and taking into account all the imponderables, an implemented project could also cause negative consequences that were by no means intended.

Not quite as dramatic, but with consequences that we did not have in mind, we implemented a project in northeastern Montenegro. In the mountain villages there, it was a big problem for the children to get to school, as it was sometimes up to 10 km away and only accessible on foot. The idea was therefore to procure some minibuses so that at least those students from remote villages could be transported to the school. Together with the school principals, we therefore worked out detailed timetables, made an agreement with the responsible ministry that it would cover the costs for the drivers and the maintenance of the vehicles and thus made all the necessary arrangements to ensure the project could continue in the long term. Shortly after the vehicles were in place, however, in one of the villages the school principal and indirectly we were exposed to outrageous allegations from some parents who therefore no longer sent their children to school. Because, in the opinion of the parents, the school director would have deliberately excluded them from bus transport for personal reasons. Thus, we called a parents' meeting to discuss the procedure and the problem again and to try to find a solution: about forty men were present. After I had reiterated the project and applied procedure, one of those fathers immediately spoke up who expressed his protest against the project by saying that he had forbidden his son (!) to continue going to school. He lived at least eight kilometers from the school, whereupon another person immediately protested, "it was no more than four". Said father then: "Then let's leave it to six" - in reality it was about two kilometers that we had then driven ourselves. "Are we here in the bazaar?" I interfered. Even the law stipulated at the time that only children whose place of residence was more than five kilometers from school had the right for school transport, even though there was no organized school transport in the entire region.

Not all objections and statements on our part, however, seemed the father listen to reason. Even after three hours of unsuccessful discussion, he continued to insist, visibly proud, that he would not allow his son to attend school in the future. For me, the only conclusion that remained was that you can never please everyone anyway, that we had tried our best and addressed it directly to the father that it was not he, but his son who actually suffered from the whole situation. Whether he had thought about it carefully, he only answered with a barking "So what!" Although without any visible result, most of the people present left the meeting with a smile (!) in the end. On the way out, an older man took me aside and suggested that we just swap the vehicle for a bigger one so that as many children as possible could be transported with it. Rather ironically, I replied that we had already requested various helicopters, whereupon he left with an astonished "Really?" It remains to be noted that said father later apparently showed understanding and allowed his son to go to school again - not to the same school anymore, but to one further away, where there was no bus transport at all! The poor boy!

Often enough, I have seen affected or corresponding institutions believe that we alone, the aid organization, are the panacea for solving all problems. People said "most of the time you can't expect anything from your own government anyway." It was even more difficult in the long-term development phase, in which you usually try to tackle problems together with the local authorities, but in my experience, they often shift the blame, especially in financial terms, to foreign aid organizations, ("one would have no funds available"). Actually, it is the objective of aid organizations to try to become superfluous gradually, and measures and responsibilities should be transferred to the hands of the institutions or organizations in the country. By the way, a rather paradoxical approach: as an employee of an aid organization abroad, no matter what position you hold, you are always working to get rid of your own job!

With regard to the supposed responsibility for projects and their continuation without our support, Kosovo was a striking example for me. Since the wars in the former Yugoslavia in the 1990s and at the latest the Kosovo war in 1999, all kinds of international aid organizations have been active there. While they initially concentrated on caring for the affected people, and then provided enormous reconstruction aid, the development phase had been in the fore for a long time. Nevertheless, more than ten years after the war, many people, as well as local institutions, still expected that the so-called international community would have to solve most of the problems. On the other hand, I saw numerous demonstrations against the UN and later the EU institutions in the country, especially in 2007, before the country's self-declared independence.

The immense amount of funds that flowed into the country showed the people that they were not left alone in their need. However, they also relied on it accordingly, so that very often the necessary commitment on their part, according to my observation, was very low. Certainly, the international community and especially the aid organizations were partly to blame, as the available funds had in some cases been used far too lavishly. Inevitably, this created some sort of mentality to have the right for support and corresponding demands. For example, a local colleague told me, that the aid organization she had previously worked for, regularly organized training for all staff in Egypt (!). On the other hand, a ministerial official with whom I spoke about a planned training said we should not forget to include per diems for the attendees in the budget. We should reward their attendance; after all, it used to be the norm with such projects. The director of civil protection in a community in whose school we had installed escape stairs on the outside of the building was even bolder. This measure had not been originally included in the project. However, in order to be prepared for possible claims in an emergency, the headquarters decided to install additional escape stairs at three schools in the country, which corresponded to German standards and were thus virtually unique in Kosovo. In one of the affected communities, the director of civil protection actually barked at me during a meeting with all the other representatives of the community, in a very specific, almost arrogant tone, whether the stairs corresponded to a recognized standard. In doing so, he probably wanted to emphasize his responsibility in the first place. At the same time, however, he indirectly admitted that he had not even looked at the stairs personally. I was boiling inside. Because I found it almost outrageous to ask such a question. I was about to answer that the stairs, of course, corresponded to ISO Standard X, which he would certainly be familiar with, even though it did not actually exist. Finally, the mayor mediated by expressing great gratitude for the provided support.

In addition, means of escape were marked in the school buildings, possible sources of fire such as the wood or coal store secured and, finally yet importantly, the schools should start holding fire protection exercises on a regular basis. Now the said director for civil protection informed us that there was only one authorized organization in the country to carry out such exercises and mentioned the expected expenses of several thousand euro. For a single simulation exercise by the organization together with the fire brigade! While I still knew from my own school days that the only exercise with us every year was to leave the classroom in the event of an alarm and to be at the assembly point as quickly as possible. Here, the plan was to train the students on fire extinguishers using wrecked cars. Although it did not argue for a lot of trust in the fire brigade, it was of course impossible for us to finance the whole spectacle. Before the meeting, I had already expected long discussions in this regard, but my statement that it would be out of the question for us to pay for this, the responsible person answered straightforwardly: "Then we organize it ourselves, on our own Costs!" At a second school in another municipality, the local director of civil protection did not want to accept the project because we had not installed an alarm system, which, by the way, was not included in the project. It was not expensive either he tried to convince me. A maximum of a thousand euro, to which I replied that he could then certainly take it over from his own budget!

The most surprising thing for me personally was the result of a project in Kosovo that we had been preparing for almost half a year. In order not to proceed to implement here and there, we intended to support four selected villages in the areas of health, income generation, education and infrastructure with around 300,000 euro for each. The condition was, however, that the corresponding 'municipality', would contribute a third of the amount. Then we would work out and implement appropriate projects together with the village community, depending on the needs. Therefore, in our target area, which consisted of six districts with 141 villages, we first informed all district administrations of this in order to obtain their feedback. Everyone agreed to our terms and conditions, which made us quite hopeful.

We organized the whole plan in the form of a tender. This meant that we had drafted a 20-page questionnaire in which we asked for all sorts of information and the willingness of the respective village to contribute to the intended projects, whether financially or through personal contribution. In addition, they should present some visionary aspects in the questionnaire, for example the idea of where you would see your village in five years or how you would imagine an ideal village community. This seemed to have been a bit too ambitious. However, we only intended that those who filled out the questionnaire should also bring their own thoughts and ideas, instead of just numbers. To make sure that we did not forget any village, we organized several meetings in the different areas, to which we invited all village heads to receive the application documents. In the end, all heads indeed received the appropriate papers.

Now they had about six weeks to fill them in and submit to us. During this time, we also offered a kind of consultation hour on Friday mornings, in which we were available to advise if problems occurred. In the meantime, I experienced my first disappointment. During the entire application period, not even one came to ask for our help. On the other hand, this also gave us hope that there were apparently no problems filling out the documents and that we could count hopefully on many questionnaires.

However, when the last week up to the submission deadline had begun, we still had not received a single completed questionnaire. The more nervous I got. My colleagues tried to calm me down by saying they knew their compatriots. They would certainly wait until the last second. However, the days passed until the morning of the handover day and we still had only received about 20 questionnaires. The deadline ended at 4 p.m. on the reporting date and only twelve more were submitted. One day later, we accepted a late submission, so that out of 141 villages only 33 had submitted a questionnaire.

For me personally a completely disappointing number, because I had expected a lot more. Obviously, my expectations were too idealistic. I had always imagined the result such a procedure would have had in my hometown. I had imagined that if I had been a resident of a remote village and knew that my village community had the prospect of almost 400,000 euro, I would at least somehow urge the local council to submit a corresponding application. Other expatriates in Kosovo were downright surprised at the number of 33 questionnaires submitted. They would have expected even less! I was particularly interested in the question of why the remaining 108 villages had not submitted any documents and therefore instructed a colleague to contact all village heads and ask for the reasons. To my surprise, more than a quarter of them replied that they were not interested and had no time anyway! Another fifth even claimed that the entire questionnaire was too difficult. Why they would not have made use of our office hours they answered with time problems, too!

We then selected the four communities applying a sophisticated point system and started to elaborate together with them reasonable projects, according their needs. We experienced further surprises in that process. One community wanted to build a health station in the shape of a cross with a red roof, so that helicopters could find the destination more easily. As far as I knew, there was not a single rescue helicopter in all of Kosovo at the time! In addition, they already had a functioning health station.

In another village people insisted strongly to build a sports area with a soccer, handball and volleyball field next to the primary school, even though there were already sports facilities. The third community took the cake regarding their elementary school, which had only four rooms. They wanted to buy the most modern technology, such as a projector in each room and numerous computers, even though they had no one who could use this technology at all. In any case, it was to be expected in the medium term that the school would be closed due to the shrinking number of students!

Everywhere we had to have endless discussions with the local councils because we doubted the necessity of these requests and therefore called meetings to which the population was invited. After that, the picture always looked different, so that we worked out new projects everywhere, which the residents also supported.

In addition, it happened to me often enough, especially in Kosovo, that we received requests for all kinds of support. On the one hand, understandable, since the number of foreign aid organizations operating in the country had meanwhile reduced to a few more than ten years after the war. On the other hand, those inquiries were sometimes difficult to understand. Especially if you had the impression that this was at best based on the motto: asking doesn't cost anything! Indeed, there never seemed to be an urgent need. A school principal phoned and asked if we could finance a photocopier. I asked, if the school had a device and how many teachers were there. He replied that they already had a device, but that it would not be enough for the forty teachers. Then I: at my wife's school in Germany there were about 70 teachers and they got by with just one device! The director (literally): I thought I would just ask!

It was similar for us even with local partners. Not only did we get project proposals that were either outside of our mandate, such as financing holidays for selected children on the Albanian coast. Most of such proposals were only formulated very roughly without actual needs had been assessed.

Once, in 2007, we received a request from a local Catholic organization about the construction of a vocational school. At first, the project idea sounded extremely interesting, especially since we wanted to carry out suitable measures in the field of education. On closer inspection, however, it turned out that a new building would have meant moving the old, already existing school so that a new Catholic church could be built on its site. The whole matter turned out to be highly political, especially since the majority of Kosovars were Muslim. We neither wanted to be drawn into local games, nor did we even see the need for a new school building. Hence, I rejected the project.

My motto has always been that we are not an all-inclusive organization and that we therefore expect commitment and contribution from our partners. Although in the end I was of course always interested in promoting development in the country through projects, there were still limits at which I simply had to say 'no'.

On the other hand, my experience in a rural area in Pakistan was completely different, where foreign aid organizations were neither part of the everyday picture, nor was there much support from the state. In all these years, I had not been to a poorer area. The mostly simple farming families had to struggle for survival every day, which was even more difficult by the fact that regular natural disasters, especially floods, afflicted the already troubled people. Even from the little bit that was left for them to survive, they gave something to show their willingness to be ready for action, so that, for example, a street would be paved, the construction of a school or health station would be possible. Even if this personal contribution was more of a symbolic character, within the framework of development cooperation it is the ideal prerequisite to work out and implement projects directly together with people and, in the end, to push ahead with development. Corresponding relief measures in this phase therefore take much longer than in the two previous ones. These often drag on for several years, for which significantly more funds are needed. These, in turn, are used in a wide variety of ways: Be it through training measures of all kinds, the development of state and civil society structures through to direct budget support for the country concerned. One of the easiest ways to recognize this phase is that, alongside other actors and aid organizations, a whole slew of advisors, so-called consultants, suddenly become active. The NGOs that specialize in emergency aid are now likely to be on duty again in another disaster. The consultants, mostly highly qualified and appropriately remunerated, should then help to set up or even completely rebuild functioning structures in a wide variety of areas. In general, such expert knowledge is indeed essential, especially to carry out complex measures. Because mere organization is no longer enough here. In practice, one can generally criticize the fact that too often, we proceed according to our western ideas, whereby the local culture and mentality remain in the background and therefore the affected parties are too seldom included in measures from the beginning. In particular, there are all sorts of jokes about the work and approach of such consultants. One of the best known is probably the one with the sheep:

A large off-road vehicle stops at the roadside in front of a shepherd, whose huge flock of sheep is grazing in the meadow. A young, well-dressed man in a suit gets out of the car and says to the shepherd "If I tell you how many sheep graze there, can I take one?" The shepherd accepts somewhat surprised. The young man then unpacks all sorts of technical devices, such as notebook, smartphone, etc., connects them, and clicks here and there and after a long calculation time he claims: "You have exactly 968 sheep there." "Exactly," says the shepherd. When the young man takes an animal, the shepherd makes him a counter-offer: "If I guessed your job right away, will I get the animal back?" "Okay," replies the young man. "You are a consultant" quick as a shot, whereupon the young man asks the shepherd how he would have guessed it. "First of all, you came without I asked you; second, you told me something I already knew; and, thirdly, you didn't take a sheep, but my dog. "

Admittedly, this joke does not exactly make the consultants appear in a good light and certainly does not do justice to many. However, it certainly applies to isolated consultants. I met one of them once at the airport in Frankfurt/Germany when I was flying to Montenegro. Studying a thick folder with the label 'Montenegro' in front of me, I asked him which organization he worked for and what he wanted to do there. He is traveling on behalf of the Council of Europe to facilitate workshops in various ministries, which essentially dealt with European standards and values, and to show Montenegrin officials the way to the EU. So now, I had an expert in front of me whom, since I was not a specialist in currency issues, I was finally able to ask for an explanation why Euro is the official currency in Montenegro, even though the country is neither part of the EU nor the monetary union. I would never really have understood that. Completely puzzled, he answered me: "What? Do you pay with Euro in Montenegro? "

Disregarding such surprises, I can safely say that most of the projects for which I have been responsible for have shown successful results. Admittedly, in humanitarian aid, the mere distribution of relief supplies, this is not too difficult. Of course, we were able to alleviate the plight of the people affected a little. The gratitude of the people was correspondingly.

However, I was not always employed as a mere project manager. It was precisely then that I was able to celebrate my greatest professional successes.

In Moldova, as already mentioned, my task was to provide a local organization a structure for its future work. A few years later, my protégés took part in a competition the EU had announced. They won the first prize. Although I was no longer involved at the time, my then employer attested that my efforts years earlier had laid the foundation for that success. What a feeling!

I was Head of Mission in Kosovo. That meant that I was responsible for all of the projects. In addition, however, I also had the task of getting the office certified according to ISO 9001, a quality management system. I had already mentioned various colleagues above. Nevertheless, after about a year of preparation, we actually managed to get the ISO 9001 label. In view of the circumstances, especially with regard to the colleagues, I still describe this as my greatest professional success today. This was remarkable because many, admittedly, at the beginning, I too, did not believe we could achieve it. Above all, the test run before the actual certification procedure did not give rise to optimism. After months of training, we failed miserably. My own result as a so-called management representative was quite sobering and left me somewhat perplexed at first. More surprisingly was the reaction of a local colleague to the disastrous result, which seemed to be entirely in the tradition of the 'Balkan' mentality. Instead of doing his own failure analysis, he blamed the consultant, who had trained us for almost a year. I could not believe what I heard. He acted like a student who blamed the teacher for bad grades. After the general rehearsal went completely wrong, we completed the certification audit all the more astonishingly. Namely without any error! I have seldom felt happier, because many people congratulated. Despite the difficult situation with the local colleagues there, in the end I was quite proud of them.

Over the years, I have been responsible for numerous aid projects of the most varied types in various missions, from which a large number of affected people benefited. Nonetheless, there were many situations that I was completely powerless confronted. I am thinking above all of the living conditions of the Roma in Kosovo, which were definitely unbearable. I am also thinking of that psychiatric clinic in southern Serbia, located remotely from any civilization, where the patients were all crammed together in the shower room, completely naked and staff bespattered them with a hosepipe. That reminded me of films from concentration camps. I am also thinking of those prison guards in Moldova who first served themselves from the visitors who brought food for their relatives or friends. Finally, I think of that Afghan man in a prison in Tajikistan who pleaded desperately for help, because, according to him, he was wrongly detained. Although I reported his case to the International Red Cross, I never found out what happened to him.

I have experienced such situations of my own powerlessness or bewilderment over the years as part of the project work. Nevertheless, I also had many nice moments. Especially when we completed a project successfully.

I will always remember one very personal moment: I was supposed to be the first volunteer to go to Kakanj in Bosnia, about 50 kilometers northwest of Sarajevo, for a few weeks during the war. An elderly man from the refugee camp in Croatia therefore asked me to visit his sister, a Bosnian Croat, in Kakanj, a town where the majority of the population is Muslim. Because he had not heard from her for more than two years. In fact, she was at home, where she, in her own words, spent most of the time, because she was afraid to leave her home. Therefore, we, a volunteer from Bosnia and I, were not only a welcome change for her, but also when we told about her brother she immediately began to cry with the joy of having finally received a sign of life from him after a long time.

I will also remember the words of a Muslim minister in Sri Lanka when we took part in the laying of the foundation stone for a new village; she hugged me gratefully and whispered Keep up the good work!

6. Encounters with drama

A recurring question was asked often enough at home after I had told what I did professionally and where I would work: was it not dangerous? To come to the point: In my own estimation, my life was never in immediate danger. Nonetheless, my experiences in this regard were certainly different from those of average citizens.

My international activities were mostly in countries that were by no means ordinary holiday destinations, where as a tourist you could unwind with a cocktail in hand. If at all, the best I could do was enjoying the evening in a bar that had specialized in solvent, foreign aid workers as a clientele. With correspondingly high prices, of course. All too often I have seen such locations being visited on the way home from the office and a supposedly short meeting for a beer turned into a spontaneous party for the entire community of aid workers. That was only positive for the owner of the location, while the locals took notice of such parties disapprovingly. In contrast, especially in traditional or religious regions, the population (rightly) showed no understanding at all.

In Sri Lanka, such gatherings resulted in an opportunity to threaten specifically local female employees of NGOs with false accusations: a leaflet said that they, the female employees, were only abused as sex objects at parties and that they were immediately taken to the abortionist afterwards. One day this was stuck to many of the house walls in which the employees lived (!). Therefore, without exception, everyone was asked to quit his or her job by a certain date. Otherwise, as it read in English "Your souls are in our hands." Unfortunately, in areas where people were used to acts of violence that occur every day, it was by no means mere sayings. You need to take such threats seriously. In this case, we could not do more than first ask our female employees how they assessed the situation and from then on took them to the office and back home by car. However, not directly from or to neither the house in which they lived, so that neighbors nor any other people could immediately identify them as employees of a foreign NGO. Fortunately, the threat remained unsuccessful in the further course of events.

Often it was precisely these stories that drew attention at home and occasionally made me, as a humanitarian worker, a hit at many parties: Which normal Joe took a helmet or a bulletproof vest to work or had armed guards? I had visibly impressed young people in particular: "Cool, amazing!"

Such precautionary measures were the exception rather than the rule. If it was a conflict area, the organization advised me of security measures and prepared me accordingly. During my voluntary work in Croatia and Bosnia and Herzegovina in the 1990s, this was unfortunately not the case.

Completely naive, unprotected and above all unprepared, we drove in a car from Split in Croatia to Kakanj in Bosnia and Herzegovina in 1995, where we passed Konjic, a city that was shot at every day from positions on the surrounding hills. I was at the wheel and when we crossed the market square, my co-driver, who had already driven the route several times, said casually "Now you have to speed up for a moment," as it was being targeted repeatedly. Shortly before, I remember pretty well, we had visited a teacher whom the other passengers knew. We were sitting in his living room, where the window was covered with a wooden panel, drinking coffee when he began to tell: We would certainly recognize the holes in the ceiling. These are bullet holes. Because a few weeks earlier, a former student of his had appeared in front of the house and asked him to "serve kindly his time at the front line". Apparently, he said, that soldier wanted some sort of revenge because of the bad grades he had given him. He, the former teacher, would have had no choice but to agree.

Especially since the bullet holes on the ceiling of the living room "were considered an invitation". They forced him to go along and would have done nothing other than digging trenches, which would have been quite physically strenuous. All of a sudden, I realized that it was not an excursion. Here a solid man had feared for his life. That was suddenly a reality. Immediately he was a hero to me, especially since he told all of this as if it were an insignificant event. He had certainly lived through fears that I myself had never experienced before. This was about survival. Only now did I get a feeling for what it meant to be scared to death. A few weeks later, on the way back from Kakanj, we were stuck in a traffic jam in front of the city of Mostar, because the city was "shelled", as one soldier told us! I could not see anything. However, always hear. A scary feeling when you are stuck in a traffic jam and people may have died within earshot.

In any case, the organization had never instructed or prepared us volunteers concerning security measures at the
time. The subject had not been even mentioned with a
single syllable, and no insurance had been taken. From
today's perspective, not just negligent, but more than ir-
responsible. Some aid organization did not seem to have
learned anything. If, for example, volunteers were still
working in Syria every day in 2013, in addition to the
work they had done, also blogged, and thus revealed,
their location - an invitation to potential kidnappers, so
to speak: here we are! In that case, it actually resulted in
three young volunteers having been kidnapped and only
released months later.

Although I became a little more hard-bitten over time, I
still experienced situations that suddenly boosted my
adrenaline level. Particular caution was always required at
police or military checkpoints, which existed in many
countries, regions and especially conflict areas. On the
one hand, they were not only a target for military opponents; on the other hand, one often did not know what
to expect. Usually, I would then let my local colleague do
the communication and keep myself calm.

Once it was particularly tricky when we had to pass a
checkpoint one morning in the middle of nowhere in
southern Russia. Obviously, the police officer was completely drunk, no one else in sight, and was staggering
around with his pistol. My colleague, although Ingush
born in Chechnya, was rather careful, because Chechens
were under a cloud of terrorism. The police officer yelled
accordingly and, in the end, the fact of my German passport should have saved us from worse. Nevertheless, all

of a sudden, my knees became very weak, sweat broke out and I tried to keep my gaze straight ahead, even though the police officer had spoken to or molested me directly ("What would I have to do with a Chechen?"). Under no circumstances did I want to make the person angrier with any movements or gestures. My colleague had already grasped the situation, but it was too late to turn back. Very calmly, he put up with even the wildest insults, telling me repeatedly: Keep calm and look straight ahead. We received the passports back. Then he put into first gear, drove off slowly and after a few meters, he accelerated fully. Only then, my tension did ease and even my colleague was relieved.

Many years earlier, at that time in Bosnia & Herzegovina in the winter of 1995/96, I personally, by no means an old hand, had to appease French soldiers with machine guns. Because they were approached and scanned by strange characters - a scene that could have been from a surreal film. What happened?

At that time, I visited my former volunteer colleagues and stayed in the house of the project coordinator. One morning she left the house to go to the bakery. When she did not come back after a while, I walked towards the bakery. Just around the corner, I saw the reason. A military truck drove into her car. Total loss of the car and no sign of her. One soldier told me that she probably broke a leg and was already on her way to the hospital. So, let us go there. Another volunteer informed her that we would try to take her to the German Army hospital in Sarajevo. We organized an ambulance for this after the hospital had given the green light. However, she did not want any special treatment and refused to be transferred. However, she changed her mind a little later after a doctor had examined her. Apparently, he was the one who was supposed to operate her: a man of about seventy in a white work coat with glasses, the power of which did not indicate that he could even find his way around without them. He stood in front of her bed and told her with a mischievous smile that he was already looking forward to the operation in the afternoon (!), while the patient lay in front of him, her face contorted with pain. Then we took her into the room where a temporary plaster was supposed to be put on to stabilize the leg. The nurse and colleague there put out their cigarettes and immediately took action. Then we took the patient to the X-ray and back to the room. Apparently, however, the leg had been moved while putting on the plaster. Because on the X-ray the bones were suddenly displaced, which scared our colleague. Now she agreed to the transfer, and, please, as soon as possible. Unbeknown to her, we had already arranged it anyway. A short time later, a group of French soldiers, led by a commander, suddenly marched down the hallway with a steady pace. The chief of the troop came up to me and asked me in the best German, but very firmly, where the German was? I showed them the way to the room. He, evidently a doctor, examined her briefly and informed her that he would fly her to Sarajevo immediately by helicopter.

There were many buildings on the clinic's premises, each of which housed different medical departments. Not far from the surgery was the psychiatry, which was only fenced by a small wall that any child could easily jump over. At a side entrance was the helipad, on which a military helicopter was now standing, surrounded by about five or six comparatively young soldiers. They in full combat gear levelling machine guns secured the vehicle, turning repeatedly from right to left. That did not seem to bother several people walking around. Some of them surrounded the soldiers, apparently also spoke to them, even touched them, while others stood around strangely with their heads bent to their shoulders and observed the events, some apathetically and fearfully. At first glance, you could not exactly tell who they were. It was only on closer look that you could see that they had no stockings and were dressed too airy for the time of year. Obviously, those patients from psychiatry were moving freely around the site and had come curiously to the landing site. I walked next to the stretcher with my colleague in the direction of the helicopter, puzzled by the strange scenery, too. I was able to understand fragmentarily what some of the patients who were standing very close to the soldiers said. They asked them for pens, lighters and to be photographed. Apparently, the young French did not understand a word and were visibly uncomfortable, especially those whose shirt and trouser pockets were being scanned. I told them that these people were probably harmless patients who only wanted small presents and that they, the soldiers, should better take down their weapons; after all, the war had been over for months. One of them replied that they had only been in the country for a few days and had been informed that everyone there carried a weapon. Therefore, caution is required at all times, even if it is a clinic. Again, I asked them to put their weapons down not to scare people.

One or the other was certainly traumatized anyway. Finally, they lowered their guns, helped the patient to load up, got in and flew away without taking a souvenir picture with the patient. My colleague, as I found out later, had overcome the operation successfully in Sarajevo and recovered completely. After her removal, I went back to the doctor who actually wanted to operate her to explain the sudden disappearance of his patient. Visibly disappointed, he wished all the best.

How one will ultimately behave in supposedly precarious situations, you only know when you experience them yourself. Especially in emergency relief operations, the probability is much higher that you will suddenly find yourself exposed to danger. It is therefore always helpful if, for example, the organization you are working for is prepared and conceivable scenarios are in place. The so-called security plan, which specifies various levels of risk and appropriate behavior, is one of the guidelines in the field. Starting with questions about your own accommodation: is it in a danger zone? Are there escape routes? Do you have enough provisions to be able to feed yourself for a longer period without leaving the house? Is the building secured against robberies? Where is the nearest Police station, hospital and the like? The staff should be familiar with this, as well as with the various levels and the corresponding reactions to them in conflict situations: this can start with supposedly harmless demonstrations on the streets up to armed clashes, which can result in the evacuation of foreigners. The guidelines should describe in every detail, how to get out of the office safely, who should drive which vehicle and which road should be taken to get out of the danger zone. Over time, you develop a feeling for possible dangers in your own work environment. For example, when I was working in the earthquake region in Turkey and had a look at every building I wanted to enter. Further, we parked the car always further away from it. In conflict areas, one usually avoids certain regions that are classified as particularly dangerous.

In the North Caucasus, I was notably aware of how important an emergency plan can be and should not be underestimated in order to be able to react quickly. When an apparently pleasant football evening - Croatia against England on TV during the 2004 European Football Championship - was suddenly interrupted dramatically and we literally had no plan.

My German colleague and I had just prepared beer and potato chips, turned on the television, swung into the armchair, when gunshots could be heard from outside. At first, we ignored them, assuming that another wedding would be celebrated with particular vigor somewhere. All of a sudden, however, we saw through the window that on the other side of the lake, which was directly in front of us, a building was exploding and at the same time, the power broke down. Now, in addition to the increasingly stronger gunshot noises, we could hear larger explosions elsewhere.

I rang our local coordinator, who immediately picked up the phone and began to whisper. He was lying on the ground because there was shooting around his house, which I could hear well in the background. A few bullets would have penetrated his apartment and he recommended that I turn off all the lights and go into the cellar. Apparently, several hundred Chechen rebels had attacked particularly state that is Russian, facilities and Police stations in the city of Nazran and had already killed many people.

We immediately called all possible colleagues from other aid organizations who had already been in the picture themselves. Only two Canadian colleagues, whose apartment was right next to the local office of the domestic secret service, had not yet been reached. We were very worried about them. In the meantime, the water and gas had also been turned off and my colleague and I were standing by the window in the dark kitchen on the first floor and were not sure what to do next. While I was sending a short SMS "Heavy Fights in Nazran" to the headquarters in Germany, my colleague was constantly trying to reach the two Canadian colleagues by phone. Later, the two of them said that they were already in the basement of their building at the time and every time the phone rang, a volley of rifles would have been fired into their office!

In all the excitement, I had forgotten about our guards outside in the garage, who were assigned by the Ministry of the Interior to protect the offices and accommodations of foreign aid workers. However, they were by no means battle-hardened former soldiers, even though they had a pro forma weapon in order to do their job in shifts. In private, we always called them armed door attendants.

I went to the garage, where the two guards completely dissolved; the fear was literally on their faces, pacing back and forth and not really knowing how to behave now. Thus, I offered them to come into the house. We would lock ourselves in and wait until the situation would calm down. They tried to calm me down, however, and insisted on staying in the garage - heroism was by no means appropriate now. However, I could not change their mind. A little later, in the meantime we had locked the metal grille on the front door and all the windows, I could vaguely make out a man outside in the darkness who was walking through our street with a machine gun in hand and the sound of the gunshots seemed to be getting closer and closer.

My colleague and I stayed in the basement when, before the cellular networks switched off, I received the reply to my SMS from our desk officer at the headquarters: "It's normal, isn't it!" He meant the gunfire. That was not very helpful, especially since we ourselves were getting more and more nervous. It was now well past midnight and we were on our own. We also no longer had any means of communication. We had no choice but to wait and see. The uncertainty was the most depressing for me, although, surprisingly, I remained rather calm. My colleague, on the other hand, was constantly pacing up and down. Apparently, he was particularly concerned about the two Canadian colleagues. I tried as best I could to calm him down. At the same time, I made the situation clear to him: now it is about us!

My colleague and I went through various options as to how we would proceed the next day. We did not have a security plan that could give us appropriate instructions, for example using a checklist. Hence, we would have to improvise. We decided to try, if possible, the next morning to contact other aid organizations to see how they would proceed.

Around four in the morning, the gunshot noises died down, so that we could lie down for at least a few hours. Less than three hours later, however, our local coordinator waked us up and asked us to leave the country on the same day. After all, one does not know whether there could be fighting again in the evening. Because the attackers, he continued, had withdrawn into the surrounding forests early in the morning after attacking all government institutions in Nazran. In addition to the interior minister, about a hundred more people were killed.

Meanwhile electricity and water as well as the mobile network were working again, so we first called our families in Germany. As expected, no one had registered anything. Nevertheless, we quieted them in case media would tell anything. Then our desk officer from the head office called me to apologize for his flippant SMS from the previous evening: the attack was the first message on the BBC (!), he emphasized. Immediately afterwards a representative of the UN phoned and informed me that an attempt would be made to organize an airplane from the Russian civil protection ministry for the next day. This would fly out all foreign aid workers from Vladikavkaz in North Ossetia-Alania, which was about an hour from Nazran. The costs of around 800 US dollars per person would have to be borne by ourselves. As if that was an obstacle for us!

At 9 o'clock, we had called a meeting with some other aid organizations in another part of the city. Before that, some other foreigners had already told us on the phone that they would join the UN proposal. We were now sitting in a group of about ten foreign employees, including the two Canadians. During the drive to the meeting, we could see the traces that the last night's fighting had left: Not far from our office was a large intersection with several burned-out cars. Our driver informed us that everything or everybody who had moved there had been shot randomly. A UN driver was also among the victims when he just tried to get an idea of the situation at this intersection. Across the city, which was now full of uniformed soldiers, we could see bullet holes in many buildings, from which we concluded that there must have been a large number of fighters.

We decided together with the others present in the meeting to leave the city and republic immediately and to drive to Nalchik, two hours from Nazran, the capital of the Russian republic of Kabardino-Balkaria. From a supposedly safe distance, we initially wanted to wait for further developments. The meeting point was the checkpoint in front of Vladikavkaz in two hours' time. Before that, the person in charge of the project at headquarters had told me that the decision to evacuate would be my own, as I could better assess the situation. At the same time, I should make all the necessary preparations and organize the handover to our local coordinator. I informed him that we would leave in any case. I had about 90 minutes to do everything I needed and right now, a To-do list would have been the ideal means to work through the essential points. However, unfortunately, we did not have any. Since we did not know how long we would be away, our local coordinator needed a written authorization to act on behalf of the organization. Together with him I went through other aspects: the rest of the staff should stay at home for a few days and only go back to work when the security situation allowed; our colleagues in Grozny, the capital of Chechnya, where we also distributed relief supplies, had to be informed, as our suppliers; Contracts had to be looked at to see if payments were due anytime soon, which usually required my signature. Then the finances: we calculated the financial needs of the next four weeks for rent, water, electricity, telephone and last but not least salaries as well as other project-related expenses. Accordingly, I left a sum of 30,000 US dollars that we had in the safe. I took the rest, also several thousand US dollars, because we also needed money ourselves. After we had put all of this down in writing, copied it and faxed it to headquarters, I packed my things. It was only during this time that I realized that I would not come back myself, as my employment contract would expire ten days later anyway.

Hence, there was no time to say goodbye to the rest of the colleagues. I did that at the agreed meeting point from our local coordinator, wished him and his family all the best, sent greetings to the other colleagues, sat back in the car and waved to him for a long time. No further nighttime fighting occurred afterwards, but all aid organizations had relocated their base to Vladikavkaz for several months and, above all, the foreign employees only went to Ingushetia during the day, if at all. At home, I then suggested to elaborate a security plan as soon as possible in order to be prepared for such incidents in the future – always expect the unexpected!

As it turned out, I found myself in a life-threatening situation sooner than I would like. Unfortunately, however, sometimes especially young foreign employees ignored or even downplayed this sort of danger, and viewed it more as normality or even adventure.

In Turkey in 2013, I was assigned to open a project office in Antakya as well as Aleppo/Syria for a small German aid organization, even though the war and the fighting had assumed alarming proportions. At that time, many aid organizations based in Turkey were still sending foreign aid workers to Syria on a daily basis, but only one that actually had an office in Aleppo. I talked to the Head of Mission of that organization about the dangers to which the employees in Syria were exposed and how she could shoulder it. Because in addition to the acts of war, foreigners were particularly targeted there to be kidnapped. "We just have to take the risk," was her short answer, which I strongly disagreed with. After all, this is about human lives and that is what she is responsible for, I answered. It should be clear to everyone who is active in emergency aid that there is always a certain risk, but especially those who are responsible for employees and their lives and limbs in the field should neither make negligent nor careless decisions. The irony of the story was that a little later in a car bomb attack in Turkey the office of that organization was destroyed. Fortunately, no employee was injured or killed, the manager, who was visibly shocked, told me afterwards. According to official information, the death toll was almost 80!

Years earlier in Serbia, I had learned my lessons in recklessness. In the course of the revolution of October 5 2000, which I witnessed first-hand. On that day, the Milosević regime was finally overthrown - a truly historic event.

Before, there had been demonstrations almost every day for months in the city center of Belgrade on and around the Republic Square, less than 300m away from our office. Sometimes I went there in the evening and watched the rallies on the sidelines. Obviously, I was still too unexperienced. Most of the time massive Police forces dissolved them by chasing the protesters. One or the other time I had to hide behind the corners of houses. From today's perspective, I can hardly believe that I was so reckless. I probably thought that as a foreigner, none of this would affect me. I was right in the middle of it! I cannot imagine what could have happened if I had been arrested. I was not even aware of that at the time. I had not thought of the possible consequences or dangers. During the day, it was of course inevitable that my local colleagues spoke of nothing else and that their oppositional opinion encroached on me.

Actually, as an aid worker, you are particularly obliged to be neutral and should avoid giving political statements as much as possible. Rather, those in need and the projects connected with them should be the focus and every effort should be made to fulfill this mission. Therefore, everything should be avoided that could endanger the work.

This includes political statements or attending political gatherings.

At the time, I cared little about such concerns. Today, however, I would be much more cautious, especially since over the years I have noticed how foreign employees from an aid organization suddenly were expelled from the country twice. In one case, local staff took part in political rallies. Apparently, that was enough to expel the foreigners, even though they did not take part. In the other case, authorities closed the whole organization immediately because they believed that it was part of the political opposition. In both cases, the decision was more than questionable. However, it showed what consequences could arise from supposedly harmless behavior.

On the said 5 October 2000 in Serbia, the events around us rolled over. Days earlier, another mass rally against the regime's apparent electoral fraud had been announced in the city center. The people of the whole country were called to take part. To work was out of question, as more and more people with banners passed the office to Parliament in the morning. At first, we observed everything from there and then finally went out onto the street to the Parliament building ourselves. However, there was hardly any getting through in the face of the crowds.

From a distance, we could only see demonstrators storming the parliament building and the Police immediately trying to disperse the people with the exuberant use of tear gas (by the way, the cover picture shows me covering my nose because of it). We, with burning eyes, ran back to the office, where several dozen protesters were already taking shelter in the entrance of the building. I unlocked the door, let everyone into the stairway, and brought water to wash his or her eyes. We heard shootings occasionally and smoke rose from the parliament building.

After we had recovered briefly, a German colleague from another NGO suggested that we go to his office, which was also not far from the center, because he had a television set. We made our way through a few small side streets past Parliament, stopped at a kiosk to buy a few drinks - a truly surreal scene: smoke visibly rose from the Parliament building, where the hundreds of thousands of people were non-stop chanting slogans against the regime and thus caused a deafening noise, but more and more superimposed by gunfire. However, we could not locate the direction from which they came. At the same time, it was completely quiet around the kiosk where we were now for a few moments and we bought drinks as if it was a completely normal day.

All channels reported the events and the rumor spread that the army was marching on Belgrade, which would certainly result in a bloodbath. We therefore decided to stay in the colleague's apartment for the time being and watch the events on the television. In the early evening, it was suddenly announced that the advance of the army had stopped because it refused to attack compatriots. It was clear that this was the end of the Milosević regime.

Hence, I wanted to experience the mood of the people first hand and went back to the office. A parade of vehicles celebrating the victory passed by honking their horns through the countless applauding, whistling people. Total strangers hugged me on the side of the road, handed me

207

schnapps and said a toast to the hopefully improving future. At around 5 a.m. I went to bed, completely exhausted. I could not sleep properly. I was too excited of the events and the honking on the streets seemed to continue endlessly. Only now did I realize that I had witnessed a truly historic event.

At 9 o'clock the following day, I had a meeting at the Ministry of Social Affairs, which I was even more excited about in view of the previous day. To my surprise, the Vice-Minister did not say a word about the events, but just pretended it was a day like any other and agreed a few steps with regard to a project that we wanted to implement for displaced people from Kosovo. Although we took our notes as usual, we also knew at the same time that any agreements were very likely no longer of any value, since it was to be expected that the Vice-Minister would be replaced very soon. After the meeting, my local colleague said succinctly that it might even have been one of her last official acts at all. In the end, the whole episode ended well for me, but, overall, my behavior was more than reckless.

A few years later in the North Caucasus, we practiced a completely different kind of carelessness, albeit entirely justified, when we went from Nazran/Ingushetia to Grozny/Chechnya. As already mentioned, the regulation stipulated that foreign aid workers were only allowed to move with armed escorts. In practice it looked like that even for playing cards in evening I had to be escorted by an armed guard with Kalashnikov for the 100m walk to the house of another German aid organization. The guard would never have let me go alone. If the car was needed, armed guards usually drove with me in the car and another in the car behind it. Fortunately, neither of them performed like Rambo. Rather, they remained silent in the background, for which I was extremely grateful.

Nevertheless, no matter where you were as a foreigner, whether in the market or in a café, you inevitably attracted the attention of the local population. Some kidnappings in the past had shown that it was not entirely safe. In addition to the armed escorts, there were also the house guards mentioned, so that one was in principle under observation day and night.

The short trips to Grozny, where we had our own team of local employees who distributed relief supplies, were completely different. As The Head of Mission, my task was to inspect the distribution myself from time to time. In order to be able to conduct this, one had to provide the authorities with three periods of two days each for the following month during which one was planning to travel to Chechnya. Most of the time, the authorities canceled at least one or two planned dates. Usually, my local coordinator took care of it. Besides me, only he knew about it. For good reason.

When the time came, he and I went out of the office in the morning and sat in the car of a certain driver, because he was the only one who had an almost new Volga, the Russian Mercedes. The risk of a breakdown of the vehicle was lower. My colleague informed him that we would go to Grozny right away. A second car with armed guards accompanied us to the border, but they stayed behind on the Ingushetian side. From then on, we roared at a very high speed without escort for the remaining hour and a half into the Chechen capital. Somehow, this secrecy and the whole procedure were rather paradoxical and grotesque, since Chechen territory was classified as incomparably more dangerous. However, the local coordinator had informed me accordingly.

Once, like now, he would have received an official appointment for one of my predecessors and informed a driver and some other employees about it the evening before. However, the following day, shortly before Grozny, some uniformed men suddenly stopped the vehicle who actually wanted to kidnap the foreigner. It was only thanks to his negotiating skills, but above all the lightning-fast action of the driver, who suddenly drove away with screeching tires, that everyone got away. Apparently, it was undisputed that the potential kidnappers had received a tip from an employee. Hence all the secrecy. My colleague justified the fact that we drove completely unprotected, that one would attract so much less attention, which was somehow plausible. However, the explanation did not necessarily help me to calm down my rather queasy feeling on the very first trip. This became even more uncomfortable when we passed a tank standing by the roadside, behind which an injured soldier was apparently being treated in the trench. Shortly before, there must have been a battle on the spot. A soldier motioned us with his hands up and down, indicating that we should slow down. Already we recognized quite young recruits going left and right along the road, who seemed to search the ground. My colleague just said that they were looking for mines! In any case, we past them very slowly and soon reached Grozny.

Immediately I thought of pictures of destroyed cities from the Second World War. It did not look much different there. The Russian army seemed to have done a great job. We passed multi-story buildings whose front or side facades were no longer there, so that one could see from the street into apartments, where people still lived. People were walking on the sidewalks and I wondered where they were going. At least everything appeared of a normal everyday life, which in view of the suffering and terror to which the residents were exposed from the Russian army on the one hand and the militia on the other, seemed somewhat absurd. We, on the other hand, made our way to a very specific backyard quickly. To the left of the entrance gate, there were long lists of names on the wall, from which you could see whether you were getting assistance from us or not. Among them, my coordinator explained to me, were mostly elderly people who lived in cellars or similar shelters. We passed the queue, and I felt the looks of people. I could not realize whether it was curiosity, suspicion or gratitude. Among those, waiting there could have been someone who quickly passed on the news that there was a foreigner here now. We went to our colleagues who had already been in the middle of the distribution. A short "hello" here, "good morning" there, and my local coordinator began to urge me to go back again: just don't stay too long in a certain place, who knows, who might turn up, he said nervously. However, I demanded that we should at least make a short detour through the city so that I could even get an impression of the former metropolis in North Caucasus. At first, my colleague agreed somewhat reluctantly, but then he obviously enjoyed showing me the city at least a little, since he was born and raised there himself. Later short visits were not much different.

As fast as we had driven to Grozny, we went back to Ingushetia. On the way, my adrenaline levels went up quite abruptly. At a hilltop, a Russian combat helicopter suddenly appeared in front of us at a height of just about 20 meters, and it seemed to me as if it was focusing on us. My colleague only said that he was certainly the vanguard of a military convoy searching the street and the surrounding area for fighters or other suspicious persons. In fact, we later met the numerous troop transports that were moving towards Chechnya. At the border, we met again our armed guards. Fortunately, there was never an incident either during my or my German colleague's brief visits. However, we never told, even to donors, that we went without any safety precautions or protection.

Suitable mechanisms to be able to process such terrible impressions, situations or experiences, everyone will probably have to develop for him- or herself.

Although realistic war scenarios are sometimes played out as part of preparations for operations, they are still just scenarios. I took part in one of them for the first time in Germany in 2005. There, checkpoints by militias and even a transport of relief supplies that was ambushed, including bomb explosions and the like were re-enacted. The whole spectacle was so far from reality, based on the 30 or so participants, that it was more like an adventure playground than serious training. In addition, neither the behavior of the individual nor that of the group as a whole was analyzed in detail. The organizers only said that they wanted to show the participants what kind of "situations" they could get into during relief operations. The posed scenes were also considered a kind of selection for suitable helpers, so you could have gotten an idea of the behavior of one or the other candidate. However, the criteria used to evaluate the candidates, who were wandering around completely uncoordinated in the hail of bombs, let alone observe all of them individually, I could not understand.

Ten years later I had again taken part in a security training, conducted by German military, who were specialized in preparing soldiers and civilians for missions abroad. I personally found the simulated kidnapping situation particularly impressive. I knew that the participants were going to be abducted, but nobody knew when exactly that was going to happen. When it happened, the simulated situation developed into an almost realistic scenario and in the end, everyone was happy when it was over. At least I had a feeling of how one might act in such a situation.

It is true that the terrorist attack in Ingushetia was quite dramatic and for a few hours, it was impossible to see how it would end. In retrospect, however, it seemed that only state authorities had been the actual target of the attackers. My German colleague, who occasionally paced back and forth on his cell phone like a frightened chicken, said to me incredulously how I could stay so calm in view of what was going on outside. What else should I have done? Fortunately, we could not leave the house anyway. It was much more difficult to weigh up between waiting and taking action in Turkey. In the center of the border town of Reyhanli, two car bombs exploded on a Saturday afternoon in May 2013, where one of our employees lived while we were sitting in the safe Antakya forty kilometers away. We could not reach her by phone or through other acquaintances. The constant worry went so far that some colleagues asked that we should go there ourselves to look for her personally; however, this was more than an illusion. On the one hand, there was a certain amount of chaos there and we had to assume that the Turkish security forces had cordoned off the city over a large area anyway, so that we would not have been able to get through. On the other hand, we would very likely have put ourselves in great danger. Although we did not expect the worst, but we were concerned about riots by the local Turkish population against Syrian refugees, as it was suspected that the bombs had been set off by Syrians. Nevertheless, in this case too, we had no choice but to wait and see. Towards evening, we finally reached the colleague by phone, who had been very lucky and somehow made it to Antakya by friends unharmed, so that late in the evening we could happily embrace her.

Unfortunately, in the same year 2013, a British man who had worked with me in the same organization many years earlier had a different experience. We met by chance at the Turkish-Syrian border when I was taking my colleagues to where they had to register to cross the border into Syria. Outside, my former colleague spoke to me: he had started working for an NGO two days earlier as a security officer and now wanted to go to Syria, to get an idea of the roads that could be used for aid transports. Two days later, we learned that he and an Italian colleague had been kidnapped. He was later beheaded, which made me feel uncomfortable as well as unbelieving, especially since I was possibly the last foreigner who spoke to him. Suddenly an apparently distant event hits you very personally and unfortunately also made clear how great the dangers can be in conflict areas.

7. Encounters with craftsmen

Different countries, different quality standards! It does not matter in which country I worked. Eventually repairs had to be made that needed a specialist. Most of the time, unfortunately, we did not find the master of his subject, but rather someone who, with a wrench in his hand, thought he was one.

A colleague from another German aid organization had hired a supposed expert in Ingushetia, because one day the washing machine had conked out. His driver knows a specialist who guarantees to get the device working again. It happened that a relative of his was a "master" who had repaired everything successfully by then. A phone call would have been enough. Shortly afterwards, the master appeared, equipped with a tiny toolbox as well as a drill and angle grinder. The latter tools in particular caused my colleague to be confused a bit. While work was still going on at the desks on the ground floor, according to my colleague, you could indeed hear drilling (!) and other typical artisan noises from the upper floor. Even though, those might have sounded strange, but gave the impression works went ahead. After some three hours, the master approached him and praised the work he had done in the highest tones: Now everything is ok finally! He took fifty euro, hugged the client and said goodbye. The colleague immediately carried out the rule to the test by filling the machine with laundry and powder and switching it on. After about ten minutes, my colleague went upstairs to make sure that the washing machine was running properly. Instead, he should have yelled at his driver to come up with a bucket of water. He himself would have filled an empty plastic bottle, turned off the machine, opened the drum and injected the water as best he could because the laundry in the drum was obviously on fire! After they finished the extinguishing work, he would have ordered the driver to summon the master and his wife. "Why the wife?" asked the driver. "To clear up the whole mess," said his superior furiously. The next morning the master and his wife appeared a little less enthusiastic and immediately took the washing machine with them.

After a detailed examination, it turned out that an electronic had broken, but one would have had to wait at least five days for its replacement. However, the master would have wanted to do everything on the spot by means of "a little improvisation" by virtue of his ability. When I asked where the machine was now, my colleague replied that apparently the master was operating on the open machine heart and changing the part. A few days later, the master put it back in its original place and when he plugged in, switched on the machine for another test, a short circuit happened! When my colleague told the story afterwards, we fell about laughing.

In 2004, I also had the dubious pleasure of hiring a supposed professional in Ingushetia. In this case, it was about assembling and connecting a satellite dish to the television. The following problem arose: it had to face south, that is to attach it to the front of the building. However, the living room with the TV was located on the rear side. Therefore, before I had to go away for a few hours, I instructed the 'specialist' to mount the antenna up close to the roof ridge. At the same time, this would prevent it from any damage without a ladder. The best thing to do is to lay the antenna cable under the roof to the other side of the house.

During my absence, however, he had apparently changed his mind and, in the absence of a ladder (!), had attached the antenna to the house wall at a height of about one meter. After I had instructed him again where he should install it, I went into the office, still a bit puzzled. I heard drilling noises, but tried to concentrate on my work. Suddenly I realized that these noises were coming from the bathroom, which was on the south side of the building. I feared the worst.

I did not even need to open the window. The master was now standing on the outside of a ladder, waved to me with a smile and drilled a hole through the house wall to lay the cable through. From there, he planned to lay the cable on the floor (!) in the bathroom, then along the wall, first one meter to the left in the corner, then three meters straight, again about one meter to the right towards the door, along the door frame, then again immediately a few inches to the left and then up the ceiling in the hallway to the living room and back down to the floor, where he would move it again for the remaining five meters or so. At least that was his elaborated plan, but I did not get it. According to my understanding, I repeated, he wanted to install the cable through the bathroom, across the hall into the living room, across the room. He smiled and nodded to me. However, I shook my head and instructed him to lay the cable directly under the roof to the other side of the house in order to reach the living room directly from there. He should kindly close the hole in the bathroom wall!

Again, I had an outside appointment and when I came back, he proudly presented his work to me: the antenna was now hanging higher up on the south side as intended and the cable was also hidden under the roof to the other end of the house, and outside about a meter straight down into the living room. There, however, he had attached it to the wall at a height of about one meter with countless cable clamps and run horizontally almost around the entire room to the satellite receiver - inconspicuous and professional looked somehow different.

Years later in Kosovo, we had also bought a satellite antenna and while we were still in the shop the seller proudly informed us that a specialist would install it on the same day for a small fee. Said and done. Shortly after I was back in the office, which had once again been my own accommodation, the supposed fitter appeared. First, he asked for 35 euro right away. I first had to explain to him that I would usually only pay after the work was done. I was also surprised that he did not have any tools with him. Not needed (!), he stated quite self-confidently and made his way upstairs. Once again, I feared the worst. After about two hours, I went up to see. There the supposed expert tried to tighten the screws by hand! Thereupon, I told him angrily he should go downstairs and take care of the receiver. There he claimed a little later that the device was not working. However, he had forgotten to plug the power cord into the socket! This beginner's mistake was the straw that broke the camel's back. I threw him out and went into the store the next morning. The owner assured that this time the specialist would come with his tools. He promptly appeared together with a second man who was supposed to help him. Of course, I should also pay him, which I acknowledged with a simple "no way" and left the shop. Later a neighbor installed it pro bono.

Whether I could infer the entire craftsmen community from these unfortunate individual cases in both countries was questionable, but to be feared. In Kosovo in particular, the quality of the construction sector left a lot to be desired, where even laypeople could notice serious deficiencies at first glance. Apparently, this never seemed to be objectionable to anyone. This was not only reported to me by my colleague on the basis of our own construction activities, which we carried out as part of our aid program, but I was also able to determine it personally when I moved into a brand-new small apartment as the first tenant. I immediately drew the landlady's attention to several shortcomings: the siphon in the bathroom was evidently already used and old; the door to the storage room did not fit in the floor so it would not close; the entire frame of the balcony door including the panorama window had not been attached to the floor at all; and some sockets were crooked so that you could see the holes underneath. In Germany, I suppose, hardly any housebuilder would have accepted these deficiencies. My landlady, however, only noted it with a shake of her head, since nothing could be changed anyway.

When it came to building a house in Ingushetia, however, I experienced quite a surprise. One day our local coordinator came with a German magazine under his arm and proudly announced that he was going to build his own home. Moreover, by no means one of the usual red brick houses with a wall that is five meters high around them. His one should be entirely in Western European style. He turned to a specific page of the magazine, pointing to an interior that was indeed modern. When I asked how he was going to do it, he explained it to me as if it was no big deal: he had shown his cousin the house in the magazine and asked him to draw up a corresponding blueprint. Although, his relative was no architect, but would have helped to build a few houses in the past. Therefore, they sat for weeks on the plan, which is now ready. Construction would have already started. We drove there and I saw an already standing carcass that had a lot in common with the house in the magazine.

My local colleague proudly guided me through his future home, which made a very modern impression in terms of the room layout. Since, in his opinion, there were no qualified artisans in Ingushetia, he had "found" some Georgians who should execute the construction. The whole time they lived right next to the site in a kind of construction trailer! Later, after the house was completed, I was more than amazed. In fact, it was very much like the one in the magazine. In addition, my colleague had furnished it in a very modern way, so that I could have felt completely at home, too. With one exception: a very high wall around the modern house and property, so that the view from the inside to the outside did not exactly suggest freedom.

One should be more careful now and then, if the landlord wants to lend a hand on more sensitive things in order to save the costs for an at least supposed expert. In Croatia, back in the 1990s when I was doing volunteer work, the homeowner's repair of the hot water boiler ended abruptly with an explosion! Just like in a cartoon, he, luckily unharmed, stepped, from top to bottom black, out of a smoke cloud!

"Do it yourself", a neighbor of mine apparently thought years later in Montenegro. He lived on a very narrow street that led directly to my apartment. On my way home, I passed his house, greeting him as usual, and saw that he was about to cut down a rather tall tree. The latter stood directly in front of the house and hardly any daylight could penetrate into the front rooms. Therefore, the action was quite understandable for me. In spite of that, I had reservations about how he, the neighbor, wanted to manage it, especially since I saw no ladder standing. Because I assumed he wanted to saw off the tree piece by piece from top down. Since I still wanted to work at home, I had brought a laptop and printer with me. I set everything up on the living room table and started typing. I also turned on the television to watch German news. When I went into the kitchen a little later to get some water, there was suddenly a loud bang, all lights went out, electrical devices switched off and smoke rose from the latter, the computer, printer and television. Immediately there was a scorched smell everywhere. I called my colleague, who also lived not far away, and asked if he had also had a power cut. He confirmed and informed me that no electrical devices would no longer work either. The next day it turned out that not only had the power cut in the entire neighborhood happen, but also all electrical devices were broken. The reason for this was the tree felling action. According to the principle: why make it complicated when it can be simple, namely the neighbor had sawed off the tree at the very bottom and it had fallen onto the power line that led along the street in front of his house. Fortunately, no one was injured. My defective devices, only a small part had to be replaced, cost a total of 50 euro, which I paid myself. All other affected parties, however, demanded compensation from the woodcutter, which was certainly not cheap due to the number of households. Poor man!

In Kosovo I also experienced a very impressive episode, but not of a constructional nature. One day I had a strong back pain. A local colleague therefore recommended a physiotherapist to me who was "great", even though he was blind! So I went to his practice, shared my suffering and several appointments were arranged immediately as well as the first one right away. I had not planned that, but I was glad that they took me on. I should go into an adjoining room and wait for someone to call me. Less than five minutes later the blind masseur appeared. A truly fascinating personality. In front of me was a well-established man, around 50 years old. He immediately began to tell me his life story. He has been blind since he was born and somehow, he became a physiotherapist. Though he could never see his patients, he would be more than happy to do the job. In addition, to me that sounded almost arrogant, he added that he was definitely the best professional in town, even though he could not see anything. He would never have sought pity, but rather recognition through his professional activity. This he would have achieved now. The number of his customers would be enough proof. Then he took action. The massage was very pleasant, but sometimes also painful. Nevertheless, I felt an improvement by noticeably reduced back pain, though I had felt the power he had in his hands. At the second and the following appointments, I was even more surprised. When the blind masseur came right up to me and spoke: "Aha, the German is back". How he could recognize me, especially since I had kept quiet, always remained a mystery to me.

In total, I probably had seven to eight appointments with him. At the second he already asked me, and then again and again, whether I had a job for him. On the one hand, I felt sorry for him, on the other hand I had never understood why he was looking for a job with us. I kept telling him that he should be happy to have his own business, which obviously seemed to be doing quite well. He had never really justified his wish for a job with us. In this respect, I had never understood him either. Rather, I encouraged him to continue his work, because there was no reason to give it up. Ultimately, he was obviously concerned with the supposedly low salary with which he could not support his family. To be honest, I did not believe him. He just thought that our organization would pay much higher salaries. Even if that was the case, I still could not understand him. At the end of my assignment, I gave him my exercise bike. Since I did not want to take the device home with me, I thought it would have been the right gift for him. Although he showed great gratitude, I could still see a trace of disappointment in him, since I probably could not offer him more.

In all of my assignments, I had recurring encounters with hairdressers. I still remember the Montenegrin one very well. Especially the very first time. My colleague had recommended him to me: "He cuts great, especially modern hairstyles!" he boasted. Oh well. Neither my own hairstyle allowed great changes, nor was I even ready to do so. Thus, I instructed him only to cut my hair shorter. After a snip with the scissors, he first slowly lit a cigarette and continued to cut. Then his phone rang. He picked up - there was obviously a friend on the other end - and he continued with one hand. He hung up but was evidently thirsty, picked up a glass and continued. Suddenly he sniffed his nose, put the scissors down, ran a hand over his nose, and continued. At least then, I realized that I should probably change the hairdresser. Because customer orientation and especially hygiene obviously did not seem to be his strengths.

In Ingushetia, I experienced the complete opposite in terms of customer orientation. One day when I told my colleague that I had to get my haircut, we drove into town to a hairdresser he knew. The fact that a woman would cut my hair surprised me a lot. Although my future hairdresser in Montenegro had been a woman, Ingushetia was a Muslim republic, where I would have expected that only a man would dress another man's hair or a woman would do a woman. At least that is what I later experienced in Kosovo, Sri Lanka and Turkey. In all three countries were separate hairdressers for each gender.

At that time in Ingushetia, the female hairdresser greeted me very more warmly than I had ever seen. The only thing missing would have been to have me lifted onto the chair. It quickly became apparent that I had been the very first foreigner who wanted to engage her services. That would therefore have to be captured photographically first! Therefore, she picked up a camera and so did the other employees! First photos were taken while standing, and then I on the chair. Then they offered tea. Without exception, everyone was in a high mood that I somehow could not understand. It was by no means mock friendliness. In fact, everyone seemed so pleased to have me, apparently an exotic, in the store. One employee even went out into the street and told passers-by that they had a foreign customer in the store! Those of course came in to see for themselves. My concern about simply having my haircut became almost a minor matter. At first when I entered the salon, I just wanted to let the whole thing go through me quickly. Now I not only felt flattered, but also fully enjoyed the situation. Even when the hairdresser took action, the spectacle did not stop. My colleague, who was there, could not even calm down. He translated and did not stop laughing. When I was about to pay at the end, the boss told me the haircut would be on the house if I promised to come back. If I wanted, she could come to my house, too. I gladly accepted the offer. The episode was very amusing, but I wanted a normal haircut to take a maximum of 45 minutes in the future - less than two hours! From then on, the hairdresser came to our office regularly.

In Kosovo, I had the barber shop in the house. One day I went in, but could not express my request due to a lack of Albanian language skills. Thus, I tried it carefully in Serbian. The hairdresser replied delighted, that I should sit down. Back then, you had to be very careful not to express yourself in Serbian at all, because they had oppressed the country for decades and even started a war in 1999. That is why many native Albanians did not even want to hear that language. The latter mainly affected the generation that had lived through the period of oppression. These were the age group from 25 to 60 years. Younger people apparently did not remember that time and many of them spoke English very well, but no Serbian at all. If, on the other hand, I met old Kosovars over 60, they always liked to speak Serbian to me. I could only figure out that they wanted to prove to the boys that they too could express themselves in a foreign language.

In any case, my Kosovar hairdresser was happy that he could communicate with me. While he was cutting my hair, it just seemed to gush out of him because he was talking all the time. Mostly about politics and the situation of his home country. It always sounded almost desperate what he was trying to tell me. Especially when politics was the topic, I had sworn to myself years before that I would not get involved. Hence, I listened to his lecture with a nod here and a shake of my head there. I never heard positive things from him, no matter what the topic was. Still, from then on I always went to him. Not only did he do a satisfactory job, but I could also hear the people's voice.

The attitude that people should accept things as they are, although a change is possible and thus corresponds to an improvement, came across me repeatedly, especially among older people in Eastern Europe. Instead of holding someone accountable even though they were right, they preferred to avoid possible problems or disputes. People, according to my impression, persisted in lethargy or, in the best-case scenario, improvised, which may be a short-term solution everywhere, but became a burden in the long-term.

At the beginning I personally got upset and annoyed about it again and again, although from today's perspective this was probably due to my own inexperience and, I would almost say, some sort of arrogance. Because I have often wondered how it could be that such a lethargy could be so widespread, given all the problems. People should them recognize and everyone should kindly be ready to cooperate, especially when a foreign aid organization provides support not only in terms of content, but above all financially. At least it would be like this for us: I thought, idealized and 'idyllized' the situation in Germany. Of course, it was more than unfair to people, especially since I on the one hand unconsciously blamed them for their own situation and, on the other hand, generalized my own attitude to the extent that our social model was the only real thing.

Depending on the situation, different aspects may have played a role in people's attitudes: for example, a remote geographical location; lack of infrastructure; lack of education; social structure; overall poverty or trauma following a disaster. While the democratic system offered and offers us the framework to be able to realize ourselves through rights but also obligations, a socialist or communist system only assigned most of the people apparently to certain role. As a result, any personal development opportunity was nipped in the bud and thus did not cause any feeling of responsibility. On the other hand, in Germany we learned that every man is the architect of his own fortune. Consequently, we have to bear responsibility, whether we want it or not. Why should the individual in a socialist society make an effort at all if he could not or was not allowed to do what he would have wanted. And finally: if all decisions were always presumably made by an institution, the party, right down to private life and responsibility was taken away, why should the individual develop his own efforts at all? It was not for nothing in those times that the waiters in many restaurants were anything but business-minded, since it made no difference whether you were serving two or two hundred guests. Not to mention whether the food was good or bad, since there was no real competition to fear. The remuneration was always the same and towards the employer, the state, an indifference has apparently developed over time, which at most gradually resulted in a retreat into private life, internal emigration. So, I could only explain to myself why then only the personal environment counted, which one could trust most, and so ultimately, the system promoted the lack of independence and personal egoism more than the common welfare.

In Serbia and Montenegro, at least in the early 2000s, I was able to observe this attitude very often, especially in state authorities, but even more so in companies, especially hotels that were still state-owned. In the mostly dingy buildings, which already looked shabby from the outside, usually several employees were sitting, rather bored, either at the reception desk or they were all watching TV and smoked. One only seemed to be interested in the customer's concerns after being asked to do so. However, the accommodation costs for foreigners differed considerably from those for locals. Sometimes I paid ten times more. When I asked if it was normal for the bathroom in a three-star hotel to be completely shabby, sockets almost fell out of the wall and the room overall looked unkempt, but I should pay eighty euro a night for it. The receptionist in Montenegro was rather annoyed: "Then I should kindly go somewhere else!"

My very first hotel stay in Moldova in 2006 was not quite as expensive, but it was even more amusing, in, at least in earlier times, the leading hotel in the capital Chişinău. In terms of shabbiness or filthiness, it could easily keep up with the state hotels in Serbia or Montenegro just described. In some other aspects, especially with regard to the staff, the Balkans, on the other hand, may not have had a chance. Even the reception took place in a frosty atmosphere, as if I were anything but welcome and more of a troublemaker. On each floor was a strict ticket inspector who wanted to see my room key every time I passed and who was sent to the room by the reception upon check-out to see if the guest didn't take one or the other 'Souvenir'.

When I arrived in the comparatively small room, I first had to make the bed myself. Although the sheet was folded up extremely accurately. When I took it apart, it felt like I was tearing a piece of paper. In addition, a colleague had already warned me that in order to get hot water in the morning, I would first have to run the corresponding tap for about twenty minutes (!) until the water temperature actually got higher. Incidentally, he was right about that! When the same colleague stayed later, he had turned on the tap in the morning as usual and went back to bed. Too bad that he fell asleep again and could only be woken up by knocking hard on the door. Because the bathroom was now under water and had caused considerable damage on the floor below!

I experienced the bizarre scene, however, at breakfast. Usually, three dishes alternated on a daily basis: ravioli with minced meat, sausages with rice or bread with jam. That morning, we were three; the waiter served the noodles without being asked. However, one of the colleagues tried to make it clear to her that he was a vegetarian and asked if there would also be a meat-free meal. Thereupon he only got a gruff "No"; the waiter took his plate, went to a wooden cupboard, opened a drawer, put the plate in and closed it with a strong jerk. Apparently, it was supposed to be kept warm in it. We then decided to go to the nearest bakery.

Admittedly, there is a lot to criticize about the excesses of our health system and some institutions have certainly seen better days. However, even these should be a whole lot better than the ones I saw or inspected on my assignments abroad. Those who have been able to avoid having to go to one abroad due to illness over the years can consider themselves lucky. On the other hand, who at least worked in locations where adequate alternatives to the usual local medical facilities existed, as was the case with me in Tajikistan. On my first day there, another German colleague advised me to see only a German doctor in case of illness - "here the phone number, very important!"

A few weeks later, a local colleague invited me to dinner in the countryside. Unfortunately, there was no sign in front of his house advertising that the salad would be washed with mineral water, as I had seen occasionally in the capital Dushanbe. This was to emphasize that tap water would not be used as it was not suitable for human consumption. It would have been more than unfriendly or inadmissible to ask the host whether mineral water was one of the tools in his kitchen. Of course, I dutifully tasted what was offered to me, after all it was considered an insult if I had refused. I (unfortunately) disregarded any imponderable consequences. Because I got Montezuma's revenge in the form of a severe diarrhea. After days of suffering, I had no choice but to see a doctor. At first, I had horror images in my head after what I had seen in healthcare facilities in the past. Fortunately, I remembered the German doctor's number whom I went straight to see. In no time, I was sitting across from the man in the white coat. After all, the consulting room looked like I was used to at home and I was able to articulate my suffering to him myself - it becomes more difficult if you don't speak the local language and therefore have to rely on a colleague's translation.

My suffering was initially out of question. Rather, the doctor first wanted to hear my story about why I was in the country. After I had reported in detail, it was my counterpart's turn. He has been working abroad for more than twenty years. Most recently in China, where he would provide his services especially for foreigners on behalf of an organization. Locals could not pay the comparatively high fees anyway. After all, he took time for the patient, as one would actually wish for German practices. Now we approached my suffering, which the contaminated food had caused obviously. Hence, the doctor asked me what kind of food I eat there. Well, the refrigerator certainly does not contain the groceries like at home and a cook in the office would prepare lunch, whose leftovers I would usually eat in the evening. Our conversation then went something like this:

He (completely flabbergasted): "I beg your pardon. You eat local products?"

I (a little irritated): "Yes, what else can I do?"

He (curious): "Where and what do you buy for food?"

I (astonished): "In the nearby small supermarket: cheese sometimes also sausage and fruit."

He (almost quick-tempered): "Like fruit? The one they sell here? "

I (rather intimidated): "Hmmjah, there is nothing else."

He (now louder): "Are you crazy! You cannot eat that! "

I (irritated): "As far as I know. I do it all the time. "

He (almost desperately): "But the germs and impurities! Moreover, which cheese and which sausage do you buy?"

I (now at a loss): "Well, you don't have that much choice. Mostly what looks reasonably attractive. "

He (instructing): "You are definitely not allowed to do that. Everything is dirty. Therefore, no fruit, sausage or cheese and no bread either! "

I (completely helpless): "Well, and what should I nourish myself from? How do you do it here? "

He (enlightening): "I have a parcel of groceries sent to me from Germany on a regular basis and believe me; it has never harmed me so far!"

I (puzzled): "Isn't that pretty expensive?"

He (confessing): "Yes, but it's worth it with a view to your own health!"

I (in conclusion): "What would you do then, should you ever need medical treatment yourself? Flying in a German doctor is not going to go well, does it? "

He (rather meekly): "Well ..."

After all, he had then prescribed tablets that was supposed to offer quick relief for my mishap and in fact, the improvement came within a day. However, I still bought my groceries in the supermarket.

It was very different for me in Ingushetia a few years earlier. I had lost a stopping, so I was in agony. Thus, a dentist needed to replace the stopping as soon as possible. A local colleague just said that under no circumstances should I go to a local dentist! It is much better to go to the neighboring republic to Vladikavkaz, the capital of North Ossetia-Alania. Because health care there is "much, much better". Thus, he made an appointment for the same afternoon, a Saturday, at the dental clinic. Well, I hardly knew Russian, so he took over the communication with the reception staff. Since I was a rather exotic patient, a nurse immediately guided me to the treatment room.

This was a windowless room with two sliding doors facing each other, which was completely tiled, even the ceiling, as you might imagine in a slaughterhouse. That certainly made cleaning easier. In the comparatively large room, there was only a dental treatment chair, completely lost, nothing else; no equipment or other furniture, not even a chair for the dentist, let alone posters on the wall or a heater! Admittedly, the whole area did not seem extremely trustworthy to me. So now, I was sitting in the chair waiting for my treatment. At first, however, other patients past me or had accidentally opened the door. In any case, they insisted on taking a closer look at me, the exotic, including my open throat. Even when the supposed dentist was already fiddling around in my open mouth, it went on like this. Well, was it just like this at the urologist there?

In view of her young appearance, the dentist could also have been a student, although I assumed that I should not serve as a subject. She instructed me to open my mouth and apparently immediately understood what to do and started accordingly without asking too much. At the end of the day, she said she would have used a temporary stopping that she needed to change for a permanent one on Monday morning. I could eat again immediately and after a thank you for the quick treatment, we were already on our way back to Nazran.

Less than two hours later the makeshift stopping was gone after I bit into an apple. I then told the dentist on Monday morning that her stopping would have been too temporary, which she only answered with a shrug. Although I let her put another stopping, I had secretly already decided to accompany my colleague on his next trip to Stavropol in southern Russia. In his opinion, there would be a real dentist! The price for this was more than 15 times what I had paid in Vladikavkaz, but the facility and, in particular, the treatment corresponded to what one would expect in this country. It was ultimately successful, but only against hard currency and the supposedly real dentist only ran her private practice in the afternoon, as she worked in a state institution in the morning. According to the principle: communist in the morning, capitalist in the afternoon.

For those doctors who, in addition to their normal work in the hospital, also ran a private practice, this also meant saving energy in the morning so that one could concentrate on being available to wealthy customers in the afternoon, coffee included. I had heard that quite often in Serbia and Montenegro. Thus, it is advisable to be cautious if, for example, a humanitarian organization wants to donate expensive medical equipment for a health facility. It can always happen that one or the other doctor borrows this permanently for his own purposes.

Incidentally, I still have the stopping to date. Fortunately, nothing more serious happened to me after that either. Who knows, maybe I would actually have ended up in a slaughterhouse somewhere.

8. Encounters with authorities

The reputation of public authorities is probably nowhere the best. Bureaucracy, long waiting times, service could be better and a supposed 'nine to five job' are most likely among the more harmless clichés.

Over the years, I was also able to gain experience with public authorities in other countries. Overall, they probably did not differ that much from the stereotypes that exist in Germany. Although: Sometimes I was surprised at the monsters that seemingly routine processes could degenerate into, or were solved completely unbureaucratically, with or without additional administrative costs.

During my assignments abroad, the first encounter with the host country's bureaucracy often took place before, with or shortly after entering the country. Because I usually needed a visa, a residence or work permit. There was a wide variety of procedures depending on the state. While I was able to enter numerous countries without problems and only apply for the necessary work permit or visa there, in the case of Pakistan I had to do this before I left to the country. This involved a number of train journeys to the consulate in Frankfurt/Germany. When I had the visa in my passport, at least I had passed this hurdle. During this brief assignment, I was supposed to go first to the north of the country and then to southern Pun-jab, each of which required a separate police permit. The one for the north the authorities rejected for security reasons. Later, when I was in Bakkar, in Punjab, while I was having dinner, the waiter came and told me to go to the reception. There is a call for me. Quite astonished, since I could not imagine who was calling me, I sent my translator. A few minutes later, she came back and said it was the secret service. They just wanted to check that I was actually in the hotel!

Entering Tajikistan was more complicated. Before I left, HQ told me I would get the necessary residence permit upon arrival at the airport in Dushanbe. Therefore, I queued in the waiting line for arrivals of other countries. Then I noticed that others in front of me already had a completed form in their hands. Not me. Therefore, I spoke to a uniformed man who harshly pointed at a door, where I should turn first. There was a kind of reception in the room right behind the door, where I received a form to fill out. I should take a seat opposite on the sofa next to the other people waiting until I was called. At the very back there was a large desk, behind which was apparently the person in charge and summoned the people waiting in the barracks tone to him. I sat down, started filling out the form, and was startled when someone was called again. A man got up and went to the boss. However, my neighbor, a Canadian, got up to tell the uniformed man that he had been waiting much longer and that it was now his turn. The boss acknowledged this objection with an unmistakable derogatory remark and showed the door to the person sitting next to me. I did not find out whether he finally got his visa. Shortly afterwards I, admittedly a little intimidated, went to the officer, who immediately gave me the necessary stamp. He asked for fifty-seven US dollars. Had I not read on the internet beforehand that the cost would be thirty US dollars? However, I kept it to myself as much as possible, so I paid the required amount, even though the receipt actually only showed the lower amount of thirty US dollars. Apparently, you had to pay a certain processing fee in addition. Where this was going was obvious.

I always experienced the exact opposite when I came to Serbia, when I was working in Montenegro at the time and often had to go to the Sandjak in southern Serbia. The border crossings were amusing. Because as a Western European I was considered exotic in the region, so that I always had a short chat with the border police. Whenever I showed my passport, the same old story came up: Gerhard. "Schreder?" (Schröder was meant, the German Chancellor at the time; the 'ö' could not be pronounced correctly); Klaus (my middle name)! "Kinkel (another Minister of the German Government at the time)?" Fischer, "Foreign Minister?" Somehow every border guard made a joke of it, until one day a police officer asked me whether I was related to Joschka Fischer, the then German Foreign Minister. I replied "Yes, of course!" Immediately they let me pass without further questions!

Nevertheless, of course, one or the other always tried to capitalize on me. As long as it stayed with promotional pens, like back then in Serbia, that was of course not a problem. Often enough elsewhere, however, it was about the actual processing fees, as in Tajikistan after I ended up there.

At the airport in Moscow, I always got a ticket to the North Caucasus without any prior booking. Often, however, only for a small additional fee, otherwise the flight would have been completely booked out, surprisingly. If I had resisted it, either staff would not listen or my degree of frustration would have increased exponentially within minutes. What else could I do than pay the equivalent of about five euro? Complaint? Then I would not have got a place. To approach the supervisor? Once it then went like this:

From the North Caucasus, I had to rebook a flight ticket from Moscow to Germany for a different date. That was not a problem; I should just go to the counter of the airline at the airport in Moscow, where the staff would easily do it, the German travel agency told me. When I stood in front of the woman at the airport and described my wish, she only responded by pointing out that it was now too late for that. The only thing left for me to do is to buy a completely new ticket. Therefore, I tried again, but only got the same answer. My objection that I had been told it was just a formality was ignored stony-faced. Apparently, she was hoping I would pay an additional fee for her service. Thus, standing in front of her, I called the travel agency and handed the phone over the counter, but she refused to take the call. Then I wanted to speak to her supervisor, who was sitting a few meters away from her. He, in turn, let me know that he was not responsible for it. I should go back to her who was responsible for 'processing' my request. Meanwhile the clock was ticking and the planned departure was getting dangerously closer. I turned to her again. Now I actually asked for a new ticket because my German conversation partner had assured me that in that case, he reimburse the costs. Now she said calmly that it was too late for that too. Snorting with anger, I wished her the plague on her neck in German, which a passing traveler had noticed and obviously understood. After I explained the reason for my 'compliments' to her, she at least managed to get me a new ticket. Fortunately, I had enough cash with me because my credit card was not accepted. Throughout the whole action, she just wanted to squeeze an 'additional fee' out of me, which I was by no means willing to pay. At the passport control, I had to push my way forward with a mock apologetic expression in order to catch the flight.

What was frustrating for me was the fact that such fees were, so to speak, part of the whole apparatus. Hereby everyone involved would get his or her part. In Russia, people told me that this often referred to the fact that positions in government agencies such as the Police, but also elsewhere, were only assigned, when people were well connected anyway. It was customary for the newcomer to pay a higher sum to the informant as an entry fee. Sooner or later, the newly admitted person would therefore try to recoup the expenses initially paid by means of smaller additional fees, for example during routine police checks or when buying tickets. A thoroughly corrupt system!

In Tajikistan, you had to be prepared beforehand when traveling overland. When I had to go from the capital to the southeast, my driver quickly went to change money, came back and put a wad of banknotes on the center console of the car. At first, I took note of it with complete incomprehension. He only said succinctly "for the police controls". Indeed, whenever we came to one of the frequent checkpoints, he gave the officer a note, who then opened the barrier. Once we had passed the checkpoint to drive into the village beyond, but returned a few minutes later and drove through the open barrier, whereupon a police officer protested loudly. My colleague, sticking his head out of the open window, shouted at him that we had already paid earlier and just continued.

We once received a more subtle request in Ingushetia under the cover of a supposedly official document. There, all aid organizations that deployed foreign personnel had to have armed guards at their side at all times to protect them. The organization, of course, had to pay the costs to the authorities who made the staff available. One day an official from the Ministry of the Interior was standing in front of me, waving a sheet of paper with the note that due to several legal changes, the fees for the accompanying staff ("unfortunately") almost doubled with immediate effect. In a long table there were listed the costs in connection with the security personnel, which ranged from the uniform, underwear, socks, shoes, through the weapon including ammunition to various insurance policies. In addition, all sorts of laws were mentioned which regulated all these costs. I replied to the officer that we had to analyze the matter first and I instructed a colleague to investigate a little closer.

The result was more than surprising for me. It was strange that, on the one hand, our security staff had never received anything that was on the list. On the other hand, on the contrary, apart from the weapon they would have had to pay for everything else themselves. In addition: some of the laws listed would not have existed at all or would have been dedicated to completely different topics! A few days later, I was able to avert the official's request with the lapidary hint that we had a fixed budget that would not allow any changes. To my surprise, the officer took note of this without any problems! I just thought what a brazen attempt! Later it a newspaper reported that guards had ambushed a senior official from the said ministry on the way home and that they robbed tens of thousands of rubles in cash! It is up to you whether you approve one crime because it was apparently a reward for another crime. At least one could say that the officer escaped with his life.

Personally, I found the regulations for withdrawing money from the bank in Ingushetia to be the most absurd. I always had to go to a lawyer beforehand, who assured me with a certified signature that I was the authorized person to withdraw money from the account, even though the bank employees had already known me. Of course, every certification cost. In retrospect, I thought that this was by no means official. Just another way of pulling money out of our pockets. Now one can argue about how corrupt a country may be. In any case, I personally have not seen any other region than that of the former Soviet Union where people demanded additional fees openly at every level and in such a frank way!

In the absence of the official registration, which was essential for opening a bank account, I could not even withdraw money in Serbia. Which is why getting cash sometimes resembled scenes from old gangster films. We usually picked up cash in Croatia near the border at the organization's office there. Therefore, when the cash register in the office slowly ran out or we had to pay a supplier - of course they had always preferred cash payments (!) - we would order a larger sum over the phone. Our colleagues in Croatia then withdrew the corresponding amount and made it available to us. The sums varied between 100,000 (app. 50,000 Euro and 200,000 (app. 100,000 Euro) D-mark (!) and we drove, either my Serbian colleague or I back to Belgrade without declaring the money at the border or myself. This would have been the obligation for amounts over DM 10,000. However, we did not, because one or the other police officer might have thought of informing dubious friends about our arrival. Once the same thing happened to a colleague from another organization. Shortly after crossing the border, he was disposed of at gunpoint of his cash - where did the two robbers get this information.

In any case, crossing the border was always problem-free, although my knees were weak at times. No wonder, because I used all sorts of pockets, whether for files or in my jacket, to stuff them with banknotes and at the same time to hope that the border police wouldn't bring it up. If everything went well, we usually went straight to the supplier to get rid of most of the money. It happened to my local colleague when he was driving to Croatia on his own that the border police discovered the money and tried to confiscate it immediately. However, he reacted quick-wittedly. When the police wanted to take the money, he first said that we would then not be able to carry out a project, namely the distribution of food to Serbian displaced persons from Kosovo the next day. He bluffed whether this would please the responsible deputy minister in the foreign ministry, whom we knew very well and was very positive about our activities. Hence, my colleague took out his mobile phone and began to dial the number, whereupon the border police got a bad feeling, gave him back the money and let him continue.

We always kept several thousand D-Marks for our office cash-box. The money exchange was similarly adventurous. Since banks offered a comparatively poor rate, I mostly went to a copy shop not far from the office. The seller then always opened a very small door, as you often have in older houses on the upper floors, either to stow something or to have access to the attic. There, however, the said seller always disappeared for several minutes until he reappeared with a wad of money. Either the room behind it was quite large or, as I always imagined it was the door to a secret system of tunnels below the city. Unfortunately, I never found out what was actually hidden behind it.

However, once I had to change a larger sum because we wanted to buy furniture. In the copy shop, the man rejected, because he did not have that much cash on hand. Thus, my local colleague steered me around a few blocks into a multi-story residential building, whose entrance area was monitored by video cameras. We knocked on a door on the second floor and it opened immediately. Without a word, a man in a suit asked us in with a simple nod of his head. No one spoke. The room in the background was darkened and around a small table that was only lit by a light bulb, three men were sitting and playing cards. The scenery could have come from a crime film. At my greeting, the card players only raised their heads for a moment, nodded and continued with their game. My colleague then informed our door opener that we wanted to change several hundred D-Marks, which he again only acknowledged with a nod of the head and disappeared into another room with our money in hand.

After about half a minute (!) he came back with a wad of dinar bills, which he pressed into my hand and complimented us towards the door, opened it and said goodbye. However, I opened the bundle as I walked and said that trust is good, control better and started counting. The door opener looked at my colleague, completely confused and puzzled. The latter also rolled his eyes to express that he, my colleague, was embarrassed too. Nevertheless, I counted to the end, confirmed the amount, thanked him and left. In front of the house, my colleague complained that one should never inquire such people, let alone count. That could be life threatening under certain circumstances. This time they probably tolerated because I was a western greenhorn. Whether we had been with the notorious Mafia, I replied rather jokingly. He, as quick as a shot, answered: "Of course, what do you think!" Oops! Fortunately, in the further course of my mission, this was the only encounter with such people.

Money transactions in Turkey were more curious. We had specially set up a project account at a bank and, upon request, we always received our project funds from the country office in Ankara. However, one day the bank changed the procedure. Our accountant rang me; I was

246

driving in the car, and told me I would get a call from the bank shortly. They wanted to have confirmation from me as the person responsible for the project that the transfer would be OK. Since the caller would only speak Turkish, according to the accountant, I should only say "Evet" (in English: yes) twice. In fact, a short time later I received the call and did as I had been told, whereupon the transfer was made. I did not understand a word. A few days later, I received another call. This time I was sitting in the office with my Turkish colleague. Again, I only heard Turkish, However, this time I said only "Double evet" (evet means yes). While my interlocutor replied "Tamam" on the phone, my colleague almost fell off her chair with laughter!

Speaking of Turkey: my assignment in the earthquake area in 1999 was still in the days of the old Turkish Dinar. At that time, one D-Mark was equivalent to around 250,000 dinars! Back then, when we went to the bank to withdraw money, we were always prepared. Because then we always went out with several bags of billions. Unfortunately, we all too often had to tell those waiting behind us that there was unfortunately no more cash to pay out! Contrary to what I expected, so-called bureaucrats were sometimes able to act completely unbureaucratically, although I would not have thought it possible. In Serbia at that time, as almost everywhere in Europe, one paid motorway tolls. With the difference that in the early 2000s vehicles with foreign license plates had to pay much more than local ones. In addition, only D-Mark was accepted as a means of payment, although at the same time it was officially forbidden to pay with foreign currency in shops or stores. In fact, it once happened to me that I did not have D-Mark, but only dinar. That is why I was forced to turn back at a pay-toll station to change money. I replied that at the latest when I left the motorway, I would face the same problem again. Because I would not have seen an exchange office anywhere before. You would not be in the Balkans if there had not been a solution for that too. Because the man in the cabin looked at me almost pityingly, winked at me, just as if I were now being shown his infinitely great mercy, leaned a little over to me, a quick scrutinizing look to the right and left, and offered me his help by suddenly sniffing and mischievously whispering with a hand held out to me. It just so happened that he had enough dinars with him, which he could exchange privately to the rate so and so. I replied that it was extremely bad, hoping to be able to negotiate a bit. Lamenting did not help; the drivers in the vehicles behind me were getting impatient. My counterpart did not give in to my request, so I put up a brave front and agreed.

Shortly afterwards, however, I learned how we could avoid such situations in the future, namely by applying for a special status for humanitarian organizations in the Ministry of Transport. With that, we would pay the same as local vehicles and in dinars. Now the surprise came into play.

At first the possibility sounded very good, but it also seemed to imply a lot of bureaucratic efforts with applications, certifications, local registration documents (which were not available at the time due to the lack of law): possibly like the visa with a confirmation of one local partner, translated statute from Germany; German

248

registration certificate; official declaration by the German management that I am authorized to act on behalf of the organization; of course everything also translated; description of our plans in Serbia and so on and so on. Nevertheless, I sent my local colleague to the ministry to find out exactly how to proceed. He returned in less than two hours. I immediately asked, but he weighed that we would not need anything. I thought we would not be able to get a permit. All he said was "Yes!" To my utter astonishment, he proudly showed me the document that should save us some trouble and, above all, costs in the future. All of this without a lengthy application process, even my personal appearance as head of the organization, not even my signature was required! As I had learned over many years in the Balkans, anything is always possible: in the positive as well as in the negative. I myself, although not involved at all, booked this as a great success for us at the time. Somehow, I did not just feel like an all-rounder to carry out projects, but saw myself back then as a hero who had achieved the almost impossible. The corks popped accordingly, of course.

On the other hand, simply picking up a parcel from the Belgrade Post Office in Serbia was an almost insurmountable hurdle. A few days before Christmas 2000, I found a notification in the office that a parcel had arrived for our organization that was stored at the post office. The next morning, we drove to the post office as it was on our way to the field anyway. I thought that this was just a formality and that we could take the package with us immediately. Far wrong!

Initially, all clerks were on the coffee break! We should come back the next day if we could not wait. In fact, we did not want to wait. Hence, we went back on foot the following day. A clerk referred us immediately to his superior's office. We quickly realized that his cautious explanation referred to the area of additional processing fees. Our head office had sent us a package containing stickers for aid packages. These were by no means fancy advertising material; rather, each package that was to be distributed usually had to be tagged in order to show the recipient who would have financed the content and who would have distributed the package. For the sake of simplicity, it was one of our first aid projects in Serbia at all, and for reasons of time, they had the said stickers sent to us from Germany. At the pick-up, I wanted to take the wind out of the sails of the suspicious officer by pointing out that it would only be stickers for food packages. Instead, I seemed to have piqued his pedant fantasy. In order to be able to hand it over, we had to present the following documents, in the original: the registration certificate of our organization from the Ministry of the Interior, after all, we are a non-governmental organization; the registration document from the Ministry of Foreign Affairs, after all, we are a foreign organization. Too bad that there was no registration procedure at one or the other of the ministries, which the post office clerk vehemently denied. Further, I need confirmation from the Ministry of Agriculture, after all, the relief supplies are food; the confirmation of the Ministry of Social Affairs, under whose aegis all activities in the country with regard to internally displaced persons were carried out; and finally, a customs certificate, since the package came from abroad. The officer sternly ignored my objection that the content of the parcel was only stickers. Then I asked him, after almost two hours and several cigarette breaks, whether he also needed confirmation from the Ministry of Waste, because, people would very likely throw away the packaging after the distribution! "No," he replied coolly, without even having understood my poignant sarcasm. I was rather angry now. I just could not believe that simply picking up a package could cause such difficulties. The officer asked us to leave the room, saying he had to make a phone call. With that, he obviously wanted to signal to us that he cares. In fact, we now had the impression that he wanted to soften us up so that we would pay a processing fee in the end. After about twenty minutes, he asked us to enter again. Obviously enjoying the patronizing moment, he sat in a superior manner and informed us that the probability of receiving the package was very high. Obviously, in anticipation of the 'extraordinary processing fee', I replied to him instead that I wanted to forego the package. He could do whatever he wanted with it! Touché! Because now he was sitting there completely perplexed. Totally taken by surprise, his bureaucratic instinct now seemed to advise him to withdraw; otherwise, he might have to justify leaving the parcel at the post office in the clutches of his own administrative apparatus! Suddenly smiling, but more putting up a good face to the matter, he was ready to hand over the package. However, he had to keep a sticker for his files as confirmation of the content. I pressed three of them into his hand, emphasizing that the rest would be a present! When we went back to the counter, I was supposed to pay the equivalent of about 65-euro cents, gave the officer about one euro and insisted, now having kittens, on a receipt and change and marched out of the building. Since the package weighed some fifteen kilos, we wanted to take a taxi back to the office. However, the route was too short for the first taxi driver, so he refused to take us with him. Only the third taxi took us, which I was annoyed by now, as this whole affair had lasted more than three hours. I was ready for the Christmas holiday...

Just as complicated, if not more grotesque, was the episode when we were donated a vehicle in Montenegro and wanted to register it. The EU Humanitarian Aid Office (ECHO) ended its mission in the country. Therefore, the plan was to donate the entire equipment to non-governmental organizations. The office manager had informed me about this at a meeting. I immediately said we were particularly interested in a laser printer. Then I asked casually what was going to happen to the vehicles. Because I thought that these would certainly be handed over to another ECHO office in the region. There is a possibility of getting a Land Rover Discovery, said the office manager, but some repairs are due and we have to give assurances that we will not sell the car. We should apply for all of this in writing. Of course, we agreed beamingly. The logistician then showed us the vehicle in question, which looked impeccably. However, he, the logistician, strongly advised us against it. The engine is no longer the best; the air conditioning does not work like all sorts of other things, especially the clutch. We roughly estimated the costs, which would add up to around 3,000-4,000 euro. Nonetheless, the vehicle was definitely worth to us. In retrospect, we found out that many cables, including the one for the air conditioning, were cut. Now we also understood why the logistician had strongly advised against it. Apparently, he had speculated that he would get the car himself and had obviously 'prepared' it accordingly. Now the adventure of registration began. Because the vehicle previously had a diplomatic license plate, but had been deregistered. We wanted to register it with the authorities in Berane, in northern Montenegro, where we had our office. To do this, however, we first had to bring it from Podgorica to Berane. However, how without license plates? The competent authority in the capital Podgorica informed us that they were not responsible for it. We should turn to the appropriate office in Berane. There they said they have to see the car first! There did not seem to be temporary license plates existing. Hence, we finally drove the 140km with no license plates, hoping the police will not stop us. In fact, we passed this hurdle. The next one then seemed insurmountable. Because we were supposed to prove that, the vehicle had been imported into the country. Although we had a corresponding letter from ECHO, the authorities did not accept it.

Even several visits to the authorities seemed to have been in vain. Finally, the police (!) suggested that we cross the border to Kosovo, which is about 60km away, "leave and re-enter" immediately. Then we would have the necessary stamp. How should we do that without license plates and, above all, vehicle registration? Which document needed a stamp? We did not have one! The Police do not know either! "We should just try it!" Then my colleague got furious and snapped at the police officer that it was apparently easier to report a stolen vehicle in Montenegro than a legally imported one. Back then the saying went: Come on vacation to Montenegro. Your car is already there! The latter pointed out the many vehicles stolen in Western Europe or brought into the country through insurance fraud. Indeed, it was. Because such vehicles (suddenly) received legal, officially issued documents!

Apparently, the police officer had sympathy with my colleague and assured us that he would now speed up the process. In fact, we finally received the long-awaited documents; after all, it had taken almost three months. Thus, we were able to use the off-road vehicle in the mountainous area. The car drove for another 15 years and in the end, it had over 700,000 km (!) on the tachometer when the then colleagues scrapped it. The vehicle turned out to be not as bad as the logistician had described at the beginning.

Very often, intentionally or unintentionally, I encountered the police on the street. What we set up for dedicated search measures was often part of the everyday picture, precisely because of the precarious security situation: police checkpoints that you could only pass presenting the ID or an appropriate permission. At first, I was always excited. Over time, however, I got into a certain routine. That is why I always sat quietly afterwards and let the local colleague, who was usually there, have the floor. Even if I was approached personally and possibly still able to communicate in the respective language. An innocent air was still the best thing to do.

Vehicles of aid organizations, most of which were identified by appropriate stickers, were very often stopped by the police for a wide variety of reasons anyway. Often out of curiosity, to see who was in the country, to admire the all-wheel drive vehicle or to have a little chat. In Kosovo, although I wore the safety belt, police stopped me several times with the instruction that I should buckle up!

In the Balkans in particular, eventually we inevitably were caught in one of the numerous mobile radar checks. Even when we thought, we would know their usual locations after a certain time. In Serbia, the penalties for excessive speed were still comparatively low at that time, so that the usual five D-Mark, i.e. 2.50 euro, were quite bearable and we then gave the police officers to understand that we were certainly the fastest aid organization present in the country, in view of our frequent fines! At first, it still helped to say that I was working for a humanitarian organization and that I was on my way to an "enormously" important meeting, where it was about the concerns of the whole country, to avoid paying me. Later, when the authorities had increased fines significantly in the whole region, I could not talk my way out of it and therefore I better adhered to the prescribed speed.

Once I was on my way from Croatia to Serbia and was actually in a hurry because a local colleague had called me. I should come immediately because there is a serious problem with one of the organization's trucks in southern Serbia. That's why I was racing at completely excessive speed when suddenly a few kilometers before the border crossing to Serbia a policeman with a manual radar device jumped out of the ditch, gesticulating wildly to signal me to stop. However, I was driving so fast that I only could stop after about 200 meters. In the rearview mirror, I could see the police officer shaking his head as he approached my vehicle. With an air of innocence, I turned down the window, whereupon he broke loose, completely furious, how dared I, at permitted 80 kilometers per hour, to speed almost 150 (!). For this, a fine of around 140 euro was due. I immediately started the usual sermon. I am on the way to Belgrade for an important meeting, which deals particularly with support for the Croatian border region. A completely absurd reason, because why should Croatian issues be the topic in Belgrade, that is, Serbia, the former enemy. I continued to say that our organization had already implemented many projects in the region for the benefit of the residents of the area, which summed up to millions! Visibly impressed, he let me go and wished me a safe journey!

Anyone who knew the route from the capital Podgorica to the north in Montenegro, at least in the early 2000s, knew that it was on that undeniably very picturesque drive through the Morava canyon and then almost to Kolašin with the numerous tunnels. However, there were not many opportunities on the single-lane to overtake. Especially when some trucks in front of you were only driving a little faster than walking speed, you had to be patient, especially if you were in a hurry.

As so often, my colleague and I drove north again. I was at the wheel. Even before the route got uphill and winding, there was a relatively straight part after one of the tunnels that was well suited for overtaking. Three trucks were in front of me, which I then overtook. However, they obscured my view completely, where a speed control was. A little later, police waved me out and I stopped at the roadside. My colleague immediately said I should just be quiet. A police officer came to the driver's side and asked me to turn down the window. He claimed that I drove more than 90 km an hour and sternly looked me in the eye. I kept quiet and my colleague replied with the usual words, he, pointing at me, is always stressed and thus in a hurry, probably thinks he is on a German auto-bahn, just knows the streets here not so good. We had a long day at work and just wanted to go home and that is why we are a little faster. In addition, he, the police officer knows, now it has become a bit more personal that after this section we would have to crawl after the trucks. He should turn a blind eye. The police officer, who had been looking at the center console between the two front seats, where my cell phone was, replied, whether he could have my cell phone? My colleague and I looked at each other completely puzzled, wondering why. The police officer, wanted to see the case. I had just bought this "no-name" case in Germany for around five euro. I gave him the cell phone and he asked if he could have the case in exchange for his - an original case! I agreed, so we exchanged and he let us go empty-handed!

One night in Kosovo, I even drove straight to a radar control because I needed the help of the police. However, they waved aside, started their engine and sped off in the opposite direction. A few minutes earlier, I had already passed the said police car. Due to a military convoy, both lanes were moving very slowly when a car suddenly swerved out of the oncoming lane and collided with me on the rear driver's side. Without stopping, the driver of the car continued his journey! I stopped for a moment, checked the damage, turned around and drove back to the police car. When it raced off with blue light, I followed and soon realized that the officers had apparently noticed the damaged vehicle of the person who had caused the accident. A few kilometers later, they got him and I joined the scene as the victim. Obviously, the driver, about 60 years old, was completely drunk. He just babbled to himself. Unfortunately, the officers did not have a breathalyzer with them, so they asked for reinforcements and three more police vehicles with about twenty officers (!) suddenly appeared. I had a lot in mind, especially since I did not understand the conversations due to a lack of language skills. Would they rip me off because I was a foreigner and the other driver was one of their compatriots? In any case, I had the feeling that the police investigated something. While the person who caused the accident continued to babble that he was not guilty of anything, even my hint that a part of my bumper was stuck in his fender did not seem to dissuade him from his innocence. The officers were not interested in my vehicle or me. It took about two hours for them to come up to me and ask for my ID and vehicle documents. I tried to make it clear to them that my car was a brand-new vehicle.

Some two weeks earlier, I had personally driven the newly purchased vehicle to Kosovo, which the police officers did not seem to understand even on the second attempt. When I showed them the year of manufacture in the vehicle registration document, the same policeman said to his colleagues astonished that the car was only four weeks old, hard to believe! That was exactly what I had been trying to explain all along. After I had filled out a few forms, they allowed me to drive home - it was now almost three o'clock in the morning. As if the whole matter had not been stressful enough, less than ten minutes later I actually got into a radar check at completely excessive speed. The police immediately looked curiously at my damaged car. I assured them that I had just spent several hours with their colleagues. Thereupon they let me drive on advising me not push the pedal to the metal.

Fortunately, nobody was injured in the accident, but the trouble happened afterwards when it came to the insurance process. Claims settlement in a very special way.

According to the police, the question of guilt was undisputed, so that the insurance company of the person responsible had to pay in any case. Hence, his insurance company initially offered me two options: I could take my damaged vehicle to a workshop commissioned by it, which would repair the damage covered by the insurance company. That was of course out of the question. Anyone who has already spent a long time in Kosovo will know that, in addition to good artisans, trustworthy workshops were more the exception than the rule. Who knows whom they would have referred me to and in what condition I would have got the car back, especially since it was brand-new? Therefore, I requested the complete restoration of the original condition by an appropriate authorized workshop. The agent replied I could also choose option two. Namely, bring the vehicle to a workshop of my choice, present the invoice to the insurance company and it would decide on the amount of the reimbursement itself. I refused. I insisted that we take the vehicle not only to an authorized workshop, but that the insurance company also had to pay the entire bill. Well, one might have heard that insurance companies are reluctant applying all means, especially in the event of damage, if people had to claim costs!

The car had been repaired in the nearest authorized workshop in Macedonia. However, I had to admit that I had a bad feeling, especially since the workshop targeted a good five days for repairs. In addition, since it was almost a brand-new vehicle, we feared that used ones could replace one or the other part in the engine. There would have been enough time. In order to prevent such hustle and bustle, it was common for car owners to take days off for an upcoming repair or inspection of their vehicle in a workshop, in order to look over the shoulder of the mechanic in the truest sense of the word.

Fortunately, my fears proved unfounded when the vehicle was back in our yard. The colleague who picked it up even brought the broken parts with him, which I initially thought was completely nonsensical. What should we do with it? I would certainly have left them in the workshop. When we presented the invoice to the insurance agent the next day, he suddenly asked about the replaced parts that he needed for a proper handling of the case. We would have left these at home. So, we returned a day later. Under the arms the approximately two-meter-long plastic bumper and the damaged fender, we marched straight into the office of the said insurance agent and, who looked a bit puzzled, placed this and all the other small parts right in the middle of his desk. We stressed that here was the evidence he asked for! In spite of this, the insurance company initially refused to reimburse the entire invoice, which it then finally made up for after a good three months under threat of legal action.

I was unable to say whether the insurance's refusal was initially because I, or the organization, was a foreigner whom one could force through some harassment to accept one's own conditions. That was what I suspected at first. However, the fact that my local colleague had brought the damaged car parts spoke against it. He simply said to me "this is probably normal"!

Nonetheless, I observed in the region that as a foreigner, especially as a Western European, one actually got frequently into situations in which I had the feeling that people considered me only as a rich milking cow who could or would not defend himself.

Starting with renting apartments, where the rent for foreigners was usually much higher, or manual work, for which, although mostly anything but professional, people suddenly applied German tariffs as well as tenders in the context of aid activities. Appropriate offers sometimes differed by a factor of two or even three.

It also happened to me several times that I fell for the old trick of manipulating gas pumps at petrol stations, especially in Serbia and Montenegro. The petrol pump had not been set to zero, so that in the end you paid a lot more than you had actually filled up. Once I was supposed to pay more than 70 liters of fuel, even though the vehicle's tank held a maximum of 60 liters! I refused, saying that this was street robbery and I would call the police immediately. After that, I just had to pay for the actual amount of diesel.

I later experienced a real robbery, albeit a minor one, in Montenegro. Once again, two representatives of the donor from Kosovo had announced that they would be visiting us. After the long drive, I advised them to park the vehicle right in front of our office, where it would be safe overnight. So far, nothing has happened. However, the next morning I saw several police officers from afar in the parking lot with notepads in hand. About ten vehicles had been broken into and while ours, which incidentally had a Montenegrin license plate, was the only one to have stolen the radio; our visitors' vehicle was the only one that had apparently remained untouched. Later at the police station, the officer told me that the car radio had also been "removed" from his car the previous year. However, a few days later a plastic bag containing the car radio was hanging on his front door. Apparently, the thief or the thieves had noticed that it was a police officer's car. Unfortunately, I did not find a plastic bag on our office door afterwards.

At the end of every assignment, I usually said goodbye, especially to the local institutions and authorities with whom I often had to deal with. Even if the collaboration had not always been cooperative, I thought, regardless of where I had been I should thank. The above-mentioned Montenegrin police officer whose radio had been stolen even said that I was the first of foreign aid workers to say goodbye to him personally. He was visibly moved by my farewell visit. Moreover, he invited me also to his home whenever I would be back in town.

Although the farewells were more formal elsewhere, people always appreciated my work, mostly in the form of a gift or a certificate. One could argue about the taste of the present, but it was the mere gift ultimately counted.

In Ingushetia, it was just that. A few days before my final departure, the mayor of a city had given me a very special souvenir that was very popular there: a much-decorated curved dagger and scabbard as well as a corresponding certificate. I pointed out again that the dagger was a gift, so it was legal to carry it with me, which the mayor himself had confirmed again with a handwritten signature at the end of which he stamped it. The customs, to whom the letter was primarily addressed, probably heard the news, but apparently, there was no belief. In any case, they took the dagger at the airport in Nazran with the instruction that no weapons were allowed on the plane. I could still have understood that in hand luggage. However, in normal luggage and with an official declaration? So I returned the gift with a somewhat surprised expression, asking the customs officer how one would win tourists if they were not even allowed to take souvenirs from their country home? Well, judging by the look on his face, he had probably heard the word tourist for the first time...

It was almost the same regarding my personally bought souvenirs. I had packed three bottles of vodka with all sorts of clothing wrapped in the suitcase so that they would survive the trip unscathed. Due to the amount of alcohol, actually a matter for German customs, the police at the airport in Nazran wanted to take action and confiscate the vodka. I replied that these were souvenirs for friends in Moscow, whereupon the officer, surprisingly, immediately stopped and let me go. Somehow, I had the feeling that the officer wanted to meet the border guards' own needs.

I had also received a special farewell present in Serbia a few years earlier. As part of a school renovation, which we co-financed, I was once on the construction site and discovered a very old, large portrait photo of Josip Broz Tito, the much-revered former head of state of Yugoslavia. The workers had put it aside and probably wanted to throw it away. Nonetheless, I was particularly interested in the wooden picture frame. I left it with mere interest, however. After the project was completed, the school director organized a celebration to mark the renovation of the building, to which he invited me as a guest of honor, as usual. Apparently, the headmaster had registered my attention to the picture of Tito at the time and presented it to me as his personal gift at the festival.

How could I take the picture home with me at the end of my assignment, at least about 60x80 cm? By plane not possible since I would have a lot of luggage anyway. Therefore, I went to the office of a private parcel service in Belgrade to find out what it would cost to send the picture - it should not be too expensive. At least that is what I thought.

In any case, the 20-year-old employee initially reacted completely disturbed to my request. I was unable to determine whether she had even recognized the Tito depicted. However, she was rather derogatory, what do I want with the old photo? Anyway, it would be best if I took out the photo, rolled it up and disassembled the frame into four parts, which would be the cheapest. It was precisely the framework, I emphasized, that made up the value for me and that should therefore by no means be broken, let alone taken apart. Then she took off the dimensions of the picture, typed a little on the calculator and told me that the delivery would take about three days, for the price of 270 D-Mark, i.e. about 135 euro! For the money I could hire someone, put him on the bus to Germany and would get the picture even faster, I replied, whereupon she immediately asked if she could play the personal messenger!

Even when I got into the bureaucratic mills on site as part of my work, I could see that they sometimes grind much finer than ours, but in one or the other case they also have very unorthodox solutions ready for us, again hardly imaginable had. At the same time, however, I also recognized that bureaucracy and thus rules are fundamentally part of it, and often are even positive, especially when one acts in supposedly unlawful areas.

In terms of service, I certainly had to cut back in the countries in which I worked, after all. Mostly, these were by no means tourist destinations, but I did experience one or two surprises, such as being in the middle of Islamabad in a bookstore and could very well pay with a credit card ("Of course!"), although I had not really expected it. In addition, especially as a German, at least in the countries in which I had worked to date, I was shown such an appreciation that it is just diametrically different from my own perception at home. I advise complainers to think outside the box. Only then, people will really know how to appreciate the place they come from. In the context of disasters, that a lot of what we sometimes call a problem at home is downright ridiculous elsewhere. In addition, even the often-maligned German over-correctness of the bureaucrats can take over strange forms elsewhere - including unforeseen surprises.

Back in the days of the Milosevic regime, I came to Serbia alone to open a project office in Belgrade. That meant having the organization officially registered first and foreign staff needed a corresponding residence permit, which I had to apply to the Ministry of the Interior. Both needed support by a local organization that acted as an advocate, so to speak. In our case, a church aid organization, with which we worked together on two distributions of aid, had promised to take the necessary steps. After about two months, I suddenly received the message on a Friday that I should go to the police, assuming that they finally hand over my visa to me.

In fact, the officer stamped the residence permit on my passport, which I put in without looking at it and drove straight to Croatia, because until then I could not leave the country and we urgently needed money for various suppliers. Being on the motorway, I opened my passport and was completely amazed that I could now leave Serbia and re-enter as often as I wanted. However, the end date of the visa was February 30, 2001, a day that did not exist at all. I immediately called the German representation office in Belgrade, who advised me not to leave the country under any circumstances. Since we urgently needed project funding, I decided we would go ahead and see what would happen. Fortunately, the border official did not notice it when he left the country. I was all the more excited when I came back a few hours later, especially since the policeman had examined my ID very carefully, but surprisingly stated that I had to be a VIP because I had a six-month visa, which was everything else but usual in those days. With mock nonchalance, I said yes. On the following Monday I went to the police again, where my now well-known officer greeted me somewhat blankly with the question of what else I wanted, since I had my visa after all. I told him there was a little "problem". "Which one?" He asked, completely surprised. "Well, it's valid until February 30, 2001," I replied. "And?" He snapped at me, whereupon I could literally see the heads of the other four officers sitting in the office smoking. Until suddenly one of them started laughing and enlightened the others. My friend just snapped: "That's really German, isn't it? Everything must always be in order", took my passport, disappeared with it and came back with a new stamp in the passport - including a schnapps to toast!

9. Encounters with leisure

It seemed to be common practice in headquarters of aid organizations that they expected constant availability around the clock when working abroad. Different time zones did not play a role, because I was often contacted long after my actual end of work. Further, an upcoming weekend did not seem to prevent the headquarters from making extremely urgent inquiries on Friday afternoons that I had to answer immediately. This happened all the time, especially when I was working in Belgrade. Almost jokingly, we expected the e-mails on Fridays with the remark that they would always switch on the internet shortly before the weekend. At first, I actually answered, which sometimes cost me a weekend or two. Until I realized, at some point, that colleagues would not read my messages until Monday anyway. At headquarters was weekend, too. Thus, certainly none of the colleagues there wanted to be available longer than necessary on Friday. Over time, I also realized that I needed the weekend to relax. At home, people actually never asked how I used to spend my free time abroad. Unless I talked about rather unusual activities, like in Serbia, where I spent almost every weekend paragliding, especially in the second half of my assignment.

Originally, I wanted to spend a long weekend in Montenegro with my local colleague, the aforementioned teacher who had been a hobby pilot before the Bosnian war. I had heard a lot about the beauty of the country. However, I had never been there and was really looking forward. On the way, it was already getting dark; we suddenly saw paragliders in the sky in Zlatibor (Central Serbia). My "pilot" at the wheel was immediately excited and suggested driving up the mountain. Said and done. He asked one of the paragliders without further ado whether we could fly with them. Sure, said one of the aviators, who spoke broken German, but still quite understandable. However, it was about to get dark, so that only a single tandem flight would be possible. Since I had never flown this way before, my colleague gave me the honor of being able to take part in this last flight and at the same time my first ever.

While I received various instructions on what exactly I should do, everyone else asked who we were and where we were from. We would work for an aid organization in Belgrade and would be on our way to Montenegro. There on the coast in Budva there would be a "perfect" take-off point for flying, you could spend the night here with us and we will go there together tomorrow, said the paragliders. Deal. These few minutes later helped me not only to varied weekend activities, but also to friendships outside of everyday life that I never met again. From then on, we drove to Zlatibor almost every Friday in the late afternoon and did not return to Belgrade until Monday morning. When the weather allowed, we spent the days paragliding on the mountain, including a campfire, and evenings together in the café. When it rained, we either played table tennis or went on excursions in the surrounding area. New people kept coming in, but I was the only foreigner among the paragliders. What was particularly interesting was the fact that, apart from my colleague and myself, all of them had not worked in our area of work and had no idea about our job. While we permanently saw in our everyday life the misery in the country, my new friends just wanted to have fun and so I realized for the first time that there was also a 'normal' life apart from poverty in the country. From today's perspective, it was certainly the best way to spend my free time that I experienced in all of my assignments. Not only did I spend most of the day outdoors on Saturdays and Sundays. I also enjoyed the company of recreational athletes. They did not ask this or that about work. Rather, at least that was my impression; they were only interested in me as a person. Those days were so relaxing, quite the opposite of my normal everyday life, where I was really just stressed out all the time.

Since we had a few days off, we immediately agreed that we would start a paragliding course for beginners on the way back from Montenegro to Belgrade. The next day we drove to the coast and indeed the flying was impressive. Started at about 800m above sea level and landed directly on the beach. On my first flight in a tandem, I went on weak on the knees, especially when I touched a bush with me feet at the start. My colleague had reassured me beforehand by saying that I should just lean back during the flight and imagine I was going to have a coffee. Since an airport was not far away, paragliding was forbidden at this point. My new friends did not seem to be interested. The police came straight away as we were about to load the paragliders into the car on the beach. My new friends immediately signaled to me that I should go to the car. Apparently, they wanted to avoid the police encountering a foreigner. Not only for my own protection, but also for theirs. Who knew what questions would have been asked? I could not tell whether it was only through persuasion or otherwise, for example a payment in the form of baksheesh. In any case, the flights continued!

We then started our basic course and on the third day, I was able to complete my first solo flight. Admittedly, the mountain was actually a harmless hill. Still, I was pleased as Punch. From then on, I only flew alone, with my 'teacher' giving me instructions over the radio on how to steer. Although he spoke little German, I only understood to some extent. However, some kind of miscommunication actually led once to my crash!

One day we wanted to take off from a departure point that was new to me. Therefore, I asked my teacher to fly first so I could see how many times he would glide left and right since the landing point was out of sight from above. From there he should then instruct me by radio. After he landed, I took off. A short time later, I saw him standing on the ground giving me the orders. All of a sudden, he began to shout "to the right, to the right, to the right", first very calmly, then more and more excitedly. Even though I was getting dangerously close to a power line, I trusted him thinking he knew what he is doing. Nevertheless, when I got too close to the line, I broke off the flight and fell from about 10m, fortunately only spraining my ankle. Immediately the instructor came up to me gesticulating wildly and screamed why I had not obeyed his instructions. Only then did he realize what was on the right for him, was on the left for me! He immediately apologized. I should not tell anyone about it, otherwise he might not be able to teach someone else. Since the fall traumatized me, I should immediately go back up to the start and fly again, he advised me. I did not, because on the one hand, my foot hurt and on the other hand, I wanted to go to work the next day. A week later, I flew again!

Towards the end of my assignment in Serbia, my friends did me the honor to become member number 24 of the paragliding club that they were about to establish. Although according to the law at the time, foreigners could not become a member of a local association! The constituent meeting proceeded entirely in accordance with the kind of mentality that I had learned after a year in the country: no problem at all (nema problema!). A lot of discussion about nullities, little about importance. As the only foreigner present, they asked for my opinion several times, but did not consider it seriously. Nevertheless, it was a legendary gathering for me personally.

At least there was an agenda at the beginning, but of course, they did not follow it. I tried in vain to encourage those present to discuss first the goals of the association, but they ignored me. First, they elected the chairperson who was by far the most experienced paraglider pilot, my instructor, and a good-hearted man. At the same time, however, he was by far the worst organizer. Now that it was almost unanimously determined, they discussed the amount of the annual membership fee at length without a final agreement and delegated the elaboration of a website to those who knew how to use computers best. Again, I threw in that they first have to know the basic goals and content in order to achieve anything at all.

However, as before, my objections got lost in the general palaver. The now elected chairperson only mentioned the goal of trying to find sponsors so that at least the best pilots could take part in a competition in Chile (!) in the following year. Thunderous applause from everyone present! I mentioned that I found this goal quite illusory. Because in the end it was like a paid vacation only for selected pilots. Therefore, the four-hour session ended with no real results, but with frenetic applause.

Apart from the election of the chairperson, who asked those present to think about the amount of the annual fee until the next meeting, there were no real results. He took me aside, put his arm around my shoulder, hugged me like a father and sighed: "It will be fine, nema problema (no problem)". Oops, there it was again, the ever-present "no problem", where not only I, but also actually most of the people there knew exactly at that moment that there would be problems after all. Years later, I went to visit my paragliding friends and, as if it were a matter of course for them, they explained to me with a smile that the affair with the club had fizzled out at some point. Then maybe no problem turned out to be a problem after all.

Somebody once told me that you would develop a special relationship with the country where you had your first assignment abroad. In any case, that applies to me completely. We worked a lot, but I especially enjoyed the weekends with my paragliding friends, so that on Mondays I could always start the new week relaxed. The freedom of movement certainly played a major role, because

I was not subject to any security restrictions, as I learned later in Ingushetia in 2004.

Going around the block to get some fresh air or going to a pub or restaurant was not that easy. People considered it far too dangerous to leave home alone. Hence, we had constantly armed escort. In addition, cafes, hotels and the like were classified in terms of security. That is why the UN divided the good into the pot, the bad ones into the crop. That meant that many localities were taboo. The selection of those places where I could possibly have ended or spent the evening was therefore quite manageable. All other aid organizations had to meet the same requirements. As a result, almost all expats, like me, spent most of the evenings at home.

Nevertheless, there were a few restaurants, which we could visit. The advantage of that was that I mostly met employees from other organizations that I had got to know in the course of work and so rarely had to enjoy my after-work beer alone. We could not avoid talking mostly about work again, but often-such informal meetings provided not only good information, but also, I was able to discuss the one or the other problem more in depth. Finally, yet importantly, you can do very good networking for yourself, because you never knew what happened after your employment contract expires.

The downside of such establishments, however, was mostly that they not only developed into a locality exclusive only to foreigners, locals couldn't afford the prices anyway, so that the evenings often ended in excessive drinking which was anything but welcome among the local population and left a corresponding negative reputation with regard to the aid workers. In addition, it was often precisely those meeting points, as they were mainly frequented by foreigners, who were the first to be declared a 'no-go area' by the so-called Risk Management.

When I served an internship at an aid organization in Sarajevo in 1999, my colleagues naturally went to the same pub after office hours to ring in the end of the day with plenty of beer. It seemed to be the custom that someone, as soon as he had to go to the toilet, quickly ordered another layer for the table at the bar, so that it happened that you had two, three or more unopened bottles of beer in front of you. My constant objection, especially to those who had to drive to consider this, have mostly commented that police would not stop vehicles from aid organizations anyway. In the end, we drove home rapidly, which would probably have resulted in a police operation including a chase and loss of the driver's license in Germany. In fact, police never checked us!

Most of the time, however, the precarious security situation restricted our own freedom of movement to such an extent that sometimes, as in Sri Lanka, it was usually decided on Fridays by a higher authority whether we were allowed to go to the seaside at the weekend or not. There, image issues of the organization played a more important role, especially since we would then have used a vehicle with a sticker from the organization. Finally, you should not attract negative attention in any way or give the local population the impression that you would spend your vacation there, while they themselves were vegetating only after a fashion. That is why our weekends were regularly spoiled by the fact that we were never allowed to leave our location while most of the other aid organizations had allowed their employees to go to the seaside. Because a change of location would blow away the cobwebs. We, on the other hand, could not do so during my entire stay! As a result, I mostly spent the weekends with colleagues I saw every day anyway. However, lamenting did not help. In the end it turned out that, the person who had banned us from any weekend excursions did so because his organization banned it himself. In any case, the working week always ended for me on Friday, after the said meeting, in such a way that he made a pig's ear out of the weekend.

That is why I found my own way of spending free time. Years earlier in Serbia, a colleague had asked me whether I would try to get a doctorate (!) while working abroad. What I initially considered to be a completely absurd idea, however, later led to the fact that I actually thought that it could certainly not be wrong to continue my education in the evening. It did not necessarily have to be a doctorate.

While I did not have any time for it in Serbia, I decided to do it for future assignments. Therefore, I completed a distance-learning course in accounting and bookkeeping in Montenegro, especially since responsibility for finances was one of my tasks anyway. After I had later repeatedly read in job advertisements that a degree related to development cooperation was a plus for applicants, I began a distance learning study in 2003 leading to a Master of Science degree in Development Management at an English university. The course should take three years, that is six semesters, whereby you did not have to complete it continuously, but could take a break. I hoped that this would improve my chances on the job market. In addition, I thought that I could also improve my English significantly, because it is the generally valid lingua franca in the areas of humanitarian aid and development cooperation.

It was not always easy to discipline yourself after particularly long working days in order to actually 'study' in the evening. Nevertheless, in addition to the learning effect achieved, it was ultimately also a way of getting away from daily business. However, I also had to make a lot of effort to stand it actually. The study was designed in such a way that before each semester I knew exactly when I had to submit a so-called tutor marked assignment, which was usually the case every six weeks. Therefore, the days immediately before the respective submission date in particular were by far the most labor-intensive. In addition, except for the last semester, I had to pass a written exam at the end. After all, I graduated in 2008 and achieved my third degree.

Since then, no one has never asked explicitly about this degree; so that I now have my doubts that it is actually a necessary degree with personal benefit. Not to forget the costs: after all, it cost me around 10,000 euro.

In 2009, I took a break to study so that I could specialize more. Because by then I had developed into an all-rounder. In addition to two advanced training courses (organizational development and evaluation in development cooperation), which were organized as modules for a whole year, I took another correspondence course in quality management ISO 9000 and 9001. Again, associated with high costs, I was able to implement at least the latter later when I went to Kosovo, where the organization had set the goal of attaining ISO 9001 certification.

I think that I can now call myself an expert on distance learning courses, including studying. After all, I completed three. From today's perspective, I would by no means do this again, although all the courses in terms of leisure activities were a thoroughly pleasant type of activity. Above all, however, I would try much longer to find out what the individual training courses would actually bring me in professional terms.

On the upwardly open sadness scale with regard to leisure activities, Ingushetia should not have been afraid of unpleasant competitors from my professional experience: UN had classified cafes and restaurants with regard to potential dangers, so that the selection was rather limited. The locations classified as positive, however, offered anything but the prerequisite for enjoying an after-work beer or a pleasant evening, which mostly ruined the ambience alone. Because next to a few tables standing around was usually some sort of cubicle, behind, which, separated from the dining room by a curtain, especially the locals sat. Not to mention the possibility to enjoy the sun outside like in a beer garden or street café.

A local colleague who had already opened a café there wanted to open a small cinema right next to it - the first in the country -, which many people had apparently wished beforehand. Hence, he purchased three dozen armchairs, which he had installed rising like in a cinema and showed DVDs on the opposite wall in large format by means of a projector. Entrance price about one euro. However, to his own surprise, it had to close again after a short time due to lack of interest. Apparently, many visitors had complained that there were no separate cubicles, although it was usually dark during the film! Whether the film was actually the focus of interest, one could only guess...

Consequently, we foreigners mostly invited each other in the evening. There were always birthdays, an occasion for a spontaneous party was easy to find or just a joint dinner. The latter was the favorite activity of my German colleague, so that our house had already achieved a legendary reputation, which became even more legendary after a very special meal.

Baked fish and vegetables were on the menu. The guests had gathered around the table in eager anticipation when the food came on the table. The cook, my colleague, however, noticed that he did not know exactly which fish it would be, especially since the smell from the oven was rather repulsive and not necessarily suggestive of fish. Two apparently particularly hungry British colleagues had served themselves immediately, one of whom put the first bite out of his mouth onto the plate in a flash and the other had to go to the toilet immediately. When asked where he had bought the supposed fish, my colleague replied that he had been to the market that morning with a driver. He would have asked at the counter what the tender white meat in the midst of the fish was and had been told it was Baran - "after all, that sounds like fish even to the unfamiliar with the language, doesn't it?" Those who understood Russian immediately burst out laughing and with tears in their eyes made it clear that it would generally be mutton and, in particular, a bare fat appendage on the rear part of the same. Normally people would cut it into wafer-thin slices and serve with vodka, as the fat would soak up the alcohol more quickly. In any case, our main course and sauce ended up in the bin. After all, the vegetables were reasonably enjoyable.

From then on, whenever my colleague invited guests to dinner, he always had to answer the all-important question, whether fish would be on the menu!

Nevertheless, I also learned in Ingushetia that local culinary specialties or those that were foreign to the locals were not always immediately accepted. On my own birthday, I promised our staff in the North Caucasus homemade potato dumplings. Eyed by the curious and stern looks of my female colleagues, I started preparing in the afternoon, since I had to serve around thirty people. As is customary there, the men took care of the meat and grilled delicious lamb and sturgeon on long skewers, so-called shashlik, over the fire. At the table, I took the first bite of a dumpling, signaling to my colleagues how to eat them. The general feedback on the taste was definitely positive. Then I went out into the garage, where the other colleagues, drivers and security staff were sitting, to see whether the dumplings had tasted good. To my surprise, however, I saw that the bowl was still on the table, untouched. Even after I asked them to help themselves, none of those present served themselves. Only when I took a meanwhile cold lump and took a bite did they take it too.

Usually, the meals together with the foreign employees of other NGOs in Ingushtia developed into full-blown parties until late at night and we often made plans for the weekend, which we used one or the other to go to breathtaking mountains for hiking, picnicking together or skiing in winter to Mount Elbrus. Without a doubt, these experiences in the great outdoors compensated for the more than dreary everyday life in Nazran, even if we foreigners and work colleagues, who we have seen each other often enough anyway, still spent our free time together.

I have special memories of the very first excursion to the North Caucasian Mountains to a completely deserted village, which consisted exclusively of residential towers, which, in earlier times protected the residents from intruders or wild animals. Since the northern part of that region, bordering Georgia, was a restricted military area, we first had to drive south almost to the Georgian border to a checkpoint, and then come back in the opposite direction. Obviously, visitors and foreigners like us were all too rare individuals. While our driver went with our passports into the little house of the police station, a police officer asked us who we were, where we were from, where we were going and whether we had weapons (!)? After he had also thoroughly inspected our car, he leaned against the barrier directly in front of us and kept sticking a match in the barrel of his pistol and firing it. When he hit a comrade, we all laughed, which he found not so funny. Because when our driver came back from passport control, the gunman made us wait a full hour in the car until he opened the barrier in almost slow motion and let us pass. When we arrived at our destination, however, the breathtaking landscape compensated for the involuntary delay and we enjoyed the whole day there with a picnic. Later I only saw a similarly impressive and above all untouched mountain world in Tajikistan.

Only when I was in Ingushetia did I learn that the highest mountain in Europe was not Mont Blanc in the French Alps, but Elbrus at over 5,600m in the North Caucasus, more precisely in Karbadino-Balkaria, a Russian republic. In the winter of 2004, some employees of the international NGO community in Nazran decided to take a weekend skiing trip there. While some Czech colleagues from other organizations were almost professionally equipped, I had neither suitable clothing nor professional skiing skills. Nevertheless, I decided to go and as usual, we set out with a whole group of vehicles including our armed guards.

The hotel we all rented, like the whole place, had proba bly seen better days. It was more like a simple mountain hut with only shared rooms. We were given a more than warm welcome from the owners, since we - about fifteen 'tourists' in total - were probably a rather unusual group and otherwise hardly any others could be seen. So after our arrival in the afternoon, they served us a hearty meal including various vodka bottles - on the house - after all, according to the owner, our presence should be celebrated!

The next morning, we drove to the nearby lift. The evening before we had already learned that there were two slopes that you could ski up to. One started at a little over 3,000m and the other higher up, which only experienced skiers should take.

A Dutchman, an American and I decided the next day to try the first descent. Everyone else went up with the gondola. When we got out of the car, we got quite uncomfortable, because it felt like minus 25 degrees Celsius. That is why we wanted to warm up with a cup of tea in a hut by the lift. Although there were only a few other skiers, we must have made a pitiful impression, only dressed in jeans and anorak. The landlady insisted that I couldn't go down without a hat and therefore gave me one!

Afterwards, we started our departure. Too bad that we could not even see the slope due to the freezing wind. We decided to wait until someone would go down so that we could roughly guess the route. However, nobody came. After not even 100m careful gliding down the completely icy and above all steep slope, we wanted to return to the hut and take the gondola back down to the valley. Suddenly a Russian ski instructor joined us who had been watching us from a gondola going up and offered to guide us down safely.

We got there after more than two hours including various falls and completely frozen out, although, according to our guide, experienced skiers would complete the descent in less than 15 minutes! The Dutch colleague, who by far had 'kissed' the snow most frequently, then asked rather ironically whether we should try the whole ordeal again. We both said no in unison, hence we decided to wait for the others in a café and talk about our adventure. Hours later, they gradually rolled in and really had an even bigger story to tell. Because one of our colleagues from another aid organization was on the way to the hospital, he probably broke his leg!

No matter where I worked abroad, sport was an essential part of my leisure time. That is why I have always tried to either encourage regular football games myself or join in with others. In Sri Lanka, we always played on Sundays on a real soccer field, where we sometimes had to give way to a herd of buffalo before we could kick and later had to turn around many piles while playing. After all, we enjoyed at least part of the otherwise very boring weekends. Once we even played against a local team. In Sri Lanka cricket was the absolute number one among the sports and after that, there was nothing for a long time. Unlike ours, soccer was more of a shadowy existence, so it was even more surprising for me that our town even had a real soccer field. In any case, the extremely young local team entered the field fully dressed, including appropriate footwear, while my team was a motley bunch of players of all ages from France, Belgium, Finland and Germany and some local employees, who could at least be recognized by a similar top, a white T-shirt.

To our surprise, even the referee was properly dressed and had a whistle, so we had to assume that the opposing team would take the match seriously. The players were clearly superior to us in terms of fitness, but to our amazement, we took the lead with two goals at halftime. Fortunately, the opposing team scored two more goals in the second half, so the game ended in a draw. We had feared that in the event of a victory, we would no longer be able to continue working in the neighboring town from which our opponent came and where we were carrying out a number of projects.

I had also played football regularly in Ingushetia and Kosovo. Once or sometimes twice a week we foreigners met in the North Caucasus, depending on the weather, outside on an artificial lawn or in the gym of a nearby school. The latter was particularly bizarre to look at, as the bodyguards mostly played along in the locked hall, while their Kalashnikovs leaned against the walls within easy reach. In Kosovo, on the other hand, we played on the typical and very numerous courts available there, mostly covered artificial turf fields that looked more like an ice rink from the outside and most of which were probably only built after the war in 1999. Especially in winter we experienced local adversities, because it was not only bitterly cold in the halls, but also our game had to be interrupted one or the other due to the frequent power cuts. Then we stayed in the pitch-dark place until the generator switched on. At first, a local colleague had organized weekly games against other teams. He later changed jobs and, now that my own employees apparently did not feel like it, I joined him and his team, which consisted without exception of players who had no connection whatsoever to humanitarian work. So at least some days a week I had the opportunity to forget about the extremely stressful working days, at least for a short time.

Back in 1995, during the war in Bosnia, playing football was less my own leisure activity than of doing something with the young people who lived there and were mostly bored, so that we played almost every day. As a highlight for all of us, I contacted the French UNPROFOR soldiers stationed near the city, the so-called international peacekeepers, and asked if they were interested in a game against the young people. At first, they accepted enthusiastically, but had to cancel a short time later because they were on alert due to the events of the war and no longer allowed to leave their accommodation. However, suddenly we found a man who had always watched our daily game and asked if we wanted to play against the local team, which he said was playing in the Bosnian first league (sic!). Of course, we enthusiastically agreed, because in addition to the sporting challenge, we also secretly hoped that the displaced young people could perhaps establish an expanded contact with local players. The man who had arranged everything agreed to train and prepare us appropriately for the opposing team. However, an incident blurred my initial enthusiasm.

I usually went on a trip to a nearby river with the youth from the camp once a week. In addition, everyone, mostly around twenty people (!), jumped into the loading area of our Mercedes minibus! Fortunately, it was a closed vehicle; otherwise, we would have had problems with the police even there. Some bathed in the river, the rather cold water of which, at least for me, had anything but bathing temperature. Others washed the car, which I always found strange, but at the same time, it showed me that they were just happy to be able to do anything at all. When we wanted to go to the river again, some suggested driving through the forest to a certain village. It was safe there, so I agreed without hesitation and had the route explained to me. I stopped at the entrance to the village, the doors opened and everyone suddenly seemed to swarm out in a purposeful manner. Strangely enough, there was no one in the street there and I understood that

286

it was a city of the dead, from which the entire population had been chased away or fled during the war. For me it was truly an eerie feeling.

I wondered what happened to the residents. Except for a few bullet holes, I could not find any real battle marks. At least I hoped they had all got away safely. The first people came back to the car with household items and I suddenly realized why we were going there. So that the youngsters could loot! I immediately started to horn to signal that everyone should get back to the car. Apparently, everyone understood why I was honking my horn. They took their prey into the car. Incredible for me! I felt misused and personally could not tolerate such behavior. How could they do that? It was easy for me to talk. On the other hand, who knows what the youngsters went through? Still, I did not want to be part of such an action. When everyone was back in the car, I drove straight back to the camp without saying a word and suddenly everyone else was mute. When we arrived at the camp, most of them left the looted items in the car. Apparently, they had understood the message. I told our trainer the whole thing and right before the next training session he gave an impressive speech to the young people: Such behavior is unforgivable. Would they have thought of the people who would have lived in the houses? Are they criminals? Did their own eviction justify their behavior? What do you think they would say if the same thing happened in their home (which very likely happened)? Are they proud of their looting? In particular, according to the trainer, they should treat a foreigner with respect, regardless of what they have experienced themselves, and not use him as a henchman who would be available for their raids. "Admittedly, a lot of bad things happened in this war, but this does not justify acting in the same way." The whole speech lasted almost half an hour and afterwards everyone brought the stolen items to me and apologized personally for their behavior! I thanked the man for his words, hoping my boys would take it to heart too. I thought so, especially since they all looked crestfallen.

Then the day had come: we played against the supposedly overpowering opponent. He even brought jerseys for us! Because most of us did not have any sportswear. Well, there was one difference: they all had soccer shoes while we played in normal street shoes.

Despite the alleged first division club, the audience interest was more than manageable. Most of them were our people, so to speak, that is, those from the camp. In the end, we lost 6-1, but celebrated our consolation goal as if we had won. Afterwards we sat down with some of our opponents, who then revealed to us that their goal was to play in the Bosnian premier league one day. Although the opponent turned out to be the one we had expected, namely not a first division, we were still the heroes in the camp for the next few days!

In addition to soccer, table tennis has always been one of my sporting activities abroad. In Tajikistan, was even a table tennis table in the inventory of the compound where I stayed. Hence, of course, I immediately asked who was going to play there. The local employee, with whom I worked closely every day, replied that actually no one used the table. Because he is by far the best player in the organization, against whom no one has the slightest chance. That is why nobody would want to play against him anymore. It is too boring for him. Well, I was not a professional by any means, but at least I always thought that I could play reasonably well. Therefore, I immediately challenged him. Our first match turned into a catastrophic defeat for my opponent, which visibly annoyed him. On the other hand, it increased his respect for me. From then on, we used almost every lunch break to play a digestive match after lunch. He had never won a single game! It was the other way around in Kosovo, where I played with some locals on Sundays and never had the slightest chance.

Whether it was table tennis or soccer, no matter where I played both, the locals in particular took every game as seriously as if it were about the World Cup. For me, the mere sporting activity and contact with people were more in the foreground. When I played table tennis for the first time with my Serbian colleague, - we both were at about the same level - and I only narrowly won the entire match. In the end, he was sitting like a pile of misery over the coffee that followed. When I asked what was wrong with him, he replied that he was still thinking why he had made so many mistakes and lost. I told him not to take it so seriously, it was just a game and, above all, fun. I guess my approach was the right one, he said, and insisted on rematch. I would like to offer him that. However, I replied with a wink, "only if he was a little better trained", whereupon he started to laugh too.

In Montenegro, I only played football once during two years. Right at the beginning, I asked my local colleague if there was an opportunity there to join recreational football. We met in a sports hall. We played four against four with two brothers chosen on each team. After admittedly an over-harsh foul of one against the other, an initially loud verbal argument developed into a solid brawl, followed by a doctor's visit by the two! I then made it clear to the athletes that I would only play for fun. That was the last time for me!

Nevertheless, sport was always a welcome activity for me when I was abroad, as it actually enabled me to switch off. For the other people I was therefore not only the 'foreigner', but also always the exotic because of my job - just like at home when people asked and ask about my occupation.

Especially when I was studying by means of distance learning courses alongside work, my colleagues even considered me to be exotic. While their value did not necessarily pay off in professional terms, despite all the efforts, they always made me feel good in the end that I had achieved something. I think that is exactly what counts in the end: namely, that you have a good feeling, no matter where you work and that you do not feel bored.

10. Encounters with return

Before each return was a farewell, mostly in the form of a party. The one in Serbia was one of the most emotional. For me personally, probably because it was my first and I had made a number of new friends. It was only through them that I started enjoying my free time there and (indeed) feeling at home. In addition, almost everyone gave me to understand that it was sad that I was going to go now. Back then, in 2001, the international community of aid workers was manageable and almost everyone had come. One of them, a German from another aid organization, had suggested celebrating and barbecuing in his garden. I had been on Revolution Day on October 5, 2000, when we went to his apartment to watch the events on TV through the person. His office, meanwhile he had moved, which was also his accommodation, was right next to the villa of the now imprisoned ex-President Milošević. People danced and partied until early next morning. In the end, we all hugged each other and talked almost melancholy about the experiences of the past year, especially the dramatic events surrounding the overthrow of the government in October 2000.

On my departure from Serbia, when I checked in my luggage at the airport, I asked rather mischievously at check-in whether smoking was allowed on the plane. The employee replied "Of course!" When the seat belt signs disappeared later in the plane after take-off, the entire crew first went back to smoke a cigarette!

Two years later, at the end of my assignment in Berane/ Montenegro, I invited some colleagues from various aid organizations from other parts of the country and informed them of the way to the venue by email: up to a parking lot in Berane, from where you could take the subway to the restaurant. In the whole of the former Yugoslavia, there was no subway at all. Still, some of them asked where the train stopped!

Even a former colleague from Serbia was present, Mladen and his partner, for which I was more than thankful. In addition, some mayors from surrounding villages appeared, so that the party almost got an official character. Everyone thanked me for my commitment in a short speech, wished me all the best for the future and hoped that I would come back. Years later, when I worked twice in Kosovo, I went to Berane very often and in fact, I met one or the other. A greeting here, a handshake there. Many recognized me and usually invited me straight away for a coffee. I had the feeling that I would still somehow belong to the community. In any case, I fully enjoyed the recognition given to me.

The same applied years later in Sri Lanka when I left in June 2006. In order to be able to move around the city of Ampara without any problems, we had hired an employee and his tuk-tuk, the three-wheeled taxi that is common there. The driver was the one who had been threatened by another colleague. During my stay I had often said, "I would like to take a tuk-tuk through town myself." Now the driver rang the doorbell and simply said "Sir, now it is your turn and pointed to the driver's seat." Said and done. He sat in the back seat and I at the wheel. Hierarchy the other way around. While he proudly waved to his compatriots, signaling to them at the same time: Look who is at the wheel, I drove him through the streets, laughing and waving. Truly an unforgettable afternoon.

At the subsequent farewell dinner with the colleagues, one of the locals said that I should come back in any case. "But then as a politician!" I could not understand whether he was indirectly criticizing my management skills or referring to my skills in all the disputes among colleagues. Then he went one: he would invite me to his wedding in September next year. I replied that I had not even noticed that he was in a relationship. He replied, "No, he still has to find a suitable (!) wife".

Whenever I sat home on the plane after all the goodbyes, I could never immediately realize that this was actually my farewell to the mission and my colleagues. Most of the time there were still projects that were still ongoing so they kept going through my head. With some employers, there was a so-called debriefing at the head office, in which we discussed again aspects of my work and the evaluation of it. After that, I closed the respective chapter.

When I got home, I suddenly moved from my professional world to the private one. Although: I did not even have my own apartment after the first two assignments abroad, so I always stayed with my girlfriend and later wife. Loaded with three suitcases, I arrived from Serbia and now lived in a two-room apartment that she shared with another student. In any case, I could not really stretch myself out, just took the essentials out of the suitcases and stowed the rest in the basement. During my assignment in Montenegro, her professional life began, so she moved to a larger apartment in another town. At least I had more space there, although I spent most of the evenings in the kitchen because she still had to work in her room.

Although the periods of my flights home from initially several months to a few weeks became shorter and shorter over the years - I tried, if it was possible, to fly home at least once a month or after six weeks at the latest. Now suddenly I was at home for an indefinite period. I no longer had a regular working day. My wife did. Therefore, I always had to get used to a life as a couple again. Now I had someone again with whom I could communicate at home and whom I had to get used to in my own everyday life. Ignoring the household chores, as I had partly done abroad, was no longer possible. There this was primarily due to the long working days, so that I just wanted to put my feet up in the evening. Now I had no excuses because I had no obligations. Still, it was always quite a conversion for me.

I was most likely to notice this at home, as I did not immediately know where the cups, plates or the like were. On the other hand, when I was cooking: forgetting the spices here and there, which she often acknowledged with "so-so". When I was abroad, I was just used to my own taste. At home, the bar was (unfortunately) much higher. Suddenly the phone rang in the evening, which I did not experience so often abroad. Most of the time I picked up the phone and passed the phone to my wife. Occasionally I got calls too. Nevertheless, over time, I realized that my own social network had dwindled. I used to have quite a large group of acquaintances and friends. It is completely normal for this to change depending on where you live. Former classmates and friends geographically were widely spread, so that the contacts were no longer the same as before. During my time abroad, personal encounters with them when I was at home decreased even more. Of course, I wanted to spend time with my wife at home. Friends or acquaintances were then only in the second row. Although I stayed in regular contact with some of my friends over the years, they were not as close as they used to be.

In addition, there were everyday occurrences. Very often, when I wanted to withdraw money from the machine, especially after previous missions, I suddenly forgot my PIN and always had to apply for a new one. At the time, I replenished my wallet with cash every time I stayed at home. Fortunately, I later received money abroad with my EC card. Shopping! Often when I was shopping in the supermarket, I found myself forgetting items because I was probably still used to the sometimes-limited assortment abroad. I may often just feel overwhelmed by the offer. At the same time, I got frequent complaints from my wife that I had forgotten this or that.

I had never mentioned a certain period of settling-in to her. She probably would not have understood it anyway, since I was now bursting into her regular everyday life. Instead, she had always assumed that I would acclimatize immediately. In the end, I always accepted that because I felt guilty to a certain extent for leaving her alone at home. That is probably the fate when you try to live in two worlds.

On my return, I came across one or the other chapter headings mentioned above. In the household, I was now the one to keep things tidy while my wife went to work. Replacing a lightbulb, pushing out the garbage can or sweeping the street were still easy tasks. Cooking was more difficult, as I mentioned earlier. While I was used to the simple kitchen, I found myself exposed to direct criticism. Often not positive!

Occasionally we needed real professionals, mostly for electrical, heating or painting work. Unlike abroad, the quality of the work was mostly satisfactory. The bill less. Quality has its price. When I once told a master painter at home that I would recommend him at any time, he strongly replied, "Please, do not!" he had enough work to do anyway. That corresponded to my own observation abroad, namely that the good artisans might have been fully booked. In spite of that, I had never found one there.

Encounters with culture? After all these years abroad, did I still feel like I belonged to my home country? I have by no means forgotten the German mentality - look at all the disputes abroad. Nevertheless, I think that the years of experience abroad have made me much more relaxed. Not only has my patience lengthened significantly, but also I can take on alleged inadequacies in Germany much more easily, especially delays.

My own safety no longer mattered. I was able to move freely and go where I wanted. I was able to communicate properly again, which in some countries had not been the case at all. I was able to enjoy homemade bread every day again, which I had always missed everywhere abroad. Finally, I was able to follow the political events in this country, which I was often unable to do abroad due to a lack of language skills. In retrospect, I am surprised at how little I kept up-to-date about it in the respective country. The assignments in different countries opened my eyes in many respects and showed that it is good to think outside the box. Because when there is a debate in Germany about the admission of refugees, which is very often populist, one or the other should look at the situation elsewhere. Nobody leaves his or her home country just for fun.

Leisure? Admittedly, at home I suddenly had a lot of it. However, I did not spend it with other colleagues (how?), but with my wife and (mostly) her friends and colleagues. At first, I joined them, but over time, I felt strange. Because the topics revolved around their everyday life, which did not correspond to mine. That is why I looked for my own leisure activity, especially in the form of studies alongside all the caretaker activities.

Official meetings? There were essentially two offices that I dealt with, but whose interest in me was diametrically opposed.

One was the tax office, to which I submitted my annual return of tax. Just filling in these turned out to be a challenge every time. I could not do it without external support, because my case was not an everyday one. When I worked in Kosovo from 2010 to 2012, the situation was even more complicated. As a German, I worked for a Luxembourg organization in the small Balkan country. After an advisor had assisted me with the tax return, questions from the tax office arose almost every week. Apparently, word had not yet got around that Kosovo had been an independent state since 2008. Because the question was what kind of state, it was. It was interesting to know which tax law actually applies there. A number of new laws had come into force since independence, replacing old ones. However, not all of them. How should I know? Therefore, I should get confirmation of my status as a working foreigner from the authorities there, even though I was no longer in the country. Surprisingly, I received this within a few days and sent it to my responsible tax office together with the tax law, the English version of which I had downloaded from the Internet. Afterwards there were various phone calls with the tax advisor, which were probably still not sufficient.

Finally, I should declare on oath that I was only doing one job in Kosovo. How it had come about was not apparent to me. As if, I had time for a part-time job at all. I found this last question in particular to be a mere joke. In the end, I received a tax refund. However, I had to transfer almost all of these to the tax advisor.

The other office that I kept coming across was the employment agency. Because I always had a fixed-term employment contract, it was inevitably my first way there after my return. Although I had a very unusual résumé, people regularly said that they could not help me. Actually, I had not expected this anyway, at least with regard to a job abroad. Rather, I was hoping for support in finding work in this country. Because that was my real goal, at least at the beginning of my career abroad. In the medium and long term, I wanted to work at home and by no means spend my life abroad.

You are always smarter afterwards. Because what was initially planned as a mere international experience became a continued deployment abroad. At some point, it became clear that I no longer had a chance of finding a job on the domestic market. For too long, actually much too long, I hung on to the idea that the more professional experience, in addition to that in different organizations, regions and contexts, the easier it would be to gain a foothold in Germany. However, where should someone like me work in Germany? Three university degrees, foreign language skills, all kinds of project management, personnel management, financial accounting, organizational and intercultural experience. All this labelled me as a generalist the German labor market apparently did and does not seem to demand. Interestingly enough, wherever abroad I was, people never believed me! When we achieved ISO 9001 certification back then in Kosovo, the auditor said to me that if I wanted to, I could start at his company at any time! How I would have loved to receive such an offer at home one day.

The support from the employment agency was limited to regular reminders to report the status of my situation, so that I got more and more the impression that it administered unemployed people instead of bringing them into work.

After I gradually got used to life at home again, and after that, I had sent countless applications without success, I decided to go abroad again. Only twice has it happened to me that I passed from one mission to another without a transition. Of course, abroad. Therefore, over the years, my motto has been after the mission is before the mission.

The return turned out to be never easy for me, both professionally and personally. Over time, I have learned to come to terms with it and to get used to the fact that my own perspective of how and where things will continue initially remained completely unclear. It just seemed to be clear that disasters happen repeatedly, so that this profession is to a certain extent crisis-proof and I will have further disastrous encounters, whether abroad or at home!

Epilogue

If someone asked me nowadays whether I would go the same way again, especially in professional terms, my answer would be ambivalent.

Of course, I do not want to miss all the different encounters as I described them before. Be it paragliding, where for me the focus was less on sport and more on meeting people. Be it the different cultures, traditions and ways of thinking that gave me a completely different perspective that I had not been aware of before. Be it security, although it quickly became clear to me that we in Germany are almost living in paradise in this regard. Be it the sentence of my colleague that I have changed his life and finally the encounter with fundamental problems of people, who struggle to survive, while at home we think that the smallest inconsistency threatens our existence. All of this taught me a lot. In addition, over the years I have met many people who have become a part of my life in the form of friendships.

On the other hand, I would probably not be so naive about this professional path nowadays. As part of my volunteer work, I liked the field of work and was enthusiastic; without having a real idea. Working abroad in an international context, and sometimes the focus of the media. How was that exciting at first? Sometimes I had the feeling that I had my finger on the pulse. After all, over time I had not only given many interviews, but also met important people from time to time. It took time to realize that these were mostly snapshots. I was not that important after all.

Even if I followed the same path, I would start to specialize much earlier. Because as an all-rounder, I had to cope with almost every aspect of the job in the context of all the different assignments. However, this also applies to me: although I have done everything once, I cannot really do anything! A typical sentence from generalists.

If I had to answer the question of which country I liked the most, it sounds quite paradoxical at first. Some outsiders would comment critically how I could have liked it anywhere in the face of the misery I encountered. People's need had motivated me repeatedly to work in adverse contexts. In addition, that was and still is a lot of fun for me!

In a ranking to the above question, I would still answer as follows. For me, the most beautiful landscape was Montenegro; in terms of leisure activities, certainly Serbia; and in terms of work, my team in Turkey was outstanding. Otherwise, I found the people in every country in which I had worked to be extremely hospitable, so that I could not make a ranking in this regard. Instead, I met facets of people everywhere that we also have. Whether puberty adolescents thought they were more adult than adults were. Whether those at least for my taste, had ridiculously pimped up their car in order to impress the girls. Whether it was stubborn officials or flexible ones who actually helped you. Whether it was those older people who knew how to make the world a better place by means of barroom clichés and who sometimes had haggard opinions about other people. I could go on and on with the list. I encountered all of this, just in slightly different circumstances than at home.

There was one aspect that struck me personally, no matter where I was, and that I still have to nibble on today. It is the much-praised German reliability, both in the professional environment and in private. In some countries there seemed to be no translation for the term. Whether it was the appointment with an artisan or the one with the cleaner, not to mention service providers such as the Internet provider. I always had to assume that they would not keep the deadline anyway. I experienced the peak in Turkey when my landlord told every day (!) for three weeks that "tomorrow" the air conditioning would be installed in the apartment. After four weeks, it really happened.

When I look back now, I also ask myself whether all the foreign assignments were worthwhile for me, especially for my private life. Of course, I would have loved to have a normal life with my wife. Although: I do not know exactly what this looks like. Somehow, everything had worked out so that for my wife and me, to a certain extent, the temporary separation became the normal state of our relationship: I was abroad, she at home. Even a weekend relationship would be the non-plus ultra! Unfortunately, we will not be able to do that in the near future.

In this respect, it is astonishing to me that our relationship has not only worked all these years and that my wife has endured all of that. Personally, I am glad I know where I belong. I have a home and a wife who, no matter where I work, has always been and is first priority. In the meantime, our life has leveled out so that both of us have our own, especially in professional terms. By trying to go home as often as possible, we have found a modus vivendi that continues to be astonishing to me. Anyway, we somehow came to terms with it.

Acknowledgements

Martina Schopper was the one who read the first draft a long time ago and thankfully critized it completely. Isolde Opielka picked up one of the next drafts and did not spare criticism, too. After all, it should not be a memoir, let alone a know-it-all monologue. The same applies to Yasemin Niephaus. Nevertheless, I did not allow myself to be discouraged. Giuseppe Scuto and Sabine Reuss-Hubner's comments on the umpteenth version were encouraging, saying: "You have to publish it!" At first glance, the feedback from Wolfgang Lambrecht and Thomas Kimling sounded less constructive. Although: especially their comments led me to the result that is now available - after what felt like 50 versions.

I thank my former boss and friend, Dr. Michael Feit, for his foreword. Finally, Karin Niesen, who suggested the text on the back.

Therefore, my special thanks go to all of you at this stage of the writing.

For the content, I would like to thank not only the various employers, but also above all the local and international employees as well as colleagues from other aid organizations whom I have met, got to know and loved in the course of my professional career. Most may never know about or read about this venture. Still, I take my hat off to them.

As terrible as the various disasters were, I still have to thank them. Because without them they would not have made all these encounters possible for me.

I would like to highlight Pavle Janković, my very first colleague abroad. He kindly made the photo of me in front of the Parliament in Belgrade (book cover) available to me and I spent this unforgettable day with him. Finally, Mladen Uskoković. He was the one from whom I learned almost everything during my greenhorn time in Serbia. Unfortunately, he died far too early in 2005.

In the end my wife Birgit. I would like to thank her especially for all her patience and for holding on to me, despite the frequent and long separations.

About me

I was born in 1966 and grew up in Lower Franconia in Bavaria/Germany. My study of Political Science and History led me to Heidelberg. After the degree as M.A. as well as several jobs as a driver and construction worker I went to Bochum/ Germany, where I enrolled and finished the study 'Master in Humanitarian Assistance'. This paved the way for my career to work for aid agencies. During my assignments abroad I completed the third degree as MSc of Development Management. In addition, I married and live nowadays in North Black Forest/ Germany.

In 2022, I started to work as a social worker in an accommodation for refugees in my hometown. Thus, after more than twenty years, I closed the chapter of working abroad in the fields of humanitarian assistance as well as development. I plan to publish another book about this part of my life in 2023, which shall be a critical review from my personal point of view. Moreover, I intend to complete the disaster trilogy with a third publication the content of which, however, is still written in the stars.

I admire Mark Twain, Monty Python and love the music of Rush, Iron Maiden, Deep Purple and Rainbow.

Any feedback, criticism or recommendation will be very much appreciated:

gkfischer@posteo.de

Picture credits:
Coverphoto: Pavle Janković;